JANE AUSTEN'S WARDROBE

JANE AUSTEN'S WARDROBE

Hilary Davidson

Yale University Press
New Haven and London

In memoriam Deirdre Le Faye,
with thanks for her extraordinary work
on Jane Austen, and her generosity
in sharing it

First published by Yale University Press 2023
302 Temple Street, P. O. Box 209040, New Haven CT 06520-9040
47 Bedford Square, London WC1B 3DP
yalebooks.com | yalebooks.co.uk

ISBN 978-0-300-263602 HB

Library of Congress Control Number: 2022942913
10 9 8 7 6 5 4 3 2
2025 2024

Copyedited by Jenny Wilson
Designed by Osborne Ross
Cover illustration and design: Jo Walker

Printed in China

CONTENTS

TIMELINE

1764	26 April – Marriage of Revd George Austen, rector of Steventon parish, and Cassandra Leigh, Jane Austen's parents
1765	13 February – James Austen (brother) born
1766	26 August – George Austen (brother) born
1767	7 October – Edward Austen (brother) born
1768	July–August – Austen family moves to Steventon, Hampshire
1771	8 June – Henry Thomas Austen (brother) born
1773	9 January – Cassandra Elizabeth Austen (sister) born
	23 March – Revd Austen becomes rector of Deane parish in addition to Steventon
1774	23 April – Francis (Frank) William Austen (brother) born
1775	**16 December – Jane Austen born**
1779	23 June – Charles John Austen (brother) born
1783	Edward Austen is adopted by the childless Mr and Mrs Thomas Knight of Godmersham, Kent
	Spring – Jane and Cassandra Austen are sent to live with Mrs Cawley in Oxford to be educated
1785	Spring – Austen and Cassandra attend Abbey School, Reading, Berkshire
1786	December – Austen and Cassandra leave Abbey School
1787	Austen begins writing juvenilia
1793	3 June – Austen writes last item of juvenilia
1794	Autumn – Austen possibly writes *Lady Susan*
1795	Austen probably writes *Elinor and Marianne*, later *Sense and Sensibility*
1796	October – Austen begins writing *First Impressions*, later *Pride and Prejudice*
1799	Austen has finished *Susan*, later *Northanger Abbey*, sold to a publisher in 1803

1800	December – Revd Austen decides to retire and move to Bath with the family
1801	May – Austen family leaves Steventon and settles in Bath
1802	2 December – Harris Bigg-Wither unexpectedly proposes marriage; Austen accepts, but changes her mind the next day
1804	Austen probably writes *The Watsons*
1805	21 January – Revd Austen dies suddenly in Bath
1806	October – Austen family takes lodgings in Southampton with Francis Austen's family
1807	March – Austen family moves into a house in Castle Square, Southampton
1809	7 July – Austen family moves to Chawton Cottage, near Alton, Hampshire
1811	30 October – *Sense and Sensibility* is published anonymously
1813	28 January – *Pride and Prejudice* is published anonymously
1814	9 May – *Mansfield Park* is published anonymously
1815	End of December – *Emma* is published anonymously, dedicated to the Prince Regent
1817	27 January–18 March – Austen works on a novel later published unfinished as *Sanditon*

18 July – Austen dies in Winchester early in the morning

24 July – Austen is buried in Winchester Cathedral

End of December – *Northanger Abbey* and *Persuasion* are published together, along with Henry Austen's 'Biographical Notice of the Author'

Nicholas Heideloff, 'Morning
Dresses and Half Dress', *The
Gallery of Fashion*, June 1798
(see fig. 5.6)

INTRODUCTION

What might historians of the future make of the remnants of your wardrobe left in photographs, correspondence and journal entries? Would these scraps represent your taste, or capture how you wore your clothes, and the style particular to you? This is largely the situation through which we must encounter the clothes owned and worn by Jane Austen: via pen, ink and diligent research. The greatest direct record of her life are the 161 known letters surviving from an estimated 3,000 she wrote during her lifetime (fig. 0.1). They form the basis of this book exploring what Austen wore, and what we can know about the contents of her wardrobe.

This research is the first-ever systematic delve into the author's clothing, and provides a rich range of at least 32 gowns, 11 coats and wraps, 13 pieces of headwear, 15 accessories and trinkets, four pairs of shoes and many undergarments to use as an insight into her life and style. While Austen has sometimes been accused of dowdiness, of not keeping up with fashion, what emerges in these pages counteracts that view with vigour. Austen frequently reveals herself to be alert to fashion, and how to purchase and incorporate its changes into her wardrobe, often quite promptly. She may not have been a fashion leader, but she maintained a respectable, informed balance between old and new clothes, and seems never to have actually fallen out of style.

The book explores Austen's garments and adornments by grouping together items in the way Regency clothing would have been stored, as a virtual wardrobe. The sections are chronological where possible, to gain a sense of how Austen's wardrobe grew, developed and changed over time, and in response to significant personal and historical events. The contents have been written so that readers can either follow the book from start to finish, or dip in and browse-read, as one might rummage through a closet. Relevant illustrations help bring Austen's text to life, to show what each piece might have looked like – accurate fodder for imaginative reconstructions of what the writer wore. I have also used only the two portraits that irrefutably depict Jane Austen to discuss in detail. Along the way, she is a delightful companion, her irony and amusement about clothes, shopping and taste never far from her pen, nor her tongue ever far from her cheek.

This is the first time that all the surviving material dress and jewellery objects Austen once owned have been published together, made possible thanks to the ongoing generosity of Jane Austen's House in supporting the research and sharing information. Much of what appears in these pages is interpretation or equivalent examples of the types of clothes Austen mentions. Examining her actual things allows us to understand her daily life more closely, and perceive how she specifically negotiated taste, money, consumption practices and many more social dimensions of dress and adornment.

We further see how Austen's sartorial strategies fit in with other women of her family and her milieu, based on records left by her contemporaries Mary Topham, Eliza Jervoise, Diana Sperling and more, especially Barbara Johnson, who kept an album of fabric scraps from her new clothes her whole life long.[1] Austen's letters often prove a starting point for discussion of how clothing was made and at what speed, how and why garments moved about the country, practices of alteration and updating, the effects of new technologies, the importance of textiles, encounters with retail spaces, and ways of sharing fashion and

Chawton Thursday Feb: 4.

My dear Cassandra

Your letter was truely welcome & I am much obliged to you all for your praise; it came at a right time, for I had had some fits of disgust; — our 2d evening's reading to Miss Benn had not pleased me so well, but I beleive something must be attributed to my Mother's too rapid way of getting on — & tho' she perfectly understands the Characters herself, she cannot speak as they ought. — Upon the whole however I am quite vain enough & well satisfied enough. — The work is rather too light & bright & sparkling; — it wants shade; — it wants to be stretched out here & there with a long Chapter — of sense if it could be had, if not of solemn specious nonsense — about something unconnected with the story, an Essay on Writing, a critique on Walter Scott, or the history of Buonaparté — or anything that would form a contrast & bring the reader with increased delight to the play fulness & Epigrammatism of the general stile. — I doubt your quite agreeing with me here. — I know your starched Notions. — The caution observed at Steventon with regard to the possession of the Book, is an agreable surprise to me, & I heartily wish it may be the means of saving you from everything unpleasant; — but you must be prepared for the Neighbourhood being perhaps already informed of there being such a work in the World, & in the Chawton World! Dummer will do that, you know. — It was spoken of here one morn? when Mrs D. called with Miss Benn. — The greatest blunder in the Printing that I have met with is in Page 220 — Vol. 3. where two speeches are made into one. — There might as well have been No Suppers at Longbourn, but I suppose it was the remains of Mrs Bennet's old Meryton habits. — I am sorry for your disappointment about Manydown, & fear this week must be a heavy one. As far as one may venture to judge at a distance of 20 miles

purchases with one's family and acquaintance networks – all essential aspects of the larger vestimentary Regency world the author lived in.

Like all women of her gentry class, Austen dressed to a pattern of ensemble with variations according to season and occasion. She would start with a shift (Chapter 7) next to the body, then add bust support in the form of corset or stays. These undergarments came in many variations during this transitional period, when stays moved from the eighteenth century's stiff inverted v-shape to the soft, more curving nineteenth-century style with gusseted cups for the breasts (fig. 0.2). Although it is often claimed that British Regency women discarded corsets, this is a myth. Austen never mentions stays she owned in the letters, but she definitely wore them. Over this foundation was at least one petticoat (chapter 7), the quantity and type dependent on the temperature and time of day. Next came the gown (Chapter 1) – 'dress' at the time usually meant the whole ensemble – higher-necked for day, lower-necked for evening, with textiles of corresponding quality. Some kind of outer garment (Chapter 2) was added when leaving the house, usually a spencer, pelisse or shawl. The head was covered with a huge range of caps, bonnets and hats (Chapter 3); the hands and arms by gloves (Chapter 5); the feet and legs by stockings (Chapter 7) and appropriate shoes (chapter 4). Many other small accessories (Chapters 4 and 5) and jewellery (Chapter 6) completed an outfit, and private clothing (Chapter 7) rounded out a wardrobe.

Austen rarely wrote about the cost of the clothing she mentions. Here and there are prices for specific pieces, so I have contextualised these with prices from contemporary accounts where possible. The clearest view we have of her expenditure on clothes is the record she kept of cash accounts for 1807 in the back of a diary. Austen started the year with £50.15s.6d and ended it with £6.4s.6d.[2] 'Cloathing and Pocket' was her largest area of expense, totalling £13.19s.3d, or 27.4 per cent of her annual cash. The related cost of having her laundry done was the next largest expenditure, at £9.5s.11½d (18.3 per cent). Nearly half of Austen's money was spent on clothes and their upkeep, and, as the letters show, a significant part of her energy, thought and consumption habits was too. The getting and maintenance of clothing was no trivial matter for Regency women, nor the 'frivolous distinction' Austen very ironically dubbed it in *Northanger Abbey*. It is also difficult to assess how many clothes, especially gowns, a woman had in her wardrobe at any one time. While dress acquisition is easy to trace, its disposal is not. We see some of Austen's thinking about what to do with shabby garments, but not when and how they are finally out of wearing circulation.

The names of various textiles in English can differ between countries and from what Regency people understood fabric names to mean. I keep to the period definition, with explanations where needed. The most relevant is muslin. In American English, this now usually means an unbleached plain-weave cheap cotton fabric often used for making test garments or toiles. In other anglophone places, this textile is called calico, which means a decorative printed cotton fabric in the USA. Muslin as the soft, finely woven, predominantly white textile it was in the Regency period is more commonly now called 'mull' in American English. I also do not call the characteristic high waistline an 'Empire' line, as this is anachronistic. The description was not widely applied to the style until around 1907, when French fashion designers brought back under-the-bust waists and dubbed them 'Directoire' or 'Empire' after the earlier historical periods.

Austen's niece Caroline Austen opined in her 1867 book *My Aunt Jane Austen: a Memoir*, that 'there is nothing in [the letters she wrote her family] which I have seen that would be acceptable to the public—They were very well expressed, and they must have been very

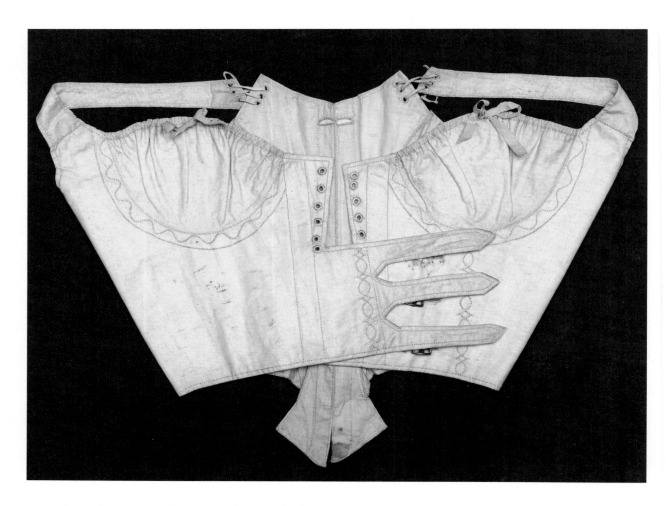

interesting to those who received them—but they detailed chiefly home and family events
… —so that to strangers they could be <u>no</u> transcript of her mind—they would not feel that
they knew her any the better for having read them— … Her letters to Aunt Cassandra
[Austen's beloved sister] … were, I dare say, open and confidential—My Aunt looked them
over and burnt the greater part, (as she told me), 2 or 3 years before her own death.'[3]
This book, among many others, is proof that time has established an opinion strongly
opposing Caroline's. I have mined Austen's epistles for the very finest of details, sometimes
mere threads, and tried to know her – or at least her wardrobe – better, having read them
extremely closely.

   These surviving letters have been edited and published as complete collections over
the last 90 years, first by Dr R. W. Chapman in 1932 and 1952, and then by renowned
Austen scholar Deirdre Le Faye in 1995 and 2011. I have used both the physical and digital
versions of the fourth edition (published online in 2015), and retained Austen's frequently
idiosyncratic spelling and capitalisation. Le Faye did a huge amount of contextual research
in her editing, and her notes have been very useful to giving more detail to Austen's

wardrobe. Given that only around 5 percent of the writer's letters survive, and they mention dress and textiles in passing, alongside many other subjects, it is remarkable how much of her clothing and accessories can be found in these partial sources. Austen was far more discursive about clothes in correspondence than in prose. All letters included here were written from Jane to her sister Cassandra unless specified: when they were apart, they wrote to each other about every three or four days. Everyone who comes to Austen through her letters must also at some point sigh wistfully and imagine what riches pertinent to their particular research perspective were rendered to ash by sisterly concern. Perhaps this adds a certain zest to the quest to wring as much as possible out of what remains.

Readers familiar with the letters will know how many clothing and textile details have been omitted. I have been strict in keeping only to those items that were clearly worn by Austen, with some back-up from the reflections of her clothes in Cassandra's wardrobe, as the sisters often had the same clothing. Some of their wider social and dress significance is discussed in my previous book, *Dress in the Age of Jane Austen*, and readers can look there for the bigger picture of Regency clothing practices. Recommendations for other books about Regency dress and textile culture can also be found in a reading list on page 227. We can only speculate about what Austen's wardrobe contained for which there is no record. There is no hint of a riding habit, the popular casual dress, for example. What did she wear to travel in? What was her favourite colour?; what exactly did her hat look like?; did she wear boots or shoes to go on the walks she loved? Unless more letters or images of the author emerge in the future, we will probably never know.

I have learned a lot while writing this book and can now delight in sharing the fruits of that labour with Austen aficionados. Please open these pages as you would pull open drawers, and I hope you enjoy peering into the wardrobe of one of the most famous authors who ever lived.

[1] See Serena Dyer, *Material Lives: Women Makers and Consumer Culture in the 18th Century* (London: Bloomsbury Publishing, 2021); Mary Topham, 'Lady's Account Book', 1810, Chawton House Library, 6641; Jervoise of Herriard Collection, Family and Estate Papers, 44M69/E13/13/3–4, Hampshire Record Office; Diana Sperling, *Mrs Hurst Dancing and Other Scenes from Regency Life 1812–23*, ed. Gordon Mingay (London: Victor Gollancz, 1981); and Barbara Johnson, *A Lady of Fashion: Barbara Johnson's Album of Styles and Fabrics*, ed. Natalie Rothstein (New York: Thames and Hudson, 1987).

[2] *Family Record*, p. 163.

[3] Cited in J. E. Austen-Leigh, *A Memoir of Jane Austen and Other Family Recollections*, ed. Kathryn Sutherland, Oxford World's Classics (Oxford: Oxford University Press, 2008), pp. 173–4. Deirdre Le Faye writes more about this in *Family Record*, p. 270.

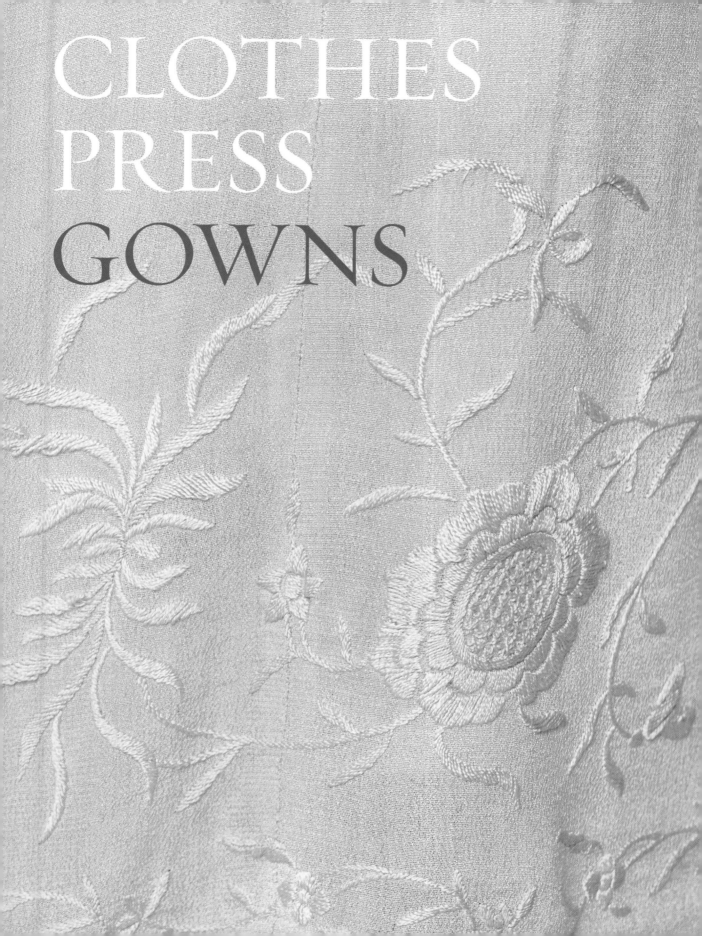

CLOTHES PRESS

GOWNS

1.1 Nicholas Heidelhoff, 'Round gown of light green muslin trimmed with an apple-green ribband', *Gallery of Fashion*, August 1796, Engraving and watercolour on paper. Courtesy of the author

1.2 Printed cotton dress, 1796. The Metropolitan Museum of Art, New York/Gift of Mr Alfred Lunt, 1955

1.3 Green plain-weave cotton dress with printed floral patterns, 1797–1800. Museum of London/ Photograph by the author

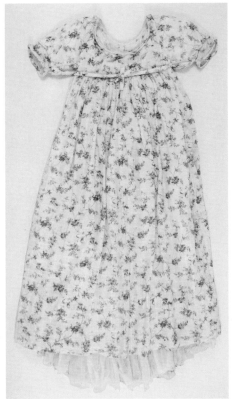

1796
COLOURED GOWN

Letter 4, Thursday 1 September 1796, Rowling [Kent]

'I am sorry to say that my new coloured gown is very much washed out, though I charged everybody to take great care of it. I hope yours is so too.'

The first garment mentioned in the letters is also the first time we hear of the two sisters having the same dress, or a gown made from the same fabric, but it will by no means be the last. Throughout their lives the Austen girls, so close in their hearts, were close in their clothing, having similar or identical dresses. What we explore through Jane's wardrobe gives a glimpse into Cassandra's.

Austen was rarely fully descriptive about her clothes. There is often a colour or textile adjective, but sometimes context is the only clue as to what a gown may have looked like or been made from – qualities equally important to Regency dressers. In this case, while she tells us that the gown is coloured, like the round gown in figure 1.1, there is no mention of its fabric. But in 1796 the only coloured cloth for a dress that could be laundered, and thus end up 'very much washed out', would have been made from cotton or a cotton-linen blend.

Cotton was the clothing wonder fabric of the late eighteenth century. It was initially an expensive import from Indian Ocean areas with a good climate for growing the fibre, but European manufacturers soon started clamouring for their own cut of the lucrative industry. Cotton's great appeal for consumers lay in its washability, colourfastness and ability to imitate decorative silks and other expensive textiles in a much cheaper form (fig. 1.2). So much did Europeans crave muslin, printed chintzes, calicoes and more, that the import and sale of these Eastern cotton fabrics was banned in Britain in 1700 and 1721 as a form of economic protectionism for domestic weavers of wool and linen, and coarser versions of the textiles. These Calico Acts were repealed only in 1774, after which imports and local manufacture, and hence the widespread use of cotton fabrics, blossomed

rapidly. British manufacturers' quests to compete with imported cotton fabrics spurred on many of the period's textile technology innovations in spinning, weaving and finishing, as part of the larger industrial revolution, until their production dominated globally by the second quarter of the nineteenth century. From the 1770s, cotton appears with increasing regularity in women's wardrobes, and was firmly established by around 1800 (fig. 1.3).

The letter incidentally affirms that Austen did not do her own laundry. It was common for middling sorts and gentry women to send washing out, or have servants do it, as it was hot, hard, heavy business. In her 1807 yearly account, Austen recorded that sending out her washing had cost her £9.5s.11½d, or 18.3 per cent of her disposable income.[1] A set of 'Instructions to the Laundry-Maid' from 1817 explains: 'As the laundry-maid is the person to whom the care of the linen is committed, it is most common for her to be brought up to it', and that 'where linen is either badly washed, or not properly got up, it soon wears; and one bad washing does more hurt than ten times using it'.[2] Who was the awkward laundress for the Austens?

[1] *Family Record*, p. 163.
[2] J. A. Stewart, *The Female Instructor; or, Young Woman's Companion: Being a Guide to All the Accomplishments Which Adorn the Female Character … With Other Valuable Information in the Branches of Domestic Economy* (Liverpool: Nuttall, Fisher and Dixon, 1817), p. 376.

1796
'SURPLICE' GOWN

Letter 4, Thursday 1 September 1796, Rowling [Kent]

'I have had my new gown made up, and it really makes a very superb surplice.'

For a short sentence, this second entry into Austen's wardrobe contains a few things to unpack. The first is that a 'gown' in the Regency period meant both the length of fabric intended for a dress, and the finished dress itself, as we shall see repeatedly through the following pages. Sometimes it can be hard to read which sense is meant in a period source. Austen's 'new gown', then, is either the fabric that has been 'made up', or the garment which was sewn from the length of fabric.

The next inference to be made is that the textile is white and light, and the dress voluminous enough to resemble a surplice, the loose wide-sleeved linen garment worn as a liturgical vestment in the Western Christian church. This tallies with fashion of the mid-1790s, newly losing its natural waistline yet retaining the volume and drapery of earlier years. The volume of fabric, with close-fitting sleeves, is shown in figure 1.4 in a c.1797 wedding dress. The effect of a dressed ensemble including typically voluminous neckerchief and fuller sleeves, more like the clerical garment, is seen in a drawing made the previous year (fig. 1.5). The remark is characteristic of the witty tone Austen's letters often take, and typical in that we cannot tell whether she thinks being a 'superb surplice' is a good thing or not.

There may be a more fashionable link being made here as well. In American English, a 'surplice bodice' has referred to a dress or top front with two parts that cross over each other since the mid-nineteenth century, and continues in use today. While I have not found any Regency usage of this term in clothing – not least because the clerical context dominates searches – there was a distinct fashion for cross-over front gowns in the late 1790s, particularly 1797–8. Although the style is in Austen's future at the date of this letter, it may be that discussion and construction were already drifting

surplice-wards at this point. Cross-over fronts continued throughout the Regency period.

The lovely red-spotted cotton dress in figure 1.6 was likely cut down and retrimmed in the 1810s from a 1790s dress, as garment expert Mackenzie Sholtz discovered in making a pattern from the object.[3] It still retains the structure of the popular crossed front from the earlier period.

Opposite
1.4 White wedding dress of nettle cloth, probably worn by Baroness Eleonora Sophie Rantzau (b. 1779) when she married Count Preben Bille-Brahe, Hvedholm, in 1797. National Museum of Denmark/Photographs by Peter Danstrøm and Roberto Fortuna

[3] *Personal communication.*

1.5 Samuel de Wilde, *A Lady,
full length, Wearing a Blue Sash and
Holding a Fan*, watercolour, graphite
and coloured pencil on paper,
38.4 × 22.7 cm, 1795. Yale Center
for British Art, New Haven, CT/
Paul Mellon Collection

1.6 Printed cotton dress,
American, 1810–15.
Private collection

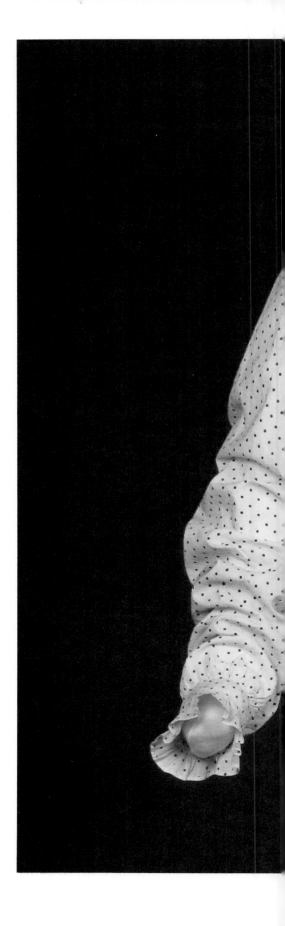

1.7 Man's waistcoat (detail), made from striped stuff with a worsted weft and cotton warp, 1810s. Courtesy of the author

1.8 Gown of cream silk and worsted stuff trimmed with silk fringing, 1805–10. Museum of London/Photograph by the author

1.9 'A Brown Stuff Gown, eight yards', Barbara Johnson's album, February 1813. © Victoria and Albert Museum, London

1798
STUFF GOWN

Letter 13, Saturday 1 – Sunday 2 December 1798, Steventon

'I find great comfort in my stuff gown, but I hope you do not wear yours too often.'

From this letter, we can see that Jane and Cassandra Austen both had stuff gowns. Stuff itself can be a difficult textile to pin down, as the name was widely applied and dates in use from the Middle Ages. In general, it was a thin, light fabric, lighter than the 'cloth' used for tailored garments (fig. 1.7), and made from plain- or twill-woven long-staple wool, known as worsted (fig. 1.8). Contemporary accounts also confusingly include silk stuffs, which can mean a textile woven from two fibres, as was common. Stuff was popular for day dress, 'undress' or 'dishabille' – the clothing one wore before formally 'dressing' for dinner and other evening events. 'Worsted' as a term for the fabric, as well as the fibre from which it was made, was slowly superseding 'stuff' by the Regency period.

Stuff was considered a plain, dependable item, as Austen's finding 'comfort' in her gown evokes. As early as 1782, the rise in popularity of cottons, calicoes and muslins caused one commentator to complain that 'the ladies think no more of woollens and stuffs than of an old almanack'.[4] Even though the *Repository of Arts* was of a similar opinion when in 1809 it pronounced stuff gowns 'completely vulgar', in 1810 the monthly women's magazine *La Belle Assemblée* told its readers that 'dinner dresses are mostly made of cloth or stuff, high in the neck'.[5] Stuff was a textile with a wide range of applications that never fell wholly out of fashion. Other period uses include men's waistcoats, servants' dress and charity clothing.

Years later, in 1813, Austen wrote to Cassandra of imagining her being 'in the Kitchen in your Morning stuff',[6] showing the sisters had gowns of the light, warm material for daywear, like the later dress in figure 1.9.[7] Being in the kitchen evokes a practicality to the woollen fibre's hard-wearing and fire-resistant qualities. Because worsted takes dyestuffs well, the gowns could have been any colour, though a shade with some depth to it would also show dirt and marks less. A sample of brown stuff bought in February of the same year is shown in figure 1.9, where 8 yards cost 2*s*.4*d* per yard at half an ell (22½ in./57 cm) wide.

[4] John Styles, 'Spinners and the Law: Regulating Yarn Standards in the English Worsted Industries, 1550–1800', *Textile History*, 44.2 (2013), p. 164.
[5] Trevor Fawcett, 'Argonauts and Commercial Travellers: The Foreign Marketing of Norwich Stuffs in the Later Eighteenth Century', *Textile History*, 16.2 (1985), p. 169. Original quote: F. Moore in 1782, cited in M. M. Edwards, *The Growth of the British Cotton Trade, 1780–1815* (Manchester: Manchester University Press, 1967), p. 33.
[6] Deb Salisbury, ed., *Fabric à La Romantic Regency: A Glossary of Fabrics from Original Sources 1795–1836* (Abbott, TX: The Mantua-Maker Historical Sewing Patterns, 2013), p. 262.
[7] Letter 80, 4 February 1813.

1.10 Nicholas Heideloff, 'Robe and epaulettes of yellow striped muslin, the whole trimmed with blue and black diamond pattern satin riband', *Gallery of Fashion*, April 1798. Courtesy of the author

1.11 Open robe of pale blue silk woven with repeating star pattern in silver thread, white silk short sleeves decorated with silk cords and gimp, *c.*1800 [record shot]. © Victoria and Albert Museum, London

1.12 'Ladies Dress Maker' (detail), from *The Book of Trades*, 1804, engraving on paper. Rijksmuseum, Amsterdam

1798
ROBE

Letter 14, Tuesday 18 – Wednesday 19 December 1798, Steventon

> '—*I beleive I <u>shall</u> make my new gown like my robe, but the back of the latter is all in a peice with the tail, & will 7 yards enable me to copy it in that respect?*'

Austen spends some time writing about her new gown, which is discussed in detail on page 27. Wanting to make it like her robe tells us she already has such a garment in her wardrobe. Robes became especially popular after the rise in waistline of the mid-1790s. They were a kind of overgown that required a petticoat skirt underneath, as they were open at the front, shorter than ankle-length, or both. The fashion plate in figure 1.10 shows a robe of yellow striped muslin with a cross-over front and open skirt revealing a petticoat also of muslin with yellow ribbon trim. The long 'tail' or train is the kind that Austen's robe has 'all of a peice' with the bodice, meaning there is no seam at the back waistline, unlike the brocaded silk example of around 1800 in figure 1.11. The cut of robes worked very well over the straighter shapes of skirts accompanying the high waistline, as they could flow down and over a form more vertical than the rounder volumes of the earlier part of the decade.

The comparison with an existing gown points to a common strategy for making Regency women's clothes: copy one that already works in the matter of fit, fashion or both. Pattern gowns, as they were called, were an effective way of building on previous sartorial success. A gown that fit well was taken as a model and copied in fabric to make a pattern for a new one. Using cotton or linen lining fabric to do this allowed the fitting bodice section, or 'body' as it was called, to be used as a lining on the finished gown. Harriet Smith in *Emma* fusses in Ford's, the local shop selling drapery and haberdashery, about where to send a package of goods based on where her pattern gown is located.[8] *The Duties of a Lady's Maid* instructed in 1825 that 'When you have once procured a pattern … which fits a lady's figure, and this you ought

to make of soft paper or cloth, you will not require to measure a fresh one for every new dress' (fig. 1.12).[9] Another advantage of pattern gowns was that the construction had already been worked out and tested at least once. The maker was copying the dressmaking process as much as the patterning.

For the strategic, pattern gowns could also offer a cheaper, material version of fashion to borrow. The Steele sisters in *Sense and Sensibility* are opportunistic and shameless about what they can get from others, as their surname homophonically implies. At Lady Middleton's, they are written as 'taking patterns of some elegant new dress, in which her appearance the day before had thrown them into unceasing delight'.[10] Copying a gown better than they could afford – possibly fresh from London – is a way of maintaining their 'very smart' dress on very small budgets, Lucy Steele being an 'active, contriving manager, uniting at once a desire of smart appearance with the utmost frugality, and ashamed to be suspected of half her economical practices'.[11] In copying her own garment, Austen was being equally practical but not at all venial.

[8] *Emma*, vol. II, ch. xi.
[9] *The Duties of a Lady's Maid: With Directions for Conduct, and Numerous Receipts for the Toilette* (London: James Bulcock, 1825), p. 318.
[10] *Sense and Sensibility*, vol. I, ch. xxi.
[11] *Sense and Sensibility*, vol. I, ch. xxi; vol. III, ch. xii.

1.13 Nicholas Heideloff, 'Evening Dress ... Pink muslin robe with
a Turkish front, the whole trimmed with white lace; short close sleeves'
(detail), *Gallery of Fashion*, August 1797. Courtesy of the author

1.14 'Opera dress ... Robe and petticoat of white or worked-coloured
muslin. Confined in front with a belt of the same', *Magazine of Female
Fashions of London and Paris*, June 1798. Engraving and watercolour
on paper. Rijksmuseum, Amsterdam/Purchased with the support of the
Flora Fonds/Rijksmuseum Fonds

1798
NEW GOWN

Letter 14, Tuesday 18 – Wednesday 19 December 1798, Steventon

> *'—I beleive I <u>shall</u> make my new gown like my robe, but the back of the latter is all in a peice with the tail, & will 7 yards enable me to copy it in that respect?'*

In discussions over three letters about how to make her new gown, Austen never mentions its colour. All that can be inferred is that it is *not* blue, as she mentions later that 'My Gown is made very much like my blue one, which you always told me sat very well' (see p. 33).[12] This addition to her wardrobe caused Austen some consternation: '—I cannot determine what to do about my new Gown; I wish such things were to be bought ready made.—I have some hopes of meeting Martha [Lloyd, a close friend] at the Christening at Deane next Tuesday, & shall see what she can do for me.'[13] Here she highlights a central aspect of Regency dress: for middle-class consumers, gowns were custom-made, whether they liked it or not. There was a thriving second-hand clothes market, but this was usually patronised by people lower down the social scale than the Austens. It was simply not possible to go to a store and buy a whole gown, all made up in the latest fashion, not least because it needed to be fitted to the individual body by the mantua-maker, or dressmaker (see fig. 1.12), as these professional women were rapidly becoming known.

All the details of clothing had to be decided from the fabric up, which is one reason why the length of fabric was also known as a 'gown'. Austen appears to have bought 7 yards and is now trying to work out if it will be enough, especially as the robe she wants to emulate (see p. 25) has no waist seam at the back, the bodice being 'all in a peice' with the train or 'tail'. The cut of the neckline, the depth at the back, the length of sleeves and any decoration of the sleeve heads, the number of breadths of fabric included, where and how to gather the skirt to the bodice, and, after all that, how to embellish or trim the finished dress: all these choices had to be considered in sewing a gown, in relationship to what suited the wearer, what she liked, and what was in fashion (fig. 1.13). No wonder Austen sought the opinion of close acquaintance and wanted 'to have something suggested which will give me no trouble of thought or direction'.[14]

She gritted her teeth and 'got over the dreadful epocha of Mantuamaking much better than I expected'. Writing to Cassandra over 8–9 January in the new year, Austen informed her sister that, after all her thought, the blue gown served as a template 'with only these variations;—the sleeves are short, the wrap fuller, the apron comes over it, & a band of the same completes the whole'.[15] A suggestion of these details is shown in figure 1.14. Using a pattern gown to copy (see p. 25) appears to have been a strategic way to help combat Austen's decision fatigue.

[12] Letter 17, 8–9 January 1799.
[13] Letter 15, 24 December 1798.
[14] Letter 15, 24 December 1798.
[15] Letter 17, 8–9 January 1799.

1798
COARSE SPOT MUSLIN GOWN

Letter 15, Monday 24 December 1798, Steventon

'that you should meditate the purchase of a new muslin Gown [is] delightful circumstances.—I am determined to buy a handsome one whenever I can, & I am so tired & ashamed of half my present stock that I even blush at the sight of the wardrobe which contains them.—But I will not be much longer libelled by the possession of my coarse spot, I shall turn it into a petticoat very soon.'

Of all the varieties of cotton fabric that were increasingly popular and available during the Regency period, muslin was without question the pre-eminent. It is the textile most associated with the Regency, and with the change in dominant fibre from silk to cotton that developed from the 1780s. The light, airy, usually white fabric (fig. 1.15) had been manufactured in Indian regions, especially Bengal, for millennia. The passion for the textile imports engendered in European consumers caused their banning in Britain until 1774 to help local manufacturers. As scholar Clair Hughes puts it, 'muslins were to the [period] what synthetic fibres were to the mid-twentieth century – they transformed life'.[16] In Britain, muslin was originally the term for finely spun cotton yarns, and the cloths were given names to identify the weave, such as cambric muslin (see p. 45) or jaconet muslin. In Austen's case, either the muslin itself, or the embroidered (fig. 1.16) or printed spot decoration, could be 'coarse'.

It was the popularity of muslin, in particular, that hastened attempts to develop a competitive equivalent product from British manufacturers, especially from the 1790s when fashion fully embraced the textile. We can see glimpses of the struggle for market dominance in myriad ways. The *Gallery of Fashion* was patriotically identifying a round dress as being made of 'British muslin' in 1798. Austen's own most famous fictional muslin implicitly centres on domestic versus imported products. *Northanger Abbey* was published posthumously in 1817, when British muslins were starting to dominate, but was finished by around 1799 at the height of muslin's popularity. Much of the novel's dealings with fashions match what Austen would have been wearing in her own early twenties and need to be read as reflecting this earlier period. Mrs Allen, fashion-minded chaperone to heroine Catherine Morland, has remarked earlier on how she is wearing 'such a delicate muslin'. When she interrupts Catherine's conversation with hero Henry Tilney, it is because a pin has torn a hole in it and 'this is a favourite gown, though it cost but nine shillings a yard':[17]

'That is exactly what I should have guessed it, madam,' said Mr. Tilney, looking at the muslin.

'Do you understand muslins, sir?'

'Particularly well; I always buy my own cravats, and

29

page 28
1.15 Thomas Beach, *Portrait of a Girl from the Burnaby Family*, oil on canvas, 71.5 × 61.5 cm, 1801. Leicestershire County Council Museums Service

1.16 Girl's dress of white Indian muslin with embroidered spots, altered from a larger dress, 1815–20. Museum of London/ Photograph by the author

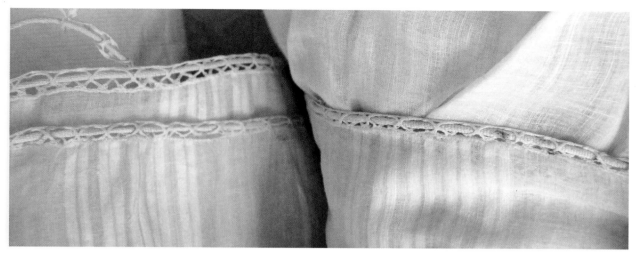

1.17 Top of a skirt gathered
with a cord through a net band,
c.1800. Museum of London/
Photograph by the author

am allowed to be an excellent judge; and my sister
has often trusted me in the choice of a gown. I bought
one for her the other day, and it was pronounced to be
a prodigious bargain by every lady who saw it. I gave
but five shillings a yard for it, and a true Indian
muslin.'

Mrs. Allen was quite struck by his genius. 'Men
commonly take so little notice of those things,' said
she; 'I can never get Mr. Allen to know one of my
gowns from another.'[18]

While Tilney might be pulling her leg, the scene
nevertheless continues with his assessment of Catherine's
gown, and muslin's versatility, 'always turn[ing] to some
account or other', and the characters keep talking on
muslins – Mrs Allen seriously, Tilney satirically – until it is
time to dance again. We too shall return to the 'subject of
muslins' throughout this book.[19]

Figure 1.17 shows an inventive way to turn a muslin
gown into a petticoat. An open-lace strip has been
attached to the top of the fabric and a cord run through it,
allowing the skirt to gather up smoothly and reducing the
bulk of a waistband or turning of fabric. See page 219 for
more discussion of petticoats.

[16] Clair Hughes, 'Talk about Muslin: Jane Austen's Northanger Abbey', in
Hughes, *Dressed in Fiction* (London: Berg, 2005), p. 36.
[17] For more discussion of this scene, see Hughes 2005.
[18] *Northanger Abbey*, vol. I, ch. iii.
[19] For scholarly discussion of muslin in Austen, see Hughes 2005; see also
Lauren Miskin, '"True Indian Muslin" and the Politics of Consumption in
Jane Austen's Northanger Abbey', *Journal for Early Modern Cultural Studies*,
15.2 (2015), pp. 5–26.

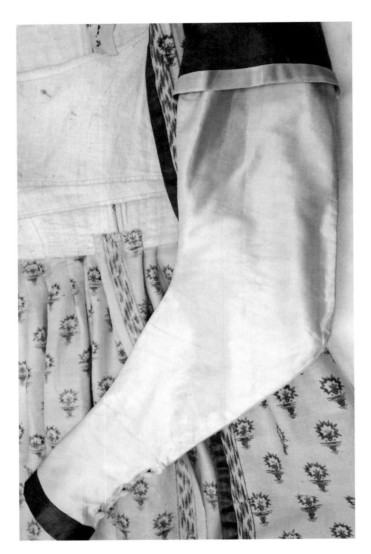

1.18 Woman's gown, English, cream silk/wool, block-printed with the pattern of an Indian shawl, silk sleeves, 1795–9. Courtesy of the author

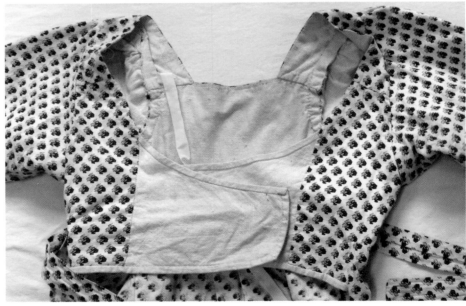

1.19 Printed cotton day dress, *c*.1805. Museum of Fashion, Bath/Photograph by the author

1799
BLUE GOWN

Letter 17, Tuesday 8 – Wednesday 9 January 1799, Steventon

'—My Gown is made very much like my blue one, which you always told me sat very well, with only these variations;— the sleeves are short, the wrap fuller, the apron comes over it'

Having looked at how Austen's new gown was both like and unlike her blue gown (see p. 27), what might that reference garment itself have looked like? If the new gown's sleeves were short, the blue gown's were most likely long. In the 1790s, long sleeves were cut from two pieces, with seams at the mid-centre front, and the same place at the back, just like men's coat sleeves. The sleeve was also cut to match the shape of the arm, with a slight bend at the elbow (fig. 1.18). This clever construction technique did a few things. First, it allowed some extra room for the wearer to move their elbow. Second, it changed the direction of the grain in the upper and lower sleeve, and thus its fit. The straight grain of fabric is the way it is woven, with warp and weft straight, and at 90 degrees to each other. But when the fabric is turned to 45 degrees, on the bias (often spelled 'byas' in Regency texts), the fabric gains more stretch and movement the closer it is to the true diagonal, as the threads are no longer restricted to their straight tension.

All of this is a technical way of saying that, by clever cutting, mantua-makers of the time could work in some elasticity to long sleeves. This made them fit more closely to the arm, with less restriction of movement. The further normal inclusion of a built-in gusset, or extra fabric under the arm, resulted in tight long sleeves with more movement in them than any modern blazer or jacket sleeve. In historic dress, what looks tight is not necessarily restrictive when worn.

Another interesting point here is how Austen speaks of 'the apron' coming over the wrap. This could be the separate garment, but because she mentions it when talking about the construction of her gown, it is the front-fall closure that developed in the late 1790s as one of the new developments in dressmaking (fig. 1.19). This is useful because, while the style was widely prevalent and is a hallmark of Regency dress, the terms 'bib-front', 'apron-front' and 'fall-front' are all modern ways to describe the technique, as it is unclear from Regency sources how they described it.

1.20 Dresses, robes and petticoats of white muslin in various styles, 'Ranelagh July 1798', *The Fashions of London and Paris During the Years 1798, 1799 and 1800,* etching and watercolour on paper. Rijksmuseum, Amsterdam/Purchased with the support of the Flora Fonds/ Rijksmuseum Fonds

1.21 'Ladies Dresses for 1799', from a pocket book or memorandum. New York Public Library

1.22 Anne Frankland Lewis, 'Collection of English Original Watercolour Drawings', plate 24, watercolour on paper 36.8 × 25.7 cm, 1799. Los Angeles County Museum of Art/Costume Council Fund/www.lacma.org

1799
BEST GOWN

Letter 19, Friday 17 May 1799, Bath: 13 Queen Square

'I am rather impatient to know the fate of my best gown, but I suppose it will be some days before Frances can get through the Trunk—In the mean time, I am with many thanks for your trouble in making it'

What 'fate' might Austen's best gown be subjected to? What might have happened on the way from somewhere to somewhere – Steventon and Bath? – in its travelling trunk that may have affected it? Is Frances the Austens' maid? Was it a 'best' gown previous to this letter, or is Austen again using the sense of 'gown' as a length of fabric? If so, was the fabric already 'best', or merely intended for 'best'? Alas, there are no definite answers. Since she thanks Cassandra 'for your trouble in making it', this could imply the reference is to a textile piece, or perhaps it means that Cassandra did actually sew up or alter a whole gown for Austen, which would be a rare example of the sisters actively constructing clothing. Two years later Austen told Cassandra, 'When you have made Martha's bonnet you must make her a cloak of the same sort of materials' – a hint of her garment-sewing prowess.[20] Other letters that did not survive may have given us a better idea to what degree the sisters engaged in making clothes. The sentence extends the thanks to include Cassandra's 'marking my silk stockings' (see p. 215), which at the very least means her sister has been writing or embroidering initials upon the legwear, and therefore doing some kind of handwork (an example of Austen's own initialling embroidery work is seen on the handkerchief on page 186.

Instead, to imagine what this dress of Austen's may have looked like, let us indulge in some pleasant speculation based upon fashion images of the time and what details were *haute ton*. The risen waistline dominated fashion (fig. 1.20) as it would do until the late 1810s. The way all the dresses in this image are described as 'robes of white muslin' shows its dominance. Trains were usual in the evening, shown attached from the shoulders and 'tied loosely on the left side, with a silk cord' on the central figure (fig. 1.20). A cross-over or wrap detail on the bodice also appears frequently in fashion illustrations (fig. 1.21). 'Short' sleeves still reach nearer the elbow than they would do in the next decade, with a little puff at the top and volume often created by draped fabric over the top of the fitted base (fig. 1.22), described as 'full epaulets' on the woman with her back to us in figure 1.20.

[20] Letter 37, 21–22 May 1801.

1.23 'Morning Dress ... Pink muslin
gown, with stomacher front laced
with cord ... Gown blue cambric,
spotted muslin; white muslin cloak
trimmed with lace', *The Lady's
Monthly Museum*, May 1800.
Public domain

1.24 'Walking Dress ... 1. Round hat
of green and white chip ... Round
dress of white muslin ... 2. Habit
of bottle green, or dark brown ...
3. Dress of white muslin; the body
made to button in front, with the
collar to button occasionally... Hat
of white chip and yellow crape',
*Magazine of Female Fashions of London
and Paris*, August 1800, hand-
coloured engraving on paper, 21.3 ×
13 cm. Rijksmuseum, Amsterdam/
Purchased with the support of the
Flora Fonds/Rijksmuseum Fonds

1800
GOWN OF
UNCERTAIN TASTE

Letter 23, Saturday 25 – Monday 27 October 1800, Steventon

'—I like the Gown very much & my Mother thinks it very ugly.'

The first we hear of this contentious gown is when Austen thanks Cassandra for buying the gown length of fabric as part of a large set of commissions from London (see pp. 151, 161 and 179). However, we can track it through some subsequent letters to find out more about its part in the Austens' lives.

A few days later, on 1 November, Austen ribbed Cassandra that 'Your abuse of our Gowns amuses, but does not discourage me; I shall take mine to be made up next week, & the more I look at it, the better it pleases me'.[21] This tells us that Cassandra has bought the same or similar fabric and, like Mrs Austen, has a touch of buyer's remorse about her choice. Austen either felt the opposite or was being contrary to amuse herself. A week later, she was still disagreeing with her sister and persuading her to like it, writing, 'I cannot possibly oblige you by not wearing my gown, because I have it made up on purpose to wear it a great deal, & as the discredit will be my own, I feel the less regret.—You must learn to like it yourself & make it up at Godmersham; it may easily be done; it is only protesting it to be very beautiful, & you will soon think it so.'[22]

Austen ploughed ahead with having her gown made up by a dressmaker called Miss Summers, who completed it by 20 November, a turnaround time of 11 days or fewer. The uncertainty about the garment continued after its construction. Although 'Miss Summers has made my gown very well indeed, & I grow more & more pleased with it', family opinion was divided: 'Charles does not like it, but my father & Mary do; my Mother is very much reconciled to it, & as for James, he gives it the preference over every thing of the kind he ever saw; in proof of

which I am desired to say that if you like to sell yours, Mary [James's wife] will buy it.'[23] A page later, though, 'Charles likes my Gown now.'

Despite the comfort of an offer to buy Cassandra's gown length within the family, meaning she would lose no money if she decided against keeping the controversial piece, she still apparently required some convincing. Austen provided this in the form of testimony from their friend Martha Lloyd, mentioning at the end of November that 'She is pleased with my Gown, & particularly bids me say that if you could see me in it for five minutes, she is sure you would be eager to make up your own.'[24] There the matter ends in the surviving letters.

We have no definite information from any of Austen's references to the Miss Summers gown as to what kind of fabric it was made from or what level of formality it fulfilled, although being made 'to wear a great deal' indicates day dress, possibly a morning or walking gown (figs 1.23 and 1.24). It therefore could appear in later letters described by colour or textile. The lack of letters between May 1801 (Letter 38) and September 1804 (Letter 39), and of any references to her own gowns before her 1808 pelisse (see p. 101), leaves a gap of seven years, by which time this much-discussed gown would likely have left or been worn out from Austen's wardrobe.

[21] Letter 24, 1 November 1800.
[22] Letter 25, 8–9 November 1800.
[23] Letter 27, 20–21 November 1800.
[24] Letter 28, 30 November – 1 December 1800.

1.25 Cotton muslin dress,
American, 1800–5. Brooklyn
Museum Costume Collection at
The Metropolitan Museum of Art,
Gift of the Brooklyn Museum,
2009; Gift of the Jason and Peggy
Westerfield Collection, 1969

1800
MUSLIN BALL GOWN

Letter 24, Saturday 1 November 1800, Steventon

'I wore at the Ball your favourite gown, a bit of muslin of he same round my head, border'd with Mrs Cooper's band— & one little Comb.'

Austen attended the Basingstoke assembly ball on 30 October, comprising 'nearly 60 people, & sometimes we had 17 couple', where she danced nine out of ten dances, although 'There was a scarcity of Men in general, & a still greater scarcity of any that were good for much.'[25] While the muslin gown may not necessarily have been a specific ball gown, it would have been fine-quality evening attire of some kind as was universally popular around 1800. Was the gown Cassandra's own favourite gown that her sister had borrowed, or Cassandra's favourite of the gowns belonging to Austen?

This dress appears just after the years when she first wrote *Susan*, which would become *Northanger Abbey*. Catherine Morland attends a public ball at the Lower Rooms in Bath, where she dances with Henry Tilney, wearing a 'sprigged muslin robe with blue trimmings' (like Austen's 1798 robe; see p. 25) and 'plain black shoes'.[26] Her chaperone Mrs Allen also wears a 'delicate muslin' to the evening event. The same novel gives an idea of how evening dress could be easily transformed for dancing when Austen writes how Catherine and her friend Isabella 'pinned up each other's train for the dance'.[27] A trained muslin evening dress is shown in figure 1.25. A further reference distinguishes between 'dressed and undressed balls' in Bath, referring to the degree of formality required in the attendees' ensembles.[28]

Mrs Cooper was their aunt, Mrs Austen's sister.[29] She died in 1783, so the 'band' Austen wears is at least 17 years old by this date. It may have been embroidered or made by the aunt, or simply a present. Austen was no more than eight years old when Mrs Cooper died, so it appears more likely the band came through her mother or sister. Figure 1.26 shows an elegant Parisian bit of muslin around the head, with lace, and figure 1.27 is a self-portrait by Anne Frankland Lewis of 1802, also in a muslin evening dress with fabric twisted around her hair, evoking Austen's appearance.[30]

[25] Letter 24, 1 November 1800.
[26] *Northanger Abbey*, vol. I, ch. iii.
[27] *Northanger Abbey*, vol. I, ch. v.
[28] *Northanger Abbey*, vol. I, ch. v.
[29] See *Family Record*, pp. 48–9.
[30] For more on this artist, see Dyer 2021.

1.28 Gown made *c*.1800, of
pink printed cotton textile, dated
c.1793–6. Museum of London/
Photograph by the author

1.29 'Walking Dress', *The Fashions
of London and Paris During the Years
1801, 1802 and 1803*, 1801,
hand-coloured engraving. Yale
Center for British Art, New Haven,
CT/Paul Mellon Collection

1801
PINK GOWN

Letter 33, Sunday 25 January 1801, Steventon

'I shall want two new coloured gowns for the summer, for my pink one will not do more than clear me from Steventon.'

Cassandra had bought Austen a pair of 'not particularly beautiful' pink shoes in October 1800 (see p. 161) and once again Austen is discussing what her sister can purchase on her behalf, though she only ends up commissioning one acquisition (p. 45). The shoes may have matched this pink gown, and at least show that the author liked the colour, although these are the only two definite mentions of pink throughout the letters. It may be that another garment or two was made of the delicate hue but is hidden by a lack of adjectives.

The clues Austen leaves about her pink dress are that it is lightweight, for summer, conjuring a garment made from a muslin or other cotton fabric such as calico or cambric muslin (fig. 1.28). The gowns she discusses with Cassandra as replacements (see pp. 45 and 49) are made from brown cambric, and a clouded silk or cotton, and the implication of everyday wear also rules out even a lightweight silk. The pink gown has apparently worn out, or is perhaps slightly too shabby for regular smart wear, indicating it is at least a couple of years old by the 1801 new year. It may be that this dress has also suffered from laundering, like her coloured gown (p. 17), and the colour is faded or the textile itself is degrading.

Fashionable colours around the turn of the century often feature pink, as well as paler, somewhat creamy greens, blues and yellows – fresh, spring-like colours that accorded well with the small, delicate, often floral motifs in fashion across textile and other pattern designs (fig. 1.28). (It was by no means all pale and pretty: dark, dashing, bold tones are also frequently found throughout visual sources and in surviving female dress). By this point, the prevailing Regency trend of wearing a white gown with coloured accessories was established. Bonnets,

caps, gloves, spencers, robes, parasols and shoes all added gorgeous contrasts to the expanses of white cottons and silks so dominating women's dress (fig. 1.29). If the whole gown was a colour, as Austen's seems to have been, then splashes of snowy textiles in the form of handkerchiefs (see p. 185), caps, gloves (p. 170–73), mittens, veils and more provided a reverse point of contrast (fig. 1.29).

1801
BROWN CAMBRIC
MUSLIN GOWN

Letter 33, Sunday 25 January 1801, Steventon

'I shall not trouble you, however, to get more than one of them, and that is to be a plain brown cambric muslin, for morning wear; … Buy two brown ones, if you please, and both of a length, but one longer than the other—it is for a tall woman. Seven yards for my mother, seven yards and a half for me; a dark brown, but the kind of brown is left to your own choice, and I had rather they were different, as it will be always something to say, to dispute about which is the prettiest. They must be cambric muslin.'

Writing in a wintry January, Austen was prudently planning ahead for her summer wardrobe while her sister was in Kent, describing some specific proxy shopping in advance of Cassandra's visit to London and asking her to get one of the two new gowns she has decided on (the second is described on page 49). They have clearly discussed these purchases already. Two weeks beforehand in Letter 30, Austen told Cassandra, 'I beleive you are right in proposing to delay the Cambric muslin, & I submit with a kind of voluntary reluctance.'[31] At the end of Letter 32, in response to a letter of Cassandra's, Austen told her on 22 January that if she wrote again soon, it would be 'to answer your [ques]tion about my Gown'.[32] Three days later, she does.

Austen mentions twice that the gowns for her and her mother must be cambric muslin. Cambric itself was a plain-weave soft linen with a slight lustre achieved by calendaring, or rolling, the surface.[33] Cambric muslin was a dense cotton cloth made in imitation of the

linen textile, rather than the fine airy fabric that muslin connotes (see pp. 29, 39, 67 and 73). Casual references to the fabrics in Regency texts can be confusing to the modern reader, but apparently contemporaries could be similarly uncertain. Elizabeth Rioby, a mantua-maker, was asked as a court witness in 1800 if 'cambric and muslin [were] the same thing?' She replied, 'Sometimes it is called cambric, and sometimes muslin.'[34]

For outer gowns like Austen's, cambric muslin was of a fine weave. The name could also refer to a somewhat coarser cloth, likewise finished with a glaze, often used for linings of garments and headwear. Although Austen asked for a plain fabric, without a pattern, the solid printed surface of a 'muslin' in two shades of blue in figure 1.37 shows how the word could be applied to a range of textiles, and the intensity of colour which could be achieved. Barbara Johnson bought 9 yards of this in 1800 at a cost of 3s.6d per yard (an ell, 45 in./114 cm wide) to make a round gown (see p. 52–3). Figure 1.30

1.31 Louis Vaslet, 'Scene I',
The Spoiled Child (detail), watercolour
with ink and wash, 1802. Yale
Center for British Art, New Haven,
CT/Paul Mellon Collection

shows an 1800 'Round gown of brown printed muslin; long sleeves with full tops'. Both Austen ladies' gowns are a little less full, with the changes in fashion, as even the gown for 'a tall woman' only requires 7½ yards – incidentally, the same amount of fabric as Austen's silk pelisse (see p. 107).

Rioby's testimony is from Old Bailey records. Other trials around this time give indications of the costs of various cambric muslins: 30 yards at a total cost of 35s, six yards valued at 7s, three yards at 4s.[35] The per yard cost was around 1s.2d to 1s.4d – cheaper, and probably coarser, examples than Johnson's and Austen's.

Brown was a practical colour choice for 'morning wear' (fig. 1.31). Dark washable colours showed less dirt and so could brush off the exigencies of poking fires, making breakfast, and similar daily house work of a morning, better than pale ones.

The warm hue was also popular throughout the couple of decades of Regency fashion. It appears throughout Johnson's album and reoccurs for Austen in her brown silk pelisse (see p. 107).

[31] Letter 30, 8–9 January 1801.
[32] Letter 32, 21–22 January 1801.
[33] Sonia Ashmore, *Muslin* (London: V&A Publishing, 2012), p. 158.
[34] *Old Bailey Proceedings Online* (www.oldbaileyonline.org, version 8.0, 24 February 2022), July 1800, trial of Ann Spencer (t18000709-86).
[35] *Old Bailey Proceedings Online* (www.oldbaileyonline.org, version 8.0, 24 February 2022), 16 September 1801, trial of Ann Gill (t18010916-6).

1.32 Peignoir, wrap-over gown of Indian *ikat*, in white with blue and red blurred warps, 1812–14. © Victoria and Albert Museum, London/Given by Messrs Harrods Ltd

1.33 Pattern book with textile samples, 'Clouds and a few satin flounces – 1792' (detail), probably made by Batchelor, Ham & Perigal, Spitalfields, London, 1792–4. © Victoria and Albert Museum, London

1801
YELLOW AND WHITE
CLOUD GOWN

Letter 33, Sunday 25 January 1801, Steventon

*'I shall want two new coloured gowns for the summer …
the other, which is to be a very pretty yellow and white cloud,
I mean to buy in Bath.'*

The second gown Austen wanted to replace her pink gown (see p. 43), in addition to a brown cambric gown (p. 45), was a 'pretty yellow and white cloud'. What she meant by this is a textile where the pattern or stripe has been dyed in the yarn before weaving.

'Cloud' was a textile technique that involved skeins of threads being formed into hanks before weaving, then being 'tightly bound round at certain intervals, previous to their being dyed, in order to prevent the parts so tied from taking the colour', as a contemporary dictionary explains.[36] The yarn itself could be a silk or cotton. Once woven, the effect of the variegated threads 'clouded' the pattern in the finished fabric. Pre-dyeing threads produces a soft and blurred effect in the pattern, most familiar in the South-east Asian textile technique of *ikat*. Figure 1.32 shows a wrap or peignoir made *c*.1812–14 of cotton Indian *ikat* woven especially to appeal to European markets.[37]

The style was better known in silk as *chiné* and was popular from the mid-eighteenth century – especially in France – as part of the increasing fashion influence of Eastern-originating design inspiration. The European techniques were inspired by silks originally woven in China. As the *New Universal Gazetteer* opined in 1798, 'the principal silks manufactured by the Chinese are … napped, flowered, clouded and pinked taffeties'.[38] Sheridan's 1797 dictionary further explains that 'cloud' also refers to the 'veins or stains in stones'.[39] Barbara Johnson's fabric album records a 'Clouded French Sattin Gown' in July 1795 – another summer gown – made

from ten yards of fabric costing seven shillings a yard, which was sewn up at Kensington. The possible effect of the yellow and white colour combination is seen in a clouded silk sample probably woven by London firm Batchelor, Ham & Perigal in Spitalfields in the early 1790s (fig. 1.33). Austen could equally have been looking for a silk or a cotton textile, perhaps with a slight lean towards cotton, as it was for summer.

As to what the finished gown may have looked like, the *Gallery of Fashion* once again presents us with a precisely dated fashion vision. Austen was looking ahead to June 1801, and figure 1.34 shows us a yellow 'round dress' with a crossed or wrap front at just this time, made of yellow muslin, accessorised by a 'Minerva helmet trimmed with a wreath of flowers', apparently made of straw, and set off with blue ribbons, gloves and shoes. Figure 1.35 is a lively rendering of a similarly light, yellow gown, with the skirt tucked up into the pocket slit to reveal the petticoat.

[36] *Sheridan's English Dictionary*, 1797, cited in Salisbury 2013, p. 68.
[37] See Victoria and Albert Museum, Peignoir, 1812–14', *Collections: http://collections.vam.ac.uk/item/O114688/peignoir-unknown/* [accessed 24 February 2022].
[38] Cited in Salisbury 2013, p. 68.
[39] *Sheridan's English Dictionary*, 1797, cited in Salisbury 2013, p. 68.

1.34 Nicholas Heideloff, 'Round dress of yellow muslin; trimming of narrow blue riband round the neck and sleeves', *Gallery of Fashion*, June 1801. Courtesy of the author

1.35 Louis Vaslet, 'Scene V', *The Spoiled Child* (detail), watercolour with ink and wash, 1802. Yale Center for British Art, New Haven, CT/Paul Mellon Collection

1.36 Nicholas Heideloff, 'Morning Dresses [left] Round gown of white muslin, short close sleeves. Ruff of cambric round the neck. [right] Jacket and petticoat of white muslin, tucks round the bottom; short sleeves; the jacket and sleeves trimmed with lace', *Gallery of Fashion*, October 1801. Courtesy of the author

1.37 'A blue muslin round Gown … nine yards, ell wide', Barbara Johnson's album, March 1800. © Victoria and Albert Museum, London

1.38 'A Callicoe round gown, nine yards, yard wide', Barbara Johnson's album, December 1798. © Victoria and Albert Museum, London

1801
MRS MUSSELL'S GOWN

Letter 35, Wednesday 6 May 1801, Bath: The Paragon

'—Mrs Mussell has got my Gown, & I will endeavour to explain what her intentions are.'

Following this opening, Austen gives her longest detailed description of clothing in the entire letters. She continues:

—It is to be a round Gown, with a Jacket, & a Frock front, like Cath: Bigg's to open at the side.— The Jacket is all in one with the body, & comes as far as the pocketholes;—about half a quarter of a yard [4½ in./11.5 cm] deep I suppose all the way round, cut off straight at the Corners, with a broad hem.— No fullness appears either in the Body or the flap;— the back is quite plain, in this form;⊤—and the sides equally so.—The front is sloped round to the bosom & drawn in—& there is to be a frill of the same to put on occasionally when all one's handkercheifs are dirty—which frill must fall back.— She is to put two breadths & a half in the tail, & no Gores;—Gores not being so much worn as they were;—there is nothing new in the sleeves,—they are to be plain, with a fullness of the same falling down & gathered up underneath, just like some of Marthas— or perhaps a little longer.—Low in the back behind, & a belt of the same.—I can think of nothing more— tho' I am afraid of not being particular enough.

What richness if she had been this particular in other surviving letters! There is a lot of clothing information here. Although there is no mention of colour, the next letter adds detail. On 12–13 May, Austen shared that she likes her 'dark gown very much indeed, colour, make, & everything',[40] and on 26–27 May, she writes 'I will engage Mrs Mussell as you desire. She made my dark gown very well', establishing it is the same one described so fully.[41]

The round gowns in figure 1.36 show what a similar style of this date could look like. A round gown was one that was closed at the front skirt, contrasting with the open front prevalent in the 1790s. Unlike the clear cross-over-front in the fashion plate, it is hard to make out quite how the front of Austen's gown was constructed, at least at a remove of two centuries. There is no 'fullness' in either the bodice (body) or the 'flap'. This could be the part that opens to allow the wearer in, yet, the front is also 'sloped round to the bosom & drawn in' to make a 'Frock front', which suggests a gathering somehow through a drawstring instead of a fall- or apron-front. The flap may therefore be part of the built-in jacket.

The inclusion of a jacket and belt describes elements of a day gown. Barbara Johnson also had a quite dark 'blue muslin round Gown' made in Bath just over a year before (fig. 1.37). It continued from her prettily patterned 1798 'Callicoe round gown' (fig. 1.38). Both dresses are for day use, and, incidentally, show the variation and patterning that can be hidden in the word 'blue'. The 'dark' hue of Austen's gown could have been anything.

[40] Letter 36, 12–13 May 1801.
[41] Letter 38, 26–27 May 1801.

1.39 Thomas Lawrence, *Portrait
of Charlotte and Sarah Carteret-Hardy*
(detail), oil on canvas, 129 ×
103 cm, 1801. The Cleveland
Museum of Art

1.40 'Afternoon Dress for July,
1801. Wingman, Dress-maker,
Hanover Street, Hanover
Square.' Publication unknown.
Courtesy of the author

1801
WHITE GOWN

Letter 36, Tuesday 12 – Wednesday 13 May 1801, Bath: The Paragon

'—I mean to have my new white one made up now, in case we should go to the rooms again next monday, which is to be really the last time.'

This letter still falls into the years reflected in *Northanger Abbey*'s clothing treatments. Austen was contemplating going to a ball at Bath's Upper Rooms, as her characters do, and we have seen so far in this wardrobe tour how white gowns dominated fashion, fiction mirroring life. 'Miss Tilney [sister of the hero, Henry] always wears white', and heroine Catherine Morland is advised to do the same when visiting her.[42] On 22 May, Austen describes the Holder ladies in Bath as 'so civil, & their gowns look so white & so nice (which by the bye my Aunt [Mrs Leigh-Perrot] thinks an absurd pretension in this place)'[43] – one wonders why.

For going out in the evening, the gown was probably made of muslin – like Austen's ball gown of the previous year (see p. 39) – or maybe a light silk (fig. 1.39). A fine-quality yet more tightly woven textile like jaconet muslin is less likely for evening. The degree of formality would encompass an 'afternoon' or dinner dress as well (fig. 1.40), the kind of versatile gown that Austen's budget preferred, and which turns up in the practical considerations of other Regency dressers needing one gown for a range of evening occasions. Austen was writing on a Wednesday and is confident her new garment will be ready by the following Monday, which provides useful information about dress construction times. While it is hard to find clear sources for how long Regency dresses took to make, this tallies with what little is known.[44]

However, a letter two weeks later expands the context of this particular white gown. Austen wrote to Cassandra that 'I will engage Mrs Mussell as you desire. She made my dark gown very well & may therefore be trusted I hope with Yours—but she does not always succeed with

lighter Colours.—My white one I was obliged to alter a good deal.'[45] Firstly, this tells us the new white gown was made by Mrs Mussell. Secondly, it further refines the delivery time of the new white gown to at least a day or two before the Monday ball, which allowed Austen to alter it, presumably by improving the fit or working on the trimmings. It sounds like Cassandra was asking her sister to bespeak the dressmaker's time to make her own new dark gown before her arrival in Bath on 1 June. There appears to be a letter of 23 May missing, which may have shed more light on the subject. No more information on Mrs Mussell has yet been found in archives.

[42] *Northanger Abbey*, vol. I, ch. xii.
[43] Letter 37, 21–22 May 1801.
[44] For more on dressmaking, see Hilary Davidson, 'Dress & Dressmaking: Material Innovation in Regency Dress Construction', in *Material Literacy in Eighteenth-Century Britain: A Nation of Makers*, ed. Serena Dyer and Chloe Wigston Smith (London: Bloomsbury Academic, 2020), pp. 173–94.
[45] Letter 38, 26–27 May 1801.

1804
BLUE DRESS

The watercolour portrait of Jane Austen seated under a tree, seen from behind, painted, signed and dated by Cassandra in 1804 is one of the only two incontestable portraits of the author (fig. 1.41; see p. 68 for the other, more famous image, also painted by Cassandra). In the early 1800s, the Austen family were living in Bath. It was their custom to go 'in the summer … to *some* sea-side. They were in Devonshire, & in Wales …'.[46] their niece Anna Lefroy wrote, 'She was once I think at Tenby – and once they went as far north as Barmouth – I would give a good deal, that is as much as I could afford, for a sketch which Aunt Cassandra made of her in one of their expeditions – sitting down out of doors on a hot day, with her bonnet strings untied'.[47] The image is in a manuscript notebook of family history still owned by the Austen family. The summer of 1804 saw the family choose Devon and Dorset seaside resorts for their travels, and 'during one of their walks in the countryside' Cassandra made the watercolour sketch.[48] Anna thought there was 'a good deal of resemblance' in this portrait.[49]

Austen doesn't mention a gown of hers in the letters between 1801 and 1808. While she had a blue gown in the late 1790s (see p. 33), this dress is not it, because of a construction detail. Although many people have lamented that this Austen 'portrait' does not show her face, its back view is possibly more useful for dress history. Down the back of the bodice is a row of buttons. This fastening method has become taken for granted in Regency and later dress, but it was new for 1804 (fig. 1.42). The change from gowns opening at the front, to those opening at the back, was one of the fundamental construction shifts in dress during this period, starting from the experimentation with new fronts in the late 1790s. Austen's gown is early evidence for the new way of making bodice openings. The detail of a smaller sleeve on top of a longer one is typical for day dresses at this point. The material, through its density and fall, appears to be plain cotton – one with an opaque weave, such as poplin or cambric muslin (see p. 45).[50] The angles of the sleeve on the lower arm reveal that section is cut on the

bias, as was common for long sleeves (see p. 32): perhaps her earlier blue dress was remade into a more modish style and kept its tell-tale sleeves.

The way her gown skirts are tucked up out of the way, to reveal the white petticoats, is also one of the many counterbalances to the persistent yet false idea that Regency women abandoned these underskirts. In fact, Austen's many skirts are quite bulky. The pose shows, too, how the gown skirt hems are carefully prevented from contact with the ground by being tucked onto the lap, giving an idea of how Elizabeth Bennet's petticoat in *Pride and Prejudice* could end up 'six inches deep in mud … and the gown which had been let down to hide it, not doing its office'.[51] A woman visiting Brighton in 1804 was painted doing the same thing (fig. 1.43), and it is also seen indoors in figure 1.35. Plain linen or cotton petticoats (see p. 219) were more easily boiled and deeply cleaned than gowns, and enduring stains more easily hideable.

The other visible undergarment in Austen's portrait is the collared neck handkerchief, or chemisette (to use the name gaining popularity). The white linen or cotton garment covered the neck, back and décolletage, visible here under the back neckline and rucking up slightly around it, including a tuck at the left shoulder. Around Austen's neck is a light and dark blue checked handkerchief (see p. 185) compressed into three folds that look like individual ribbons. On her head is a bag bonnet, discussed in detail on page 131.

[46] Caroline Austen, copy of a letter to James-Edward Austen Leigh, 1869, in Austen-Leigh 2008, p. 188.
[47] Anna Lefroy to James-Edward Austen Leigh, 20 July 1869, National Portrait Gallery archive, quoted in National Portrait Gallery, 'Jane Austen', *Regency Portraits Catalogue*: https://www.npg.org.uk/collections/search/portraitExtended/mw00230/Jane-Austen [accessed 23 May 2021].
[48] *Family Record*, p. 142.
[49] *Family Record*, p. 280.
[50] I have made a reconstruction of this gown for Jane Austen's House, and a dense cotton worked very well.
[51] *Pride and Prejudice*, vol. I, ch. viii.

1.41 Cassandra Austen, portrait
of Jane Austen from behind, pencil
and watercolour on paper, 1804.
Private collection, reproduced
with permission

1.42 Muslin dress, c.1810.
The Hopkins Collection, London

1.44 'London Fashionable
Afternoon Dresses', *The Lady's
Magazine*, April 1805, hand-coloured
engraving on paper. National
Portrait Gallery, London

1.45 'London Fashionable
Mourning Dresses 1. Plain chemise
dress of Italian gauze ... over a black
sarcenet slip; sleeves and front trimmed
with black net trimming, fastened
with bugles. 2. Dress of imperial
lustre; short sleeves', *The Lady's
Magazine*, September 1805,
hand-coloured engraving on paper.
National Portrait Gallery, London

1805
CRAPE SLEEVES

Letter 44, Sunday 21 – Tuesday 23 April 1805, Bath: 25 Gay Street

'—You were very right in supposing I wore my crape sleeves to the Concert, I had them put in on the occasion; on my head I wore my crape & flowers, but I do not think it looked particularly well.'

On 21 January of this year, Austen's father Revd George Austen died suddenly after a short illness, leaving his widow and two daughters suddenly dependent on their small personal incomes and the generosity of the remaining Austen men. That period of mourning was not yet over when the mother of their dear friends Mary (married to James Austen) and Martha Lloyd died on 16 April. Austen's crape additions to her gown therefore represent double mourning when she went out that evening. She wrote a verse – 'Lines <u>supposed</u> to have been sent to an uncivil dressmaker' – to amuse Martha about this time:

> Miss Lloyd has now sent to Miss Green,
> As, on opening the box, may be seen,
> Some yards of a Black Ploughman's Gauze,
> To be made up directly, because
> Miss Lloyd must in mourning appear –
> For the death of a Relative dear –
> Miss Lloyd must expect to receive
> This license to mourn & to grieve,
> Complete, er'e the end of the week –
> It is better to write than to speak[52]

While Martha was wearing gauze in imagination, the crape Austen wore in real life was the mourning fabric *par excellence*. The textile was a crinkled semi-transparent silk, not to be confused with plain, opaque China crepe (see p. 87). The threads were heavily twisted in the weaving, which, with the crimped finish, helped dull silk's natural lustre almost completely and make it non-reflective, and appropriate for mourning when dyed black. White and coloured crape appears frequently throughout fashion pages, sometimes being used in place of muslins, but in black it was only for periods of grieving. The fashion plate in figure 1.44 is also for April 1805, showing a 'Black crape turban, with jet ornaments; crape dress, with lozenge black velvet trimming down the front' and drawn tucker made of the white crape. The headdress, with flower added, could have resembled what Austen wore. Her sleeves were probably added as draped pieces over normal sleeves, as the plate shows. They are unlikely to be long sleeves at this point in evening fashions – indeed, Austen tells us when they become more acceptable in 1814 (see p. 93).

The Duke of Gloucester, brother of King George III, died on 25 August 1805. *The Lady's Magazine* ran a plate specifically for royal mourning fashions (fig. 1.45), featuring a 'plain chemise dress of Italian gauze; full front, fastened in the centre with a jet brooch, over a black sarcenet slip; sleeves and front trimmed with black net trimming, fastened with bugles'. Fanny Austen (Knight) recorded in her diary that 'We all went into mourning for the Duke of Gloucester.'[53] Austen merely supposed 'everybody will be black for the D. of G'. The most consideration she gave the national mourning in her dress was to ask, 'Must we buy lace, or will ribbon do?' (see p. 91 for her use of ribbons as mourning).[54]

[52] *Family Record*, pp. 148–9.
[53] *Chronology*, p. 317.
[54] Letter 47, 30 August 1805.

1.46 Richard Dighton, 'A fashionable
lady' (detail), hand-coloured etching,
1807. The Stapleton Collection/
Bridgeman Images

1.47 'London Dresses for October'
(detail), *The Lady's Monthly Museum*,
September 1808. Courtesy of the
author

1808
DYED BLUE GOWN

Letter 57, Friday 7 – Sunday 9 October 1808, Southampton: Castle Square

'—*My Mother is preparing mourning for Mrs E.K.*[55] *—she has picked her old silk pelisse to peices, & means to have it dyed black for a gown—a very interesting scheme, tho' just now a little injured by finding that it must be placed in Mr Wren's hands, for Mr Chambers is gone.—As for Mr Floor, he is at present rather low in our estimation; how is your blue gown?— Mine is all to peices.—I think there must have been something wrong in the dye, for in places it divided with a Touch...*'

Dyeing altered clothing to update or refresh it, or transform older clothes into mourning, as Mrs Austen was planning. As so many gowns started off white or pale, they would take a darker overdye well once they grew worn. The family are informed on the local dyers' skills, trusting Mr Chambers but being less sure of Mr John Wren, who worked at 76 High Street.[56] Mr Floor is to be pitied a little for going down in history as a man who ruined one of Jane Austen's gowns. However, looking at what the poor dyer's process required extends him some compassion.

Chemistry was far from being an exact science in this period. Those working with chemical substances like dyes did so based on practical experience but not physical certainty. In 1815, chemistry professor Thomas Cooper published a 'practical treatise' on dyeing. He discusses the uncertainty involved, as every dye house had its own recipes, and varying access to good-quality raw materials. His recipes lay out the complicated and hazardous processes required, and he asserts that being both a good chemist and a good dyer was required to be successful.[57]

Once again it is unclear whether the sisters' 'gowns' are completed garments or lengths of fabric. An alternative is that they too are offering up old blue gowns to be dyed black. Dyeing blue involved indigo vats, with potash or lime – harsh substances that could affect a textile's structure. Black and some blues were dyed with acidic liquors, such as iron sulphate or vitriol. Even more than blue, achieving a good black required lots of heat, and dipping and airing several times. There were many places in the process for something to be 'wrong in the dye'. After dyeing, time, light and cleaning took further tolls on the final colour.

If this was a completed garment, it could be the one in the 1804 painting (p. 56) but is unlikely to be the 1790s blue gown (p. 33). An 1807 gown is shown in Dighton's satirical drawing (fig. 1.46). Fashion plates for autumn 1808 (fig. 1.47) show day dress with increasingly puffed sleeves which a length of fabric might become.

[55] Possibly Elizabeth Knight, the sister of Thomas Knight, Edward Austen's adoptive father. *Letters*, fn. 5, p. 392.
[56] *Letters*, p. 589.
[57] Thomas Cooper, *A Practical Treatise on Dyeing, and Callicoe Printing: Exhibiting the Processes in the French, German, English, and American Practice of Fixing Colours on Woollen, Cotton, Silk, and Linen* (Philadelphia, PA: Thomas Dobson, 1815), p. viii.

Engraved for the Lady's Magazine.

London Morning & Evening Dress.

1.48 'London Morning & Evening Dress', *The Lady's Magazine*, January 1810. Los Angeles Public Library

1.49 'A Bombazeene Gown. Ten yards. 4ˢ.3ᵈ a yard. Mourning for my dear Brother Johnson', Barbara Johnson's album, February 1814. © Victoria and Albert Museum, London

1808
BOMBAZINE
MOURNING GOWN

Letter 59, Saturday 15 – Sunday 16 October 1808, Southampton: Castle Square

'—*I am to be in Bombazeen & Crape, according to what we are told is universal here...—One Miss Baker makes my gown, & the other my Bonnet*'

The sudden post-partum death on 10 October of her sister-in-law Elizabeth, married to Edward, resulted in Austen having new mourning clothing made. Cassandra was staying with Edward's family in Kent when it happened, so the letters crossed two grieving households.

Crape (see p. 61) and bombazine were the most genteelly appropriate mourning fabrics at this time (fig. 1.48), and retained their dominance in the market through to the twentieth century. In 1817, Austen wrote of a Mrs Philmore as 'chief Mourner' wearing 'Bombasin, made very short, and flounced with Crape'. Bombazine was a twill-weave fabric made from silk and worsted, or cotton with silk, or worsted alone (fig. 1.49). The sample shows the finer warp threads visible at the fraying edge. With the worsted yarn uppermost, the finished effect was matt, with the non-sheen surface desired for mourning. Bombazine can sometimes be considered a kind of 'stuff' (see p. 23) – Perry's English dictionary of 1795 gives it thus, as 'a slight stuff for mourning'.[59] Alternatively, the customs house called it 'stuffs of silk mixed with worsted'.[60] The two fabrics were also a mainstay of Norwich textile manufacture. The town specialised in crape but excelled at bombazines, and had an artificial monopoly on British production of mourning textiles, especially black bombazine.[61] 'Norwich crape' was a soft woollen textile, distinct from all-silk crape, until 1819 when a modern 'Norwich crape' of fine silk and worsted was invented, very similar to bombazine.[62] Barbara Johnson's 1814 bombazine (fig. 1.49) is noticeably finer than a textile of the same name

in her album from 1759, showing how far manufacture had improved in the intervening years. While black dominated, both textiles could be made in a variety of colours, as Austen's brown bombazine (see p. 85) shows.

The Miss Bakers are two of the few named makers in the letters. In 1803, a Mrs Baker was a milliner at Above Bar, Southampton. At the same address was a Miss Baker, mantua-maker. Mrs Baker was probably Sarah (née Missing), who married milliner and haberdasher James Baker in 1801. Their business was successful enough to take on apprentices regularly between 1802 and 1806. In 1804, linen draper Thomas Missing (presumably Sarah's brother) married Sophia Baker (presumably James's sister). Within a family business of textiles and dress, the two Ms Bakers could well have made both garment and bonnet, although a second Miss Baker located in Chapel Street was also a mantua-maker. The rest of Austen's mourning outfit comprised her velvet pelisse (see p. 103) and silk and crape bonnet (p. 133). Something of the velvet's intense black against a duller bombazine gown can be seen in the fashion plate of this year in figure 1.48.

[58] Letter 155, 23–25 March 1817.
[59] Cited in Salisbury 2013, p. 32.
[60] *Parliamentary Abstracts, Containing the Substance of All Important Papers Laid before the Two Houses of Parliament during the Session of 1825* (London: printed for Longman, Hurst, Rees, Orme, and Brown, 1826), vol. I, p. 355.
[61] Fawcett 1985, p. 152.
[62] Ursula Priestley, 'Norwich and the Mourning Trade', *Costume*, 27.1 (1993), p. 48.

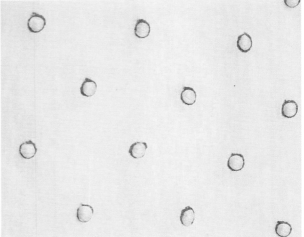

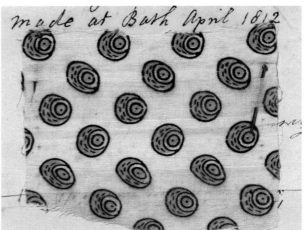

1.50 Dress of white cotton
muslin embroidered with white
cotton and red wool spots,
1805–10. The Metropolitan
Museum of Art, New York/Gift
of Mrs Frank D. Millet, 1913

1.51 Detail of white cotton
muslin dress (see fig. 1.50).
The Metropolitan Museum of
Art, New York/Gift of
Mrs Frank D. Millet, 1913

1.52 'A Blue Spotted Muslin
Gown. Six yards, ell wide. 2ˢ.2ᵈ
a yard', Barbara Johnson's
album, April 1812. © Victoria
and Albert Museum, London

1809
SPOTTED MUSLIN GOWN

Letter 65, Tuesday 17 – Wednesday 18 January 1809, Southampton: Castle Square

'I can easily suppose that your six weeks here will be fully occupied, were it only in lengthening the waists of your gowns. I have pretty well arranged my spring & summer plans of that kind, & mean to wear out my spotted Muslin before I go.—You will exclaim at this—but mine really has signs of feebleness, which with a little care may come to something.'

Muslin was a fragile fabric. Loosely woven, it caught, snagged and tore easily; it showed dirt when white; and its fluffy cotton surface could pill, or, at worst, catch fire. Once torn, even the most scrupulous and minute mending would still show on its surface (seen on Austen's muslin shawl, p. 143). Austen uses the fabric's fragility to slip a sly innuendo into *Pride and Prejudice* when the recently married Lydia declares, 'I shall send for my clothes when I get to Longbourn; but I wish you would tell Sally to mend a great slit in my worked muslin gown before they are packed up.'[63] Women complained about dancing with military officers in full uniform and having the spikes of their boot-spurs destroy delicate hems.

Like Lydia's, Austen's gown was probably 'worked'; that is, it had needlework as the form of embellishment. If it was, the spots were embroidered in, generally while a length of fabric instead of after being made up. An example of this all-over spotted design is shown in figure 1.50. The gown – of around the same date as Austen's – has raised satin-stitch white spots encircled by red chain-stitch or tambour work (fig. 1.51). It may be that the eventual demise of Austen's gown, which she appears to be pleasantly looking forward to, caused a gap in the wardrobe which she and Cassandra filled in 1811 with the purchase of a red crewel-spot muslin (see p. 72).

Decoration embroidered into muslin was called *chikankari* or *chikan* work in India, and its popularity there was influenced by the arrival of many British women during the late eighteenth century.[64] Austen's muslin could have been imported, or a British imitation, then embroidered on home soil.

Another possibility is that this gown is more prosaically made of a slightly stouter muslin, more like a cambric muslin, and was printed. A pretty muslin spotted with irregular dark and pale blue roundels formed part of Barbara Johnson's spring and summer wardrobe in 1812 (fig. 1.52). It cannot be Austen's coarse spotted muslin (p. 29) as that was already wearing out in 1798.

The other interesting point about the reference is the note concerning 'lengthening waists'. A sense of the sisters' active material participation in fashion is revealed at a point where the highest, most classically inspired waistlines of the 1800s start to give way to the slightly lower and more fluctuating waistlines of the 1810s. To keep up with these subtle changes meant moving the skirt a little further down the bodice. Any previous stitching holes could be hidden with a belt.

[63] *Pride and Prejudice*, vol. III, ch. v.
[64] Ashmore 2012, p. 23.

1.53 Cassandra Austen, portrait
of Jane Austen, pencil and
watercolour on paper, 11.4 ×
8 cm, *c.*1810. National Portrait
Gallery, London

c.1805–10
PORTRAIT GOWN

This is the most famous and only authenticated front-facing portrait of Jane Austen (fig. 1.53). Cassandra drew the undated 'scribble', as it was described in the family, probably around 1810 when Austen was in her mid-thirties, adding colour with watercolour paint.[65] There is no mention of it in the letters.

The small image is not a brilliant portrait. Anna Lefroy thought it 'hideously unlike' her aunt.[66] Later scholars called the picture a 'disappointing scratch', or more fulsomely, 'the irrelevant painted doll's face in watercolours which her sister Cassandra began and gave up as a bad job: unfortunately she neglected to tear it up and now it must be preserved for ever to salve the consciences of historians'.[67] It was first reproduced as is in the 1906 book *Jane Austen's Sailor Brothers*. James Andrews did a watercolour sketch based on it in 1869 (fig. 1.54) as the basis for the lithograph portrait by William Home Lizars (fig. 1.55) on the frontispiece of James Edward Austen-Leigh's memoir of his aunt, published in 1870. That rendering is the more famous version and now graces the British £10 note. Soon after, an unknown artist produced an engraving that expanded the small sketch with imaginary details (fig. 1.56); this often appears online with the dress tinted blue.

Andrews's image received some familial approbation: 'I think the portrait is very much superior to any thing that could have been expected from the sketch it was taken from. – It is a very pleasing, sweet face, – tho', I confess, to not thinking it much like the original; – but that, the public will not be able to detect.'[68] Another niece decided of the copy: 'there is a look which I recognise as hers – and though the general resemblance is not strong, yet as it represents a pleasing countenance it is so far a truth.'[69] The original portrait has been in the collection of the National Portrait Gallery, London, since 1948, and as they say, 'because of constant reproduction and lack of an alternative, this "very pleasing sweet face" has become completely associated in our minds with Jane Austen herself'.[70]

But what of the clothes? Working with a pencil gives the artist the luxury of sketchiness. Cassandra's original is barely worked to finish, except in the face. A line drawing traced from the portrait to clarify the clothing shapes shows the difficulty of delineating Cassandra's hazy original (fig. 1.57). Using the two together, we can break down what Austen seems to be wearing. After all, this is one of the only two ensembles we know without any doubt Austen wore, the other being the blue painted dress (see p. 56). The detail in the finished watercolour and pencil sketch of 1804 suggests that, had this one been completed, the dress details would have been more easily and precisely discernible, as Cassandra's skill distinguished between different textiles there. Austen's flesh is lightly coloured but her gown, chemisette and cap are unpainted.

The gown has a fall-front, bib or apron bodice held up by a button just below the left shoulder. The top neckline is not cut in a curve, but shows instead the tension of the fabric down from the button, pulling a straight line into a curved appearance because of the bosom. The short sleeves, worn without gloves, most likely place the sketch's completion during the year's middle warmer months, around the British summer, probably drawn indoors. The line around Austen's throat looks to be the edge of a chemisette or other décolletage-filling garment, as seen in her 1804 portrait and discussed on page 57. There is the merest hint of a frill at the neck in the pencil work.

The apron-front top is sewn into a band at top and bottom, not gathered. There appears to be a second, perhaps decorative button sitting below the first (fig. 1.57), although it may be a quirk of the pencil. Curiously Cassandra has not drawn buttons on the left-hand side – she may have been planning to do so in finishing the portrait, or perhaps they are lost in pencil haze. The smoothness of the band below the bust looks like the common detail of a sewn-in waistband. Two small areas of more mass at each outer edge of the sleeves look like drawstrings for the sleeve volume, and there are small channels around the cuff supporting this reading.

1.54 James Andrews, *Jane Austen*, based
on the sketch by Cassandra Austen
(see fig. 1.53), watercolour over pencil
heightened with gouache on card, 14.3
× 10 cm, 1869

1.55 William Home Lizars, *Jane
Austen*, based on the watercolour
by James Andrews (see fig 1.54),
stipple engraving, 1870

1.56 Engraving, based upon the
stipple engraving by William
Home Lizars (see fig. 1.55), in
Evert A. Duyckinck, *Portrait
Gallery of Eminent Men and Women
of Europe and America* (New York:
Johnson, Wilson and Co., 1873)

1.57 Hilary Davidson, line tracing of Cassandra Austen's portrait. Courtesy of the author

many clothing details which were then transferred to the lithograph. The line around the throat was worked up into a crude and ahistorical drawstring closure. Andrews also ignored the button on the left shoulder strap, instead giving a slightly awkward rounded neckline transition, and he made assumptions about the cut and fall of the sleeves, which are assigned a lot of drape within the volume Cassandra provided. The bottom of the bodice front was depicted as gathered, or with volume, instead of the original's smooth line. The waistband below the bust was turned into a creased sash, with gathers springing out from the space created by moving her solidly folded arms to trail out of frame. Austen's chest and shoulders were narrowed too. Other interpretive details include a clear and even frill on the front of the cap, and a ribbon behind it. The second lithographer (fig. 1.56) further added frills at the edges of Austen's cuffs and neckline. All three later copies reflect the aesthetics of the late nineteenth century and are distorted sources that should never be used as evidence for what Jane Austen wore.

On Austen's head, Cassandra's mass of feathery, indistinct lines indicates only her cap's volume and something like a couple of small trailing ribbons on the right. The black band at the hairline is the only clearly rendered element; perhaps a ribbon, perhaps the edging of a soft bonnet. The uncoloured element suggests it is a white indoor cap, presumably made of a cotton fabric, but it may merely be lacking colour to turn it into a cap or bonnet. The dress, too, infers whiteness, or at least a pale colour, but may have burst into chromatic life if finished.

Taken together, the clothing shows stylistic elements appearing in women's dress from about 1800 to 1810. The ensemble looks nearer to 1805–10, when Austen was 30–35 years old. Without clearer details it is very difficult to date more precisely. Nothing in the gowns mentioned in the letters before this portrait definitely matches its appearance, although it comes closest to her new gown of 1798–9 with short sleeves: 'the apron comes over it, & a band of the same completes the whole'.[71] The lack of a 'full wrap' detail disqualifies this dress. It could be one of those without a good description, such as the 1801 new white gown (see p. 55).

In rendering Cassandra's imprecision into definite lines for his vignette (see fig. 1.54), James Andrews had to make decisions about what sits where and which line connects with what, and in doing so he misinterpreted

[65] *Family Record*, p. 177.
[66] *Family Record*, p. 280.
[67] Dr R. W. Chapman, and David Piper, cited in National Portrait Gallery, 'Jane Austen', *Regency Portraits Catalogue*: https://www.npg.org.uk/collections/search/portraitExtended/mw00230/Jane-Austen [accessed 23 May 2021].
[68] *Family Record*, p. 280.
[69] *Family Record*, p. 282.
[70] National Portrait Gallery [2021].
[71] Letter 17, 8–9 January 1799.

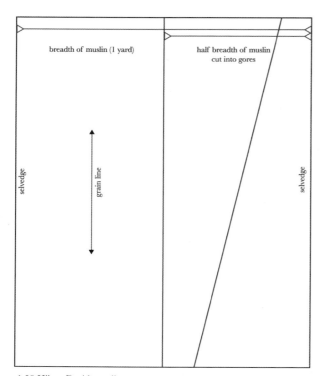

breadth of muslin (1 yard)

half breadth of muslin
cut into gores

selvedge

grain line

selvedge

1.58 Hilary Davidson, diagram
of the layout of cutting gores on
a breadth of muslin, based on
historic garments. Courtesy of
the author.

1.59 Muslin gown embroidered
with red crewel wool spots and
tan and red borders, *c*.1812.
Museum of London/
Photograph by John Chase

1.60 Length of white muslin,
embroidered in red cotton, with
regular rows of red spots, made
in Dhaka for the export market,
1855. © Victoria and Albert
Museum, London

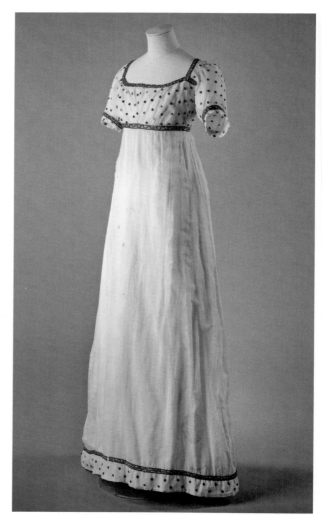

1811
RED SPOTTED MUSLIN GOWN

Letter 70, Thursday 18 – Saturday 20 April 1811, London: Sloane Street

'I was tempted by a pretty coloured muslin, & bought 10 y^{ds} of it, on the chance of your liking it; it is only 3/6 p^r y^d, & I sh^d not in the least mind keeping the whole.——In texture, it is just what we prefer, but its' resemblance to green cruels I must own is not great, for the pattern is a small red spot.'

Austen yielded to temptation during a London shopping expedition ostensibly to Grafton House (see p. 181 for more on this retailer). She ended up buying the muslin at 'a Linendraper's shop to which I went for check'd Muslin'. That article cost twice as much, at seven shillings a yard, as the red spotted one. Ten yards of the latter cost £1.15s in total. Austen had been seeking a muslin embroidered with green crewel wool (a fine, loosely twisted woollen or worsted yarn), and instead found one decorated with the opposite colour. It is probable this substitute was also embellished with crewels, though cotton thread was also an option at that very reasonable price, or even a printed pattern. A 'coloured' muslin could mean any length of the cloth with colour on it, not necessarily dyed all over.

The letter shows Austen and Cassandra are again sharing fabric, as Austen would not mind 'keeping the whole'. Therefore, she is allowing 5 yards (4.57 metres) per woman per gown. This may have been a slightly scant length, as a following letter makes clear. Ten days later, on 30 April, Austen explained to her sister that 'I mean, if I can, to wait for your return, before I have my new Gown made up—from a notion of their making up to more advantage together—& as I find the Muslin is not so wide as it used to be, some contrivance may be necessary.—I expect the Skirt to require one half breadth cut in gores, besides two whole Breadths.'[72] It is likely this gown is the red-spotted muslin, especially as the sisters are sharing the fabric. By cutting both gowns out of the one length, the cut can use the textile's full length more economically, as figure 1.58 shows.[73] Muslin was usually between around 30 and 36 inches (76–91 cm) wide.

For the fabric to be purchased embroidered or printed meant it had passed through the hands of an artisan before it reached the shop. The low price suggests it is not an Indian muslin, as they commanded higher prices for the better quality and importation costs. By the time Austen wrote, British manufacturing of muslins was becoming competitive in quality. Figure 1.59 is a gown of *c.*1812 embroidered exactly with crewel wool, red and tan. The spotted fabric is used only on the bodice, although a matching border sets off the main edges. A similar muslin embroidered all over with red spots from the mid-nineteenth century (fig. 1.60) shows the pretty effect it would have had in a gown.

[72] Letter 72, 30 April 1811.
[73] Alden O'Brien, ed., *'An Agreeable Tyrant': Fashion after the Revolution* (Washington, DC: DAR Museum, 2016), p. 176.

1.61 'London Fashionable
Morning [*sic*] and Full Dress
… 1. Full dress. —Black velvet,
ornamented with jet and bugles
… 2. Morning Dress. —Of
raven-grey silk, made tight at the
throat, with white crape ruff', *The
Lady's Magazine*, November 1810.
Los Angeles Public Library

London Fashionable Morning & Full Dress.

1.62 Diana Sperling, *Henry Van
[Hagen] electrifying – Mrs Van –
Diana, Harry & Isabella – Mum
& HGS* (detail), Dynes Hall,
watercolour, 25 May 1817.
Private collection

1811, 1813, 1814
MOURNING DRESS

Letter 75, Thursday 6 June 1811, Chawton

'Their business was to provide mourning, against the King's death & my Mother has had a Bombasin bought for her.'

A letter about putting on walking things for a visit to Austen's nearest town, Alton (see p. 115), continues into the reason for the trip. Mrs Austen confirmed this mission in a letter of June 1811 (although she heads it 'July'): 'last week I bought a Bombazeen, thinking I should get it cheaper than when the poor King was actually dead. If I outlive him it will answer my purpose, if I do not, somebody may mourn for me in it — it will be wanted for one or the other, I daresay, before the moths have eaten it up.'[74] (Note the two different spellings of the same textile.) The Prince of Wales had become Regent of the British throne on 5 February that year due to George III's mental and physical incapacity to rule. The king became seriously ill in May 1811, hence the anticipation of his death, which would not occur until 1820.

Bombazine was the normal and genteel choice for middle-class mourning gowns (fig. 1.61), as seen in Austen's 1808 dress (see p. 65). While the shopping here was for her mother, this useful fabric would not go to waste, as Mrs Austen sanguinely noted. Poor young Elizabeth Grant suffered from a similar royal panic-buying of bombazine. Her 'careful mother, fearing that black would rise in price, bought up at a sale a quantity of bombazine'. When the king recovered, she and her sisters 'just had to wear [the bombazine], and trimmed plentifully with crimson it did very well'.[75]

There are oblique dress references to Austen's own mourning ensembles in 1813 and 1814. Their cousin and sister-in-law, Eliza de Feuillide as was, now married to Henry Austen, died on 24 April after a 'long & dreadful Illness'.[76] Austen was at her bedside in Sloane Street, London, when it happened, as the two were close, and by the time she wrote to her brother Frank in early July 1813, Austen noted, 'Our mourning for her is not over, or we should now be putting it on again for Mr Thos

Leigh', showing that the mourning was of a material nature. Mary Lloyd Austen, James's wife, recorded that she 'Put on mourning' for her sister-in-law on 2 May.[77] Austen returned from London on 1 May, and so she spent the warmer months in black or dark colours, including throughout her visit to London between 19 and 26 May.

Austen was also caught out in London during a period of royal mourning. Queen Charlotte's brother, Duke Ernest Gottlob of Mecklenburg, died on 27 January 1814. The '6 weeks mourning' period started a little late, as the British court only heard he had died on 2 February. As was customary when away from home and unexpectedly in need of mourning dress, Cassandra sent Austen's up from Chawton, and it arrived on 8 March, the moment after Jane had just written that the parcel had not arrived.[78] When their sister-in-law Elizabeth Austen died, Jane sent to Cassandra, who was in Godmersham with her family, 'such of your Mourning as I think most likely to be useful, reserving for myself your Stockings & half the velvet'.[79] In 1814, Austen was making do with what she had and altering her dress to be suitable: her experiments with adding black satin ribbon to gowns (see pp. 91 and 93) are within this mourning period. Figure 1.62 shows the effects of such mourning clothes in everyday Regency life.

---

[74] The undated letter is headed July, but must have been written in June to tally with the date of Letter 75 and Anna Austen's visit. The date is therefore Friday 14 June 1811, as she talks of getting the cloth 'last week'. 23M93/62/2/13/1, Hampshire Record Office.
[75] Elizabeth Grant (Smith), *Memoirs of a Highland Lady* (London: J. Murray, 1911), p. 160.
[76] Letter 86, 3–6 July 1813.
[77] *Chronology*, p. 443.
[78] Letter 98, 5–8 March 1814.
[79] Letter 59, 15–16 October 1808.

1813
GOWN WITH WHITE RIBBON TRIM

Letter 87, Wednesday 15 – Thursday 16 September 1813, London: Henrietta Street

'4 o'clock.—We are just come back from doing Mrs Tickars, Miss Hare, and Mr Spence. … My Gown is to be trimmed everywhere with white ribbon plaited [pleated] on, somehow or other. She says it will look well. I am not sanguine. They trim with white very much.'

This is one of the few times Austen named a maker of her clothes, and we could wish she had been a little more specific in doing so. Mr Spence was a dentist, and the tribulations of his attentions to her nieces recur through this and the next letter. Mrs Tickars remains a mystery. As Deirdre Le Faye supposed, she was a 'stay maker or dressmaker'. The assumption comes from the wonderful observation Austen recorded 'from Mrs Tickars's young Lady, to my high amusement, that the stays now are not made to force the Bosom up at all;—that was a very unbecoming, unnatural fashion. I was really glad to hear that they are not to be so much off the shoulders as they were.' The comment is applicable were Austen having either stays (see fig. 0.2) or a gown made, as the bust was the defining shape for both. Further rummaging among business records, however, has to date turned up no whisper of Mrs Tickars's establishment that might guide us further as to which she was.

Miss Mary Hare is more obligingly discoverable. In 1808, she took out insurance for her millinery premises at 6 Lower Grosvenor Street in Mayfair, just round the corner from Bond Street, in the heart of London's prime shopping area.[80] Austen explicitly described buying a 'white sattin' cap from her later in the letter (see p. 139), tallying with a millinery business. Miss Hare appears to have expanded her trade into (costly) dressmaking. The next spring, in March 1814, Austen wrote:

—A grand thought has struck me as to our Gowns. This 6 weeks mourning [see p. 75] makes so great a difference that I shall not go to Miss Hare, till you can come & help chuse yourself; unless you particularly wish the contrary.—It may be hardly worthwhile perhaps to have the Gowns so expensively made up; we may buy a cap or a veil instead;—but we can talk more of this together.[81]

This may tally with records from the 1830s, in which Ann and Mary Scrivener, 'milliners and dress-makers', now have premises both at the Grosvenor Street address and two blocks away, at 3 George Street, Hanover Square (now St George Street). Miss Hare may have married, or her business been taken over by the Scrivener ladies. As *The Book of English Trades* explained, 'the business of a Mantua Maker [and] a Milliner … although in London these two parts of in fact the same trade, are frequently separate, they are not always so'.[82]

The exchange with whichever professional women it was gives a rare insight into how fashion decisions were made between client and maker. Austen is relatively passive in this transaction. The maker tells her it will look well and appears to be using her knowledge of current fashions to shape taste. Austen is dubious, yet trusts the metropolitan fashion imperative. Rolinda Sharples painted herself in a beautiful evening confection around

page 76

1.63 Rolinda Sharples, *Self-Portrait*, oil
on canvas, 31.2 × 28.4 cm, *c*.1814.
Bristol Museum and Art Gallery/©
Bristol Museums, Galleries & Archives/
Purchased, 1931/Bridgeman Images

1.64 Jacques-Louis David, *Madame David*,
oil on canvas, 72.9 × 59.4 cm, 1813.
National Gallery of Art, Washington,
DC/Samuel H. Kress Collection

1.65 Yellow muslin gown with silk satin ribbon trim, 1805–10. The Hopkins Collection, London

1814 (fig. 1.63), and figure 1.64 shows an equally pretty 1813 painted white satin gown with a gauzy ribbon pleated around the neckline. The same technique is seen in a more vivid gauze of a slightly earlier date (fig. 1.65), bedecked around neckline and cuffs.

80 Sun Insurance Records, 'Insured: Mary Hare, 6 Lower Grosvenor Street, Milliner', 1808, London Metropolitan Archives: City of London, MS 11936/440/812959.
81 Letter 98, 5–8 March 1814. Cassandra probably arrived on 12 March (*Chronology*, p. 475).
82 John Souter, *The Book of English Trades: And Library of the Useful Arts: With Seventy Engravings*, 7th edn (London: John Souter, 1818), p. 222.

1.66 Dress of dark yellow silk
and wool poplin, 1800–10
[record shot]. © Victoria and
Albert Museum, London/Given
by Mrs J. Bulkeley

1.67 Detail of dark yellow silk
and wool poplin dress (see fig.
1.66) [record shot]. © Victoria
and Albert Museum, London/
Given by Mrs J. Bulkeley

1.68 Cream poplin (wool/silk)
with figured diamond motif,
English, 1790s [record shot].
© Victoria and Albert Museum,
London

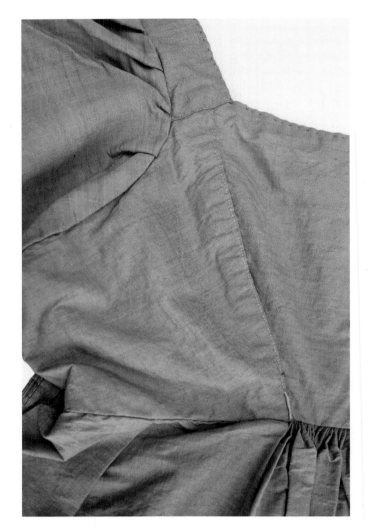

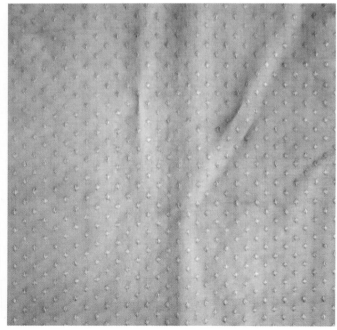

1813
POPLIN GOWN

Letter 87, Wednesday 15 – Thursday 16 September 1813, London: Henrietta Street

---

'Instead of saving my superfluous wealth for you to spend, I am going to treat myself with spending it myself. I hope, at least, that I shall find some poplin at Layton and Shear's that will tempt me to buy it. If I do, it shall be sent to Chawton, as half will be for you .... I shall send 20 yards.'

Following the death of his wife Eliza in April that year, Henry Austen moved from Sloane Street to live over his banking premises at 10 Henrietta Street in Covent Garden, from whence Austen was writing on a three-day visit. Henry's neighbours, Edward Layton and Anselm Shears, were silk mercers at 11 Henrietta Street and, like him, they lived above the shop. The shop had two names: 'Layton & Shears <u>is</u> Bedford House', as Austen explained.[83] The proximity allowed the ladies to go there 'before Breakfast' and discover 'Very pretty English poplins at 4[s].3[d].—Irish D[itt]° at 6[s].0—more pretty certainly—beautiful.'

Poplin was a textile woven with a worsted weft, and a dense silk warp that either covered the coarser woollen yarns to create a corded or ribbed effect, or was an even plain weave (figs 1.66 and 1.67). They differed from bombazines in having a higher silk proportion and were very similar to tab[b]inets.[84] Poplins came in every possible pattern and colour. Mrs Elton in *Emma* owns a 'white and silver poplin', as the poplin in figure 1.68 is patterned, and they were popular for morning and half-dress.[85] The best poplins were made in Ireland, hence the cheaper costs of the English ones. Layton & Shears's price was good too. The following year an advertisement in *La Belle Assemblée* offered 'Plain Poplins' at '4s. 6d. and 5s. the yard, usually sold at 5s. 6d. and 6s.'[86]

Austen's poplin is one of her less obvious wardrobe purchases, as her discussion is couched in terms of a gift to Cassandra. But only half the 20-yard (60 ft, or 18.2 m) piece is for her sister; the generosity is prompted by Austen's treat to herself. The fabric went down well: 'I am extremely glad that you like the poplin. I thought it would have my mother's approbation, but was not so confident of yours. Remember that it is a present. Do not refuse me. I am very rich.'[87] Austen's last comment is often interpreted as munificence from her novels. She wrote in July to her brother Frank, exulting that 'every Copy of S[ense]. & S[ensibility]. is sold & … has brought me £140 … I have therefore now written myself into £250 …'.[88] However, before the opening quote her letter reads: 'I have this moment received £5 from kind, beautiful Edward. Fanny has a similar gift. I shall save what I can of it for your better leisure in this place.' So Austen's 'superfluous' wealth is specifically a generous windfall. Twenty yards of English poplin at 4s.3d would cost her £4.5s. The 6s-per-yard beautiful Irish goods would clear her out, at £6 total, making a handsome gift indeed. This is the letter where she buys a white dress and satin cap from Miss Hare (see p. 139), so Austen was enjoying a new financial ease and finally leaving off mourning for her sister-in-law.

[83] Letter 87, 15–16 September 1813.
[84] Florence M. Montgomery, *Textiles in America, 1650–1870* (New York: W.W. Norton & Co., 1984), p. 327.
[85] *Emma*, vol. II, ch. xvii.
[86] Salisbury 2013, p. 209.
[87] Letter 89, 23–24 September 1813.
[88] Letter 86, 3–6 July 1813.

1.69 'Costume Parisien',
Journal des Dames et des Modes,
10 September 1812: plate 1254.
Rijksmuseum, Amsterdam/
Purchased with the support
of the F. G. Waller-Fonds

1.70 Linen dress, American,
*c.*1814. The Metropolitan
Museum of Art, New York/Gift
of Mrs Howard E. Cox, 1978

1.71 Selection of printed cottons
from patchwork coverlet, made
by Jane and Cassandra Austen
and their mother, *c.*1810. Jane
Austen's House, Chawton/
Courtesy of the author

1813
BLUE GOWN

Letter 92, Thursday 14 – Friday 15 October 1813, Godmersham

'—Mary's blue gown!—My Mother must be in agonies.—I have a great mind to have <u>my</u> blue gown dyed some time or other—I proposed it once to you & you made some objection, I forget what.—It is the fashion of flounces that gives it particular Expediency.'

Austen was on the money with her concern about flounces as a marker of current fashion. Flounces appear in French fashion plates increasingly through 1812–13 (fig. 1.69), but not as frequently in English plates of the same years. Slightly under a year later, Austen wrote from London to her friend Martha Lloyd in Bath of having been 'at a little party last night at Mrs Latouche's, where dress is a good deal attended to, & these are my observations from it.— Petticoats short, & generally, tho' not always, flounced.'[89] So much of the gentry middle classes' attention to clothing was concerned with 'reconciling tensions between custom and fashion'.[90] 'A degree of conformity … to preclude the appearance of particularity, is reasonable and becoming', and defined the appropriate sartorial middle ground for Austen and her status peers.[91] This passage is an example of Austen's attention to the niceties of fashion of the moment, and how to be in the general realm of what was appropriate in dress.

Knowing when flounces were coming back in, and trying to include them in her wardrobe, was part of Austen's bending her custom to fashion. She was noticing the growing trend for decorating the hems of gowns or petticoat skirts with more embellishment (fig. 1.70), a trend that would become the distinctly triangular skirt shapes of the late 1810s and '20s. A few days later, she wrote to Cassandra, 'How do you like your flounce? We have seen only plain flounces.'

Austen continued by discussing making their bombazine dresses (see p. 85) into morning gowns, and how she 'would rather sacrifice my blue one for that

purpose'.[92] Since this is the second time she mentioned a blue gown in a short space, we can presume these two references are to the same garment, and that it is a dinner or evening gown, since it is one she could 'give up as a morning gown', has a degree of fashion in flounces, and has been in her wardrobe for long enough to have grown a little worn. There has been no mention of a blue gown in the letters since the dyeing disaster of 1808, and as that one 'divided with a Touch' (see p. 63), it cannot be this garment. Figure 1.71 shows pretty blue printed cottons for dresses surviving in the quilted coverlet the Austen ladies made together.

Austen previously wrote about flounces in 1807, and of putting 'five breadths of Linen also into my flounce; I know I found it wanted more than I had expected, & that I sh^d have been distressed if I had not bought more than I beleived myself to need, for the sake of the even Measure, on which we think so differently'.[93] There is no context here for what garment she may have needed a flounce for. Perhaps it was not a garment but a furnishing textile, flouncing a bed skirt or cover.

[89] Letter 106, 2 September 1814.
[90] See Hilary Davidson, *Dress in the Age of Jane Austen: Regency Fashion* (London and New Haven, CT: Yale University Press, 2019), ch. 1.
[91] Stewart 1817, p. 168.
[92] Letter 94, 26 October 1813.
[93] Letter 51, 20–22 February 1807.

1.72 Bombazine of fine red silk warp and coarser brown wool weft, twill woven and embroidered in floral sprigs with silk twist, 1770–80 [record shot]. © Victoria and Albert Museum, London/Given by Messrs Harrods Ltd

1.73 Dark brown silk dress with a fall-front, brown silk satin strip with cord in the centre trimming round neck edge; brown satin round cuffs with cord each side; frill round hem with cord heading, 1805–15. The Hopkins Collection, London

1813
BROWN BOMBAZINE GOWN

Letter 92, Thursday 14 – Friday 15 October 1813, Godmersham

'I produced my Brown Bombasin yesterday & it was very much admired indeed—& I like it better than ever'

The brown silk pelisse (see p. 107) had been identified by descendants of the Knight branch of the family as being this dress. However, bombasin (bombazeen [see p. 65], bombazine) generally has a silk warp and a worsted or cotton weft (see fig. 1.72), and the pelisse fabric is entirely silk. Therefore, this reference must be to another gown, and one which Cassandra also owned. Two letters later, Austen hoped 'you have not cut off the train of your bombazin. I cannot reconcile myself to giving them up as morning gowns; they are so very sweet by candlelight. I would rather sacrifice my blue one [see p. 83] for that purpose; in short, I do not know and I do not care.'[94] This reference tells us the bombazine gowns are evening wear with trains (nearly out of fashion by this point), although getting on a little if the sisters are considering relegating them to morning wear. The candlelight may also have gone some way to blurring the gowns' deficiencies, flattering them like the glow does faces.

The brown bombazine seems to have had a stay of execution and retained its evening position a little longer – maybe the blue gown was sacrificed in its place. Letter 98 written in early March 1814, the next year, records how 'Almost everybody was in mourning last night, but my brown gown did very well'.[95] Austen's previous references to bombazine are to do with mourning clothing, and so it is logical to think that the 1813 bombazine and the 1814 brown gown are the same. Advertisements frequently reference coloured and black bombazines and bombazets (a cheaper version with less silk). It appears not only black signified mourning, but that bombazine was so often worn for the dead that the textile alone could signify adherence to the social etiquette. A coloured bombazine was equally appropriate for dinner or evening dress. Figure 1.73 conjures the effect of a brown gown fitting this bill.

[94] Letter 94, 26 October 1813.
[95] Letter 98, 5–8 March 1814.

1.74 Pink silk crepe dress, 1815–20. Museum of London/ Photograph by the author

1.75 Embroidered Chinese silk crepe dress, skirt constructed from three 48-cm selvedge widths, 1810–15. Courtesy of Cora Ginsburg LLC/Photograph by Rachel Robshaw

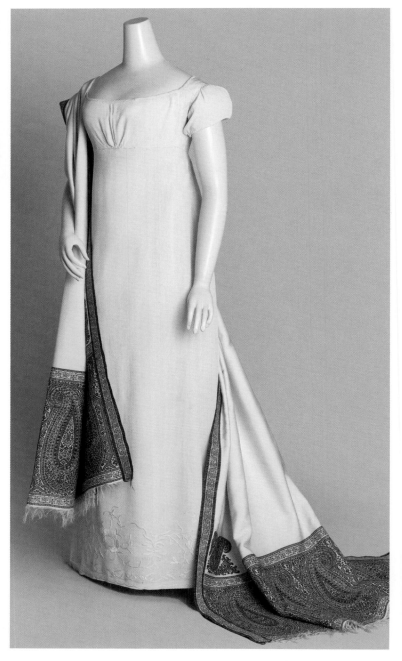

1.76 Detail of embroidered Chinese silk crepe dress (see fig. 1.75). Courtesy of Cora Ginsburg LLC/Photograph by Rachel Robshaw

1813
CHINA CREPE GOWN

Letter 96, Saturday 6 – Sunday 7 November 1813, Godmersham

'I was so tired that I began to wonder how I should get through the Ball next Thursday.... My China Crape is still kept for the Ball.'

'China' crepe or crape distinguished this textile from the semi-transparent, crinkled mourning version. Crepe weave has a high twist in the yarns comprising it, which creates a springy, soft body to the fabric, and a matte surface, as is seen in surviving gowns (fig. 1.74). It was usually used for gowns worn in the evening, to dinners, balls or the opera (fig. 1.75).

Hidden in Austen's China crape is a global textile distribution. The key to unpacking it is a letter from Fanny Palmer Austen, married to Austen's brother Charles, written from Halifax, Nova Scotia, where the couple were living in September 1810 as the northern base of the Royal Navy's North American station. 'We shall send you a part of our Brother Frank's China present', she told her sister Esther, living in Bermuda (where they were born), '& hope it will prove acceptable viz. … part of a piece of India Crape which I have had made up into a gown for you by Miss Johnson who had <u>your</u> measure'.[96] In August that year the other naval brother, Francis Austen, had sailed in an armed escort for thirteen East India Company merchant ships travelling from Canton via Madras to England. Evidently he sent gifts on to the Halifax connection.

Although crape could be woven in India as Fanny implied, Frank had started his journey in China, the traditional home of silk production. The chrysanthemum pattern on the gown in figure 1.76 indicates that it, too, may be the genuine Chinese textile. Her 'piece' meant an uncut length of fabric, sufficient to make gowns for two women. In narrow silk poplin, Austen bought 20 yards for two women (see p. 81), where ten of wider muslin was enough for the same (p. 73). Fanny sending Esther a pre-made gown she knew would fit was a thrifty move, instead of potentially wasting the valuable fabric by sending a guess at the length required for a gown.

Now, if Francis Austen went to the kind effort of sending only his sister-in-law a handsome textile present, would he not make an equal or lovelier gift to his actual sisters? It is highly likely that the references we read to the Austen sisters' evening gowns of China crape are the results of Frank's generosity after his 1810 return. In early 1813, Austen 'hope[s] [Cassandra] will wear your China Crape' at a visit to friends at Manydown in Hampshire, then 'thought of [Cassandra] at Manydown in the Drawg room & in your China Crape', before sharing the experience with her own China crape in the quote above at the end of the same year.[97] We know this gown was trimmed with ribbon because she copied the arrangement for her lilac sarsenet in 1814 (see p. 91), giving a rare idea of how Austen is embellishing her gown.

Although London shops frequently retailed 'China Crape', it is probable instead that one Austen man was the direct transmitter of the luxury textile halfway round the globe to clothe women of his family in Hampshire, Halifax and Bermuda.

[96] Sheila Johnson Kindred, *Jane Austen's Transatlantic Sister: The Life and Letters of Fanny Palmer Austen* (Toronto: McGill-Queen's University Press, 2017), p. 68.
[97] Letter 79, 29 January 1813; Letter 80, 4 February 1813.

1.77 Muslin dress, *c*.1810.
The Hopkins Collection, London

1.78 Woman's dress made of white
cotton Indian muslin, American,
c.1805. Philadelphia Museum of Art/
Gift of Thomas Francis Cadwalader,
1955, 1955-98-7a

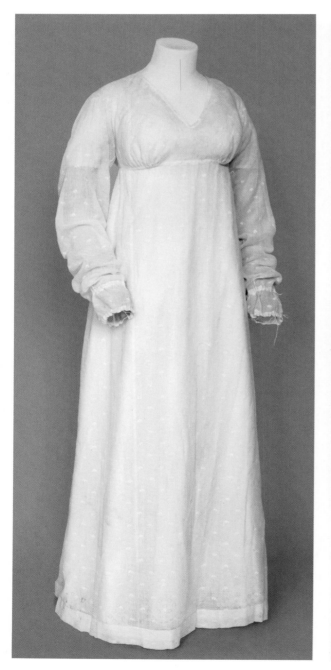

1814
OLD MUSLIN GOWN

Letter 97, Wednesday 2 – Thursday 3 March 1814, London: Henrietta Street

'—Mrs Perigord has just been here. I have paid her a Shilling for the Willow. She tells me that we owe her Master for the Silk-dyeing.—My poor old Muslin has never been dyed yet; it has been promised to be done several times.—What wicked People Dyers are. They begin with dipping their own Souls in Scarlet Sin.'

Mrs Marie Marguerite Perigord – the same age as Austen, 38 – worked in Henry Austen's house along with her mother, Madame Bigeon. The two French servants, more like family, were originally employed by his wife and first cousin Eliza de Feuillide. Jane Austen left £50 to Mrs Bigeon in her will, and Cassandra continued to give her small amounts of money after her sister's death. The 'Master', then, is Henry Austen, who appears to have paid a dyer's bill on his sisters' behalf. The lamented muslin waiting to be refreshed may have been one of Austen's earlier gowns, last seen being spotted or newly purchased. Or it could be one of the many other dresses unremarked upon in surviving letters. Even for such sparse coverage from already incidental references, it is the sixth gown she has mentioned made of the textile, further reinforcing muslin's ubiquity in female Regency wardrobes, as seen in a lovely day dress of *c.*1810 in figure 1.77 and an Indian muslin gown of *c.*1805, which would have been 'old' as a gown in 1814 (fig. 1.78).

White muslin's propensity for taking stains was immense. After a while, dyeing it another colour would have been more effective than trying yet again to restore a whiteness long lost to dinginess (explained further on p. 63). Even if this gown was one of the stouter, more tightly woven muslins (see p. 45), they lost colour through washing and general wear of the cloth, as Austen opened her letters lamenting. There is possibly a practical problem here too. Austen arrived in London on 2 March, so when did she give her muslin to the dyer? Would its lack of being finished have presented a problem for Austen's wardrobe if she had been planning on wearing her gown while in town? Had it been held over from her last London visit in November 1813, which tallies with the promises of 'several times'? In addition, what kind of silk was dyed – a skein, a piece of textile, or a garment – and when was it done?

Mrs Perigord also brought with her a shilling's worth of 'Willow', meaning willow sheets or squares made of plaited willow, sold ready prepared for hat making.

1.79 Pink silk dress with back opening, and cords round hem, 1815–25. The Hopkins Collection, London

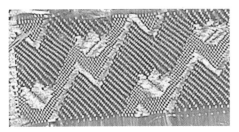

1.80 Sample of 'rich lilac-shot figured sarsnet', *The Repository of Arts*, October 1813. Los Angeles County Museum of Art/Purchased with funds provided by Victoria Corbell/www.lacma.org

1.81 'Evening Dress… A round robe of blossom-coloured crape, with demi-train, worn over a white satin slip, gathered frock back, and stomacher front; the sleeve unusually short… The sleeves and neck of the robe ornamented with puckered white satin, and a fancy border round the bottom, composed of white satin and crape, the same as the dress', *The Repository of Arts*, November 1813. New York Public Library

1814
LILAC SARSENET GOWN

Letter 98, Saturday 5 – Tuesday 8 March 1814, London: Henrietta Street

'I have determined to trim my lilac sarsenet with black sattin ribbon just as my China Crape is, 6d width at bottom, 3d or 4d at top.—Ribbon trimmings are all the fashion at Bath, & I dare say the fashions of the two places are alike enough in that point, to content me.—With this addition it will be a very useful gown, happy to go anywhere.'

In England, the penny was the measurement unit for ribbons. As an 1841 encyclopaedia explains, 'Ribbons are made according to a fixed standard of widths designated by different numbers of pence, which once no doubt denoted the price of the article, but at present have reference only to its breadth.'[98] 6d is described as $^{10}/_{12}$ of an inch wide, 3d is ½ an inch, and 4d is ⅝ of an inch. These are fine, narrow ribbons, rather than the wide bands of decoration seen in figure 1.10. Technically, it was a 'riband', but the common spelling eventually became the correct one. In the same year, another genteel woman's account book records some prices for 'sattin ribbon': London widow Mrs Mary Topham bought 5 yards of 'black Sattin Ribbon' at 8d per yard, though no width is recorded.[99]

The comment that 'Ribbon trimmings are all the fashion at Bath' begs the question: what is Austen's source of information? A friend or relation passing on fashion commentary in a letter? Her niece Fanny Knight, aged 21, had been in Bath between 19 February and 4 March, so perhaps had told Austen. The 'two places' are presumably Bath and London, not that Austen seems much bothered. And as to the 'anywhere' that this gown might be happy to go, its fabric evokes an evening or dinner dress, or at the very least an afternoon gown. Sarsenet, as seen in Austen's pelisse (see p. 107), was a common kind of silk textile, often in a twill weave that imparted a slight body to its softness. It was roughly

midway between the crispness of taffeta and the soft drape of crepe (see p. 87), shown in figure 1.80 in 'lilac', reading now as a pink. The effect of a pinkish sarsenet in a gown is seen in figure 1.79, which also has a contrast trimming around the neck, as does the 'blossom-coloured crape' gown 'ornamented with puckered white satin' in figure 1.81, recalling Austen's white ribbon-trimmed dress from Miss Hare the year before (see p. 77). Austen's wardrobe tended to be versatile, rather than overly specific, so a silk gown like this would have covered a range of social occasions.

[98] *The Penny Cyclopædia of the Society for the Diffusion of Useful Knowledge* (London: Charles Knight and Co., 1841), vol. XIX, p. 492.
[99] Topham 1810.

1.82 Detail of silk satin and gauze striped ribbons applied to the striped silk fabric of a dress, 1810–20. Museum of London/ Photograph by the author

1.83 Silk gauze dinner or evening gown, 1815. © Fashion Museum, Bath/Bridgeman Images

1.84 Silk gauze dinner or evening gown, 1815. © Fashion Museum, Bath/Bridgeman Images

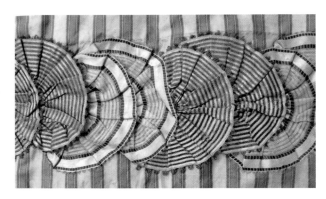

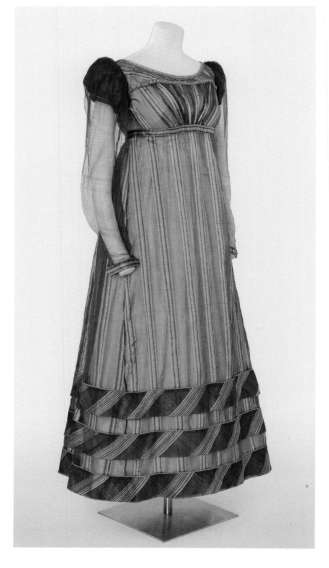

1814
GAUZE GOWN

Letter 99, Wednesday 9 March 1814, London: Henrietta Street

'—I wear my gauze gown today, long sleeves & all; I shall see how they succeed, but as yet I have no reason to suppose long sleeves are allowable.—I have lowered the bosom especially at the corners, & plaited black sattin ribbon round the top.'

This letter describing Austen's dress for dinner with the Tilson family comes straight after one in which Austen describes how she has been 'ruining' herself in 'black sattin ribbon with a proper perl edge', noting that she has been 'trying to draw it up into kind of Roses, instead of putting it in plain double plaits'.[100] What these may have looked like is shown in figure 1.82, purl edge and all, meaning the picot loops at the side of the ribbon. The second letter may be describing design choices instead of, or in addition to, this pretty embellishment. The black sattin ribbons were being added in a period of court mourning for the queen's brother (see p. 75) and may have been a quick decorative response to the required etiquette or a permanent change to the gowns.

Silk gauzes had been popular in fashion since the late eighteenth century. In the 1810s they were increasing in popularity as part of the translucent transformation taking place in garments as netting and gauze-making machines improved. A strong aesthetic trend of this decade was a see-through outer gown decorated with ribbons, flowers and other haberdashery trims, worn over an undergown or 'slip' petticoat (see p. 218), often of silk to allow the outer dress to slip easily over it. Austen's description of her dress trimming confirms its adherence to fashion at the time.

The question of whether long sleeves for evening was allowable shows Austen's concern for being in the mode of appropriate dress perhaps more than its fashion aspect. In the same letter, she returned to the subject after the dinner party, telling Cassandra, 'Mʳˢ Tilson had long sleeves too, & she assured me that they are worn in the evening by many. I was glad to hear this.'[101] Her friend's assurance of London convention put Austen's mind at rest about the niceties of evening dress etiquette, and this change after many years of short evening sleeves. By September that year, Austen was writing to Martha Lloyd that 'Long sleeves appear universal, even as Dress'.[102] By 1817, Rolinda Sharples could depict even a lady's maid in Bristol wearing gauze sleeves over short sleeves (fig. 4.32).

Long gauze sleeves are part of the gowns in figures 1.83 and 1.84. These were made in 1815, ostensibly for the Duchess of Richmond's ball on 15 June before the Battle of Waterloo on the 18th, but research has been unable to confirm this.[103] As Penelope Byrde has noted, their brown colour also tallies with the Austen sisters' preference for the hue, and they are probably dinner or evening gowns rather than ball dress. The 'Waterloo dresses', as they are known, are matching but not identical, and thus reveal a lovely insight into how the Austen sisters may have adjusted in construction the details of the same gown fabric they so frequently bought, so that their own dresses were complements to, not mirrors of, each other.

[100] Letter 98, 5–8 March 1814.
[101] Letter 99, 9 March 1814.
[102] Letter 106, 2 September 1814.
[103] Penelope Byrde and Ann Saunders, 'The "Waterloo Ball" Dresses at the Museum of Costume, Bath', *Costume*, 34.1 (2000), pp. 64–9.

1.85 'Walking Dress',
The Repository of Arts, December
1817, hand-coloured engraving
on paper. Los Angeles County
Museum of Art/Gift of Dr
and Mrs Gerald Labiner/
www.lacma.org

1.86 'Evening Dress',
The Repository of Arts,
January 1818, hand-coloured
engraving on paper. Los Angeles
County Museum of Art/Gift of
Dr and Mrs Gerald Labiner/
www.lacma.org

1.87 'Carriage Dress',
The Repository of Arts,
January 1818, hand-coloured
engraving on paper. Los Angeles
County Museum of Art/Gift of
Dr and Mrs Gerald Labiner/
www.lacma.org

1817
OLD BLACK GOWN

Letter 152, Wednesday 26 February 1817, Chawton [to Caroline Austen]

'—*William was mistaken when he told your Mama we did not mean to mourn for Mrs Motley Austen. Living here we thought it necessary to array ourselves in our old Black Gowns, because there is a line of Connection with the family through the Prowtings & Harrisons of Southampton.*'

This is the last gown Jane Austen mentioned in the letters. How much more poignant, then, that these old black gowns are mourning items, when we know the author herself will die just under five months after writing. In 1808, Jane and Cassandra had black bombazine mourning gowns (see p. 65) and nine years is long enough that we may be seeing these same gowns grown worn with the passing of time. The connection with the deceased was slight, and so there is none of the flurry of acquisition of new mourning that accompanied the significant death of a sister-in-law earlier. There is thus little point turning to fashion plates and images of this year to visualise what these garments of the Austen sisters might have looked like, which is ironic, because 1817 saw an influx of mourning attire into fashion (figs 1.85–1.87).

Austen's death from a lingering illness on 18 July 1817 at the age of only 41 was a great loss to her family and, as time would reveal, to literature. A larger and more immediately shocking loss occurred on 6 November, however, with the death in hideously mismanaged childbirth of Princess Charlotte, the pretty, witty, nationally cherished 21-year-old daughter of the Prince of Wales. The death of the only legitimate heir to the throne amongst George III's sons' children changed history, as subsequently the bachelors among them rushed to marry. The Duke of Kent won the succession race with the birth of Princess Victoria in 1819, who ascended to the throne as Queen in 1837 and ushered in the monumental Victorian age.

After Charlotte's death, 'the dark and oppressive cloud which now hangs over the dominion of Fashion, has caused her ministers to droop the head, and the mourning stole and cypress plume hang over the fair forms', as a fashion magazine put it.[104] In less florid words, dress went dark in the etiquette of royal mourning, and Norwich crapes and bombazines were once again *à la mode*. A year later, on 17 November 1818, Queen Charlotte would die, and the fashion pages darkened again. By then Henry Austen had released his sister's last two finished novels *Northanger Abbey* and *Persuasion* in one volume, including the 'Biographical Notice' that finally revealed to the world the identity of 'A Lady', to whom the four previous novels were attributed. The name of Jane Austen would grow steadily in fame from then onwards.

[104] 'Fashions for December', *La Belle Assemblée: Or, Court and Fashionable Magazine*, November, issue 103 (London: J. Bell, 1817), p. 229.

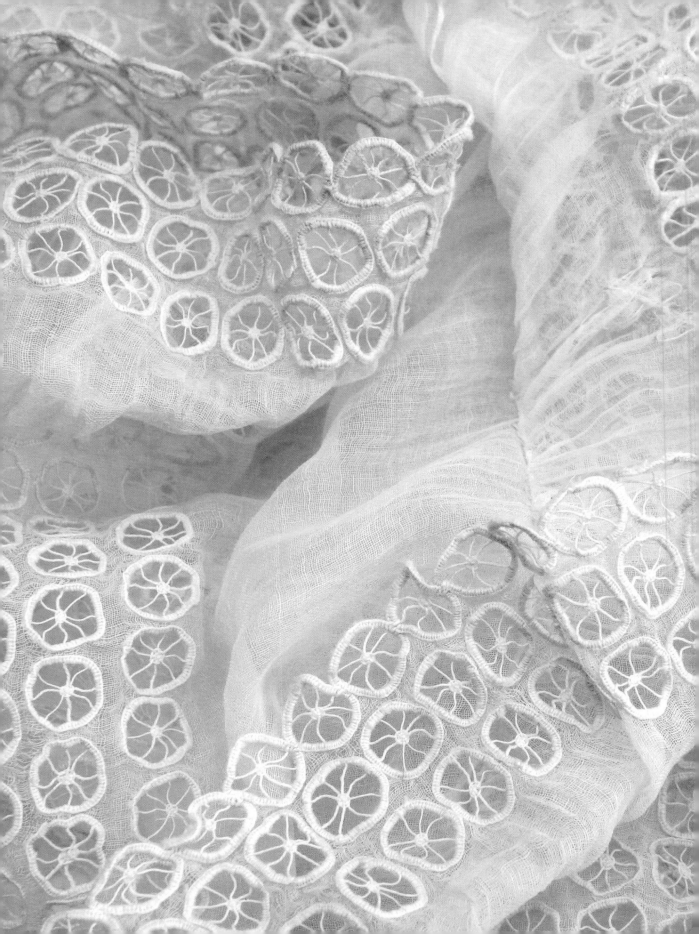

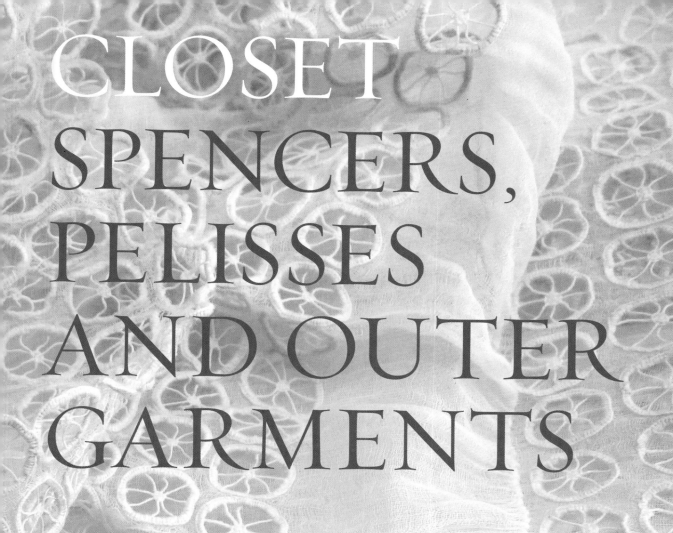

CLOSET

SPENCERS, PELISSES AND OUTER GARMENTS

2.1 Bound sample book containing different types, qualities and colours of kerseymere or cassimere cloth, English, 1795. © Victoria and Albert Museum, London

2.2 'Kerseymere Spencer' (detail), *The Lady's Monthly Museum*, February 1804, hand-coloured engraving on paper. Los Angeles Public Library

2.3 'Cossack Spencer', *La Belle Assemblée*, June 1807 (detail), hand-coloured engraving on paper, 21.9 × 12.7 cm. Los Angeles County Museum of Art/Gift of Dr and Mrs Gerald Labiner/www.lacma.org

1808
KERSEYMERE SPENCER

Letter 55, Thursday 30 June – Friday 1 July 1808, Godmersham

'What cold, disagreable weather, ever since Sunday!—I dare say you have Fires every day. My kerseymere Spencer is quite the comfort of our Even^g walks.'

Francis Yerbury of Bradford patented kerseymere in 1766 as 'cassimere' (also casimir, cassimer) by making a softer, lighter version of the long-established woollen fabric kersey, a 'thin superfine cloth for the summer season at home', as he described it, and one that was more like cashmere from which the name derives.[1] The fabric was 2/2 twill-woven from very fine yarns, preferably Spanish merino, not given a nap (raised and cut surface finish obscuring the weave), around 27 inches (68.5 cm) wide, and had the warmth and strength of the wider broadcloth but with less weight. The sample book in figure 2.1 shows the wide range of colours that kerseymeres came in, and they remained a popular textile throughout the nineteenth century.[2] Napoleon Bonaparte was also a fan. His valet recorded that the emperor's 'vest and britches were always of white casimere; he changed them every morning'.[3]

The summer season is precisely when Jane Austen is wearing the textile, rugged up against the vagaries of an English summer and its frequent rain and cold spells. Lightness in warm clothing is an underappreciated selling point for Regency consumers, when layers of thick wools in women's outer garments meant they could weigh upwards of two pounds (1 kg). An 1804 kerseymere spencer in 'Brown Egyptian Earth-color [*sic*]', worn with a tippet and matching hat, is shown in figure 2.2.

The short half-coat called a spencer was a new garment during the Regency period and became one of the era's distinctive female fashions (fig. 2.3). Even in Paris it was called a spencer instead of a French name. In 1801, Austen reported from Bath that 'black silk spencer[s], with a trimming round the armholes instead of sleeves', were much worn, noting that 'some are long before, and some long all round', describing how they were then in flux regarding the shape and style, and had a resemblance to her lace cloaks (see pp. 147 and 151).[4]

A spencer was originally a male coat, and the man who invented it was connected with the Austen family, though Jane may not have known or cared about its origination. Fashion histories often attribute the coat's invention to George Spencer, 4th Duke of Marlborough, but the earliest references in periodicals of around 1795 name the originator as his brother Charles. This gentleman 'betted some friends, that he could sport a fashion, the most useless and ridiculous that could be conceived, and that it should … be universally adopted'.[5] He did this by cutting off the tails of his coat to create a cropped jacket which swiftly moved from the male to the female wardrobe as its proportions complemented the risen waistline. Spencer was colonel of the Oxfordshire militia in which Henry Austen was a captain, and the two men were good friends.

[1] Peggy Hart, 'Cassimere: Hiding in Plain Sight', in Textile Society of America Symposium Proceedings, 2020, p. 2.
[2] See Hart 2020.
[3] Hart 2020, p. 2.
[4] Letter 37, 21–22 May 1801; see also Deirdre Le Faye (ed.), *Jane Austen's Letters* (Oxford: Oxford University Press, 2011), p. 92.
[5] *Norfolk Chronicle* (March 1795). Other, later versions of the story say a Spencer nobleman either burned off his coat-tails in front of the fire or tore one off when riding, and decided to make the truncated jacket a fashion as a way of carrying it off.

2.4 'London Dresses for April…
Pelisse of silk, made without
plaits [pleats]; a small bonnet, to
correspond with the pelisse' (detail),
The Lady's Monthly Museum, April
1808. Public domain

2.5 'Cornette de Tulle. Redingote
de Perkale, garnie d'un Effilé' [Tulle
cornette cap. Percale pelisse, with an
effilé trim] in *Elegantia, of tijdschrift van
mode, luxe en smaak voor dames*, April
1808. Rijksmuseum, Amsterdam

1808
A PELISSE

Letter 53, Monday 20 – Wednesday 22 June 1808, Godmersham

'Her very agreable present will make my circumstances quite easy. I shall reserve half for my Pelisse.'

Earlier in the letter, Austen told Cassandra that '—This morning brought me a letter from Mrs Knight, containing the usual Fee, & all the usual Kindness.'[6] The 'fee' or 'agreable present' was a gift of money, something the wealthy woman could well afford. Mr Thomas Knight was a cousin of Revd Austen. He and his wife Catherine had no children and in 1783 adopted the Austen's second son Edward as their heir. He went to live with them at their main property, Godmersham Park in Kent, and legally took the surname Knight after Mrs Knight's death in 1812 (Thomas died in 1794). After he married Elizabeth Bridges in 1791 and commenced creation of their 11 children, Edward's sisters often went to stay with the family in Kent, where Austen wrote this letter home. At this point Mrs Knight was living nearby in Canterbury.

The name and first concept of the pelisse was a borrowing from masculine martial dress, where the garment was a fur-lined, braid-decorated half-coat essential to regimental Hussar uniforms. However, female fashion soon ran away with it as a kind of coat-dress or overgown made in inventive variety. Pelisses appear in early nineteenth-century fashion in every kind and weight of fabric, from sheer cotton muslins to fur-lined luxury, worn indoors and out, in all seasons, and reaching anywhere from the wearer's knees to her ankles (fig. 2.4). They were also spelled pellise and pelice. Pelisses were vehicles for fashion, situated between the essential gown and the hardier warmth of redingotes (see p. 115), mantles and cloaks. Where eighteenth-century women added warming garments underneath, like quilted petticoats, the slimmer lines of Regency fashion encouraged their addition on the outside (although flannel undergarments were also used; see p. 213).

Pelisses could be cut with a separate skirt piece, like gowns (this was the more common construction), or they could flow uninterrupted from shoulder to hem, as Austen's surviving silk pelisse does (see p. 107). Some pelisses had cutaway fronts revealing the skirt below; some enveloped the neck in high rolls. The garment was a staple for women in Austen's dressed world. In *Persuasion*, Captain Wentworth likens his ageing ship to the ubiquity of pelisses: 'I had no more discoveries to make than you would have as to the fashion and strength of any old pelisse, which you had seen lent about among half your acquaintance ever since you could remember, and which at last, on some very wet day, is lent to yourself.'[7]

Austen already had a black velvet pelisse by this point. She was looking for a new one three months earlier than she describes refreshing the previous one, and mentioned, 'I am sure I shall have no occasion this winter for anything new of that sort.'[8] This implies the new pelisse considered here would have been more of a spring or summer garment (it may be that the windfall did go to the cost of remaking the black velvet one, as is explored on page 103.) One windy June day the next year, Cassandra got a white (likely cotton) pelisse muddy when visiting Wye, so it may be a similar garment that Austen bought to wear that summer (fig. 2.5).[9]

[6] Letter 53, 20–22 June 1808.
[7] *Persuasion*, vol. I, ch. viii.
[8] Letter 59, 15–16 October 1808.
[9] *Chronology*, p. 369.

2.6 'Costume Parisien', *Journal des Dames et des Modes*, 31 December 1807: 'Toque et Redingote de Velours, garnies en Satin' [Cap and pelisse of velvet, trimmed with satin], plate 860. Bibliothèque nationale de France, Paris

2.7 'London Walking & Full Dress… Black velvet pelisse, with a stand-up collar, trimmed with plaited net, and fastened on the right breast with steel ornaments, and down the front; to match round the bottom with swans-down', *The Lady's Magazine*, November 1805

2.8 'London Fashionable Walking & Full Dress', *The Lady's Magazine*, 1808. Los Angeles Public Library

1808
BLACK VELVET PELISSE

Letter 57, Friday 7 – Sunday 9 October 1808, Southampton: Castle Square

'We must turn our black pelisses into new, for Velvet is to be very much worn this winter.'

Clearly, the new pelisse Austen contemplated buying three months earlier (see p. 101) was to supersede or complement the black velvet pelisses already in her and Cassandra's wardrobes. We can assume they were made *c.*1802–7, given how often Austen updated her wardrobe. At this time nearly all velvet was made of silk (cotton or woollen velvet was more often called plush), meaning the original black pelisses would have been a significant financial investment in the sisters' attire. This refreshing of an existing article of clothing is tucked in at the end of a letter in which Austen was glad to hear of their sister-in-law Elizabeth's 'hitherto happy recovery' from the birth of her eleventh child, from Cassandra who was staying with that part of the family. Unfortunately, the poor woman died on 10 October; Austen had heard the news by the 13th (Letter 58). The black velvet pelisse became suddenly enlisted as part of the mourning dress about which she hoped Cassandra could give her 'some direction', and which resulted in the addition of a new gown (see p. 65) and bonnet (p. 133).

Austen went into more detail two letters later, on 15–16 October. She assessed that 'My Mourning however will not impoverish me, for by having my velvet Pelisse fresh lined & made up, I am sure I shall have no occasion <u>this winter</u> for anything new of that sort', showing a mindfulness of economic use commensurate with her finances.[10] Black velvet pelisses appear in fashion plates across this time (figs 2.6–2.8). Their coloured trims and accessories signify that these are not ensembles for mourning. When Austen accessorised hers with black crape and bombazine, the social meaning of her pelisse would shift into the memorial. Accompanied by bright shawls and lively headwear, as per the plates, the velvet coat-dress would return to its state as a fashionable winter garment.

Letter 59 shares further cost-cutting strategies for revising this pelisse. Austen was going to 'take my Cloak for the Lining—& shall send yours [to Kent] on the chance of its' doing something of the same for you', though Cassandra's pelisse 'is in better repair'.[11] The only two cloaks Austen has mentioned so far are the lace ones of 1799 and 1800 (see pp. 147 and 151). It may be that the body of the latter was made from a light silk such as persian that would also be suitable for lining a pelisse, just like her surviving pelisse is lined (see p. 107). Perhaps after eight years the lace was tattered and the silk shabby. The high probability of the cloaks being black, based on fashionable usage, means the lining fabric they could lend was the right colour for this black garment. However, Austen may have had another, fuller or wider cloak of a different colour she deemed sacrificable. As to being in 'better repair', velvet often loses its pile with wear, especially at the edges of garments such as cuffs and collars, and it is harder to clean when dusty or spilt upon. Recutting, shaping, binding or trimming would give the opportunity for tactically hiding any existing wear and tear.

[10] Letter 59, 15–16 October 1808.
[11] Letter 59, 15–16 October 1808.

2.9 Cotton print pelisse with buttoned front and neck frill, *c*.1815. Brooklyn Museum Costume Collection at The Metropolitan Museum of Art, New York/Gift of the Brooklyn Museum, 2009/Gift of Florence Inniss, 1970

2.10 'An Autumnal Pelisse', *La Belle Assemblée*, 1 September 1812, hand-coloured engraving on paper. Los Angeles County Museum of Art/Gift of Dr and Mrs Gerald Labiner/www.lacma.org

2.11 R. Sands, 'London Dresses for March ... A pelisse of green merino cloth, buttoned down the front and up the arm with small gold buttons, the collar and cuffs of white or green velvet; an ermine tippet', *The Lady's Monthly Museum*, March 1811

1811
PELISSE WITH
BUTTONS

Letter 70, Thursday 18 – Saturday 20 April 1811, London: Sloane Street

'—Our Pelisses are 17/S. each—she charges only 8/ for the making, but the Buttons seem expensive;—are expensive, I might have said—for the fact is plain enough.

This is now the third pelisse Austen has mentioned in her letters. She had one in 1808 (see p. 101), bought another the same year (p. 103), and will have another *c.*1812–14, the only known clothing of hers to survive (p. 107), which, because it has no buttons, is not this pelisse. This was roughly a new pelisse every two or three years, overlapping in use and presumably warmth, and status, as they get a little shabbier through wear. This pelisse was bought in London at the same time as a straw riding hat (see p. 135), as Austen was keeping up with current fashion in her new purchases while in the capital. There is no clue as to what the garment's fabric might have been, and the range of materials used for pelisses was so broad it could have been nearly any textile.

The letter is the only time Austen mentions a cost for making a body garment, in a way that merits some explanation as to how Regency dressmakers divided their bills. The final price was the total for sewing the garment, its textile, lining and trimming, with all parts itemised separately. Eight shillings for making was a fairly standard price in London, for both gowns and pelisses, and only starts to rise to ten shillings around 1815. Therefore, nine shillings comprises the cost of the buttons, the lining and applying and/or supplying a trimming. Clients could bring their own fabric to the dressmaker, as they then had control of the selection, colour and quality. Since Austen bought so many gowns in piece, this is what she would have done here. Her buttons could have been functional, to hold the garment closed (figs 2.9 and 2.10), or decorative, used as trimming as in figure 2.11.

We know there is a trimming – which may have been the buttons – because of a further letter. On 30 April, Austen was somewhat grumpy: '—I do <u>not</u> mean to provide another trimming for my Pelisse, for I am determined to spend no more money, so I shall wear it as it is, longer than I ought, & then—I do not know.'[12] It sounds as if something has gone awry with her new pelisse and it is not as expected. Her phrase 'longer than I ought' is ambiguous, though intelligible to Cassandra. Austen could mean that the hem length is too long, or she could mean the duration of wear. It is also possible to read the passage as referring to an older pelisse which has been altered or updated somehow. It is tempting to infer that this mildly dissatisfying pelisse carried Austen through until she obtained her beautiful brown silk one a year or so later.

[12] Letter 72, 30 April 1811.

2.12 Front of Jane Austen's silk
pelisse, 1812–14. © Hampshire
Cultural Trust

2.13 Back of Jane Austen's silk
pelisse (see fig. 2.12). © Hampshire
Cultural Trust

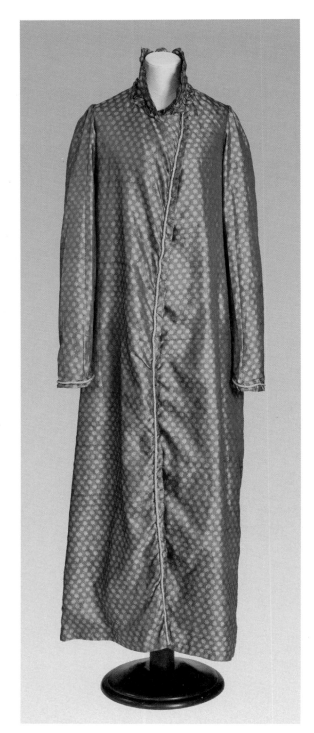

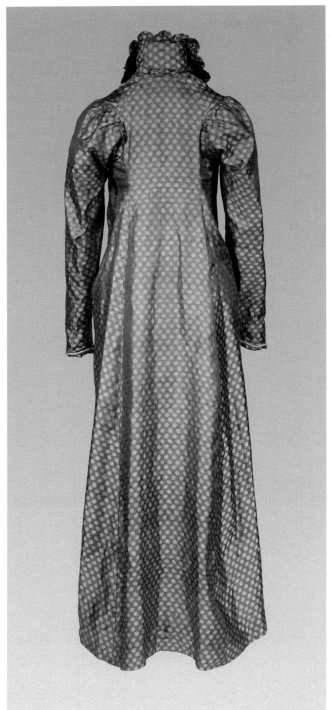

1812–14
BROWN SILK PELISSE

Letter 105, Tuesday 23 – Wednesday 24 August 1814, London: 23 Hans Place

'Henry ... has once mentioned a scheme, which I should rather like—calling on the Birches & the Crutchleys in our way. It may never come to anything, but I must provide for the possibility, by troubling you to send up my Silk Pelisse by Collier on Saturday.—I feel it would be necessary on such an occasion'

The indisputable star of the surviving wardrobe items once belonging to Austen is a silk pelisse coat dated 1812–14, the only body garment among the memorabilia (in the collection of Hampshire Cultural Trust; figs 2.12 and 2.13). The reference from this letter is the only one that could describe the piece. Austen's identification by no other descriptor than 'silk' implies that she had only one such garment at the time of writing, suitable for an occasion, though she had other pelisses (see previous pages). If another pelisse made from silk was in her possession, other qualifying adjectives about colour or textile would have been needed.[13] It cannot be the pelisse of April 1811 (see p. 105), since this one has no buttons and can be dated stylistically one to three years later. Based on the style, Austen acquired the pelisse not before 1812, and potentially as late as the year she wrote the letter.

The pelisse is made of an expensive brown twill silk sarcenet, patterned with falling oak leaves woven in pale gold, lined in white silk (fig. 2.17), sewn with yellow silk thread, and adorned with more silk cord (figs 2.14 and 2.15). The fact that it is a garment contrasts with the jewellery and accessories forming all that is known of Austen's dress relics (see Chapter 6, and pp. 143 and 187). Because Regency clothing was bespoke, surviving garments reflect the body they were made for, and so this pelisse has been a template to help understand Austen's physique. To do so, I have made detailed reconstructions of it, looking at every aspect of its production and context

in close detail. This work revealed new information about Austen's bodily appearance and has been published in more detail in an open-access academic article,[14] and an exhibition catalogue.[15]

How do we know it was hers? The provenance is strong but not watertight, and the short answer is we will probably never know for certain. The longer answer is that everything about the coat's qualities, construction and especially its size supports the story that Austen did indeed wear it. A descendant of the Knight family donated the pelisse to Hampshire County Museums and Archives in 1993. The donor inherited it from her grandmother, Mrs Winifred Jenkyns (née Austen-Leigh), who had received it from Eleanor Steele (née Glubbe, b. 1857). Miss Glubbe had visited the Knight family as a young lady of eighteen, around 1875, and was given the garment by Miss Marianne Knight (a descendant of Jane's brother Edward Knight), along with other mementoes 'now mislaid'.[16] At the age of seventy-three Mrs Steele felt the pelisse should return to the Austen family and sent it to Jenkyns, the great-granddaughter of Jane's elder brother James Austen. Mrs Steele's note accompanying the parcel reads: 'I missed the little coat for a long time but lately it turned up. I cannot remember if it was "Jane's" but it seems probable.'[17] If Mrs Steele had known what difference her 'probable' made to the certainty of attribution, she may have used different phrasing, or perhaps she had no certainty herself. Mrs Jenkyns wrote: 'Mrs Steele in 1930

2.14 Side collar and front with silk cord of Jane Austen's silk pelisse (see fig. 2.12). © Hampshire Cultural Trust

2.15 Detail of inner cuff of Jane Austen's silk pelisse, with silk cord (see fig. 2.12). Hampshire Cultural Trust/Photograph by the author

could not positively state that this dress had been Jane's own, but knew it belonged to one of the Austens.'[18]

My more technical article on reconstructing the pelisse outlines its many congruencies with what we know of Austen's bodily shape. In particular, the pelisse matches closely descriptions of her long, thin figure, which range from an unkind neighbour's 'a thin upright piece of wood or iron' to a 'tall, thin *spare* person with very high cheekbones', 'tall and slight, but not drooping', and the more complimentary 'slight and elegant'.[19] Austen herself considered that she was 'a tall woman'.[20] Based on measurements and testing the replicas on a range of people, the pelisse's wearer was also tall and thin, with long arms and a round chest. Her vital statistics were approximately 31–33 inch (79–84 cm) bust, 24 inch (61 cm) waist, and 33–34 inch (84–86 cm) hips; she was between five feet six inches and five feet eight inches (168–173 cm) tall, which is categorically tall for a woman in the early nineteenth century.

The silk for this pelisse would have been a major purchase, which would have made sense to carry out among London's plethora of retailers. It is of English manufacture, as French silk imports were banned. While Regency people merrily and frequently smuggled cloth, in this case its origins are verified by a tiny visible section of selvedge. Stripe patterns in silk selvedges were distinctive to particular areas and manufacturers, and can be a useful way to pinpoint a textile's origins. The more complicated the weave, the more labour involved, and so the more it cost. A decorative silk, such as the sarcenet, would have represented a considerable outlay for Austen.

Unfortunately, only one of her letters survives from late 1812, the first point it is likely the fabric was bought, and we have no record of any purchase by her that matches this cloth. Austen had made some money from her writing by this time; the pelisse could have been a sartorial indulgence. At any rate, it is dated to the period when for the first time she has some independent financial means. In July 1813 she could record, 'I have … written myself into £250.'[21] Her first trip to the metropolis since achieving some income appears to have been May 1813 but no textile purchases are recorded, maybe because she was in mourning for Eliza Austen.

Barbara Johnson's album of textile pieces is once again useful to interpreting Austen's material life. Johnson purchased plain, twilled and figured (patterned) sarcenets in the early nineteenth century. Two entries evoke the Austen pelisse. The first is an unfigured or plain 'Brown

French Sarsanet Pelise, nine yards, six shillings a yard, half ell wide made at Bath March 1811' (the attached silk sample is tabby weave with a black warp and brown weft). A March 1809 entry for a 'figur'd Sarsnet Gown, ten yards, half-yard wide made at Bath' has a sample of silk attached which is very like the pelisse fabric (fig. 2.18). The twill textile has an identical warm brown ground, with a stylised leaf-like pattern woven in silvery-grey silk in opposing twill. It cost nine shillings and sixpence per yard. A similarly scaled small-leaf-patterned sarcenet is used in an 1807 pelisse now in the collection of the Fashion Museum, Bath. After replicating the Austen pelisse, I calculated it would take seven and a half yards of silk to make – just the amount Austen requested from Cassandra to make her brown gown a dozen years earlier (see p. 45). Silk fabrics had much narrower widths than cloths of other fibres, running from half a yard (18 in./46 cm) wide to around 22 inches (56 cm). Accordingly, silk not only cost more per yard, but the purchaser also needed more of those yards to make into clothing. Even using cheaper sarcenet, the financial investment in materials for such an item emphasises the quality and importance as an article of clothing of the pelisse. I estimate it to have cost somewhere around £5.11s.6d total, including the labour of the maker, who may well have been based in London.

Sarcenet was a popular clothing fabric, and Austen had a lilac gown of the material in 1814 (see p. 91). Initially, I thought the pelisse's white plain-weave silk lining (fig. 2.16) was also a sarcenet. However, the lining's softness, its light weight, slight shine and translucency combine to identify it as persian, an even commoner fabric, popular for its relative cheapness. Austen delighted in a letter from her niece Anna Lefroy describing a shopping expedition for persian: 'I was particularly amused with your picture of Grafton House; — it is just so. —How much I should like finding you there one day, seated on your high stool, with 15 rolls of persian before you.' (Grafton House is discussed in more detail on page 181.) Almost twenty years earlier, Austen had admitted to spending all her money on 'white gloves and pink persian'.[22] Persian was around half the price of sarcenet, recorded as costing 2s.6d per yard in 1812 and 1813, and 2s.4d and 2s.9d in 1817.[23] This economy would have suited Austen's always straitened purse more comfortably. So significant an investment as the pelisse would also have run the gauntlet of family opinion, like her new gown in 1800 (see p. 37).

Austen's sarcenet purchase may have held further

2.16 Printed cotton cambric swatch matching the design on the figured sarsenet of Jane Austen's pelisse (see figs. 2.12–2.15), *The Repository of Arts*, May 1812. Courtesy of the author

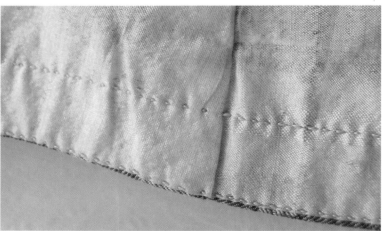

2.17 Detail of stitching on the lining of Jane Austen's silk pelisse (see fig. 2.12). Hampshire Cultural Trust/Photograph by the author

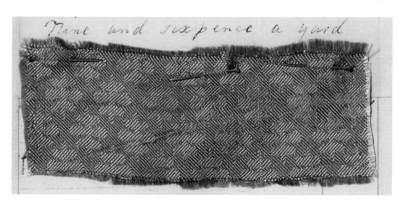

2.18 Figured silk twill sarsenet, March 1809, from Barbara Johnson's album. © Victoria and Albert Museum, London

family significance. The pattern identified as oak leaves had strong associations with Britain's naval prowess during the sustained Napoleonic conflicts of the early nineteenth century, a navy in which two of her six brothers served. From the official Royal Navy march 'Heart of Oak' (1760) to the profusion of oak-tree-laden mourning memorabilia produced for Nelson's funeral (1806), the oak leaf and acorn motifs expressed a patriotic Britishness invested in the navy. The 1809 Johnson album silk hints at the popularity of small, stylised oak-leaf or acorn-like motifs, as seen in the pelisse silk. A printed cotton cambric dated May 1812, included as a swatch in *The Repository of Arts*, is an exact match for the pelisse textile (fig. 2.16).[24] There must be a manufacturing or copying relationship between the silk and cotton designs because they are identical, the golden leaves being precisely the same size, scale and colourway as the silk – a congruence I have not yet found in any other textile pattern. The cotton puts forward an 1812 manufacture date for the silk, because the background of diagonal printed brown lines imitates the silk's woven twill lines, implying it was designed after the silk. It could have retailed any time after this, however.

Could Austen have made this pelisse herself? Her sewing was excellent, as her embroidered handkerchief and she herself attest (see p. 187). But among gentry women it appears that even those in poorer circumstances availed themselves of mantua- or dress-makers for gowns and other long body garments. Given the absence of definite references in the letters to Austen making gowns, and the tendency for women not to make outer garments, especially in an expensive silk that required careful handling, this pelisse fits into the category of professionally made clothing. In support, its professional origins emerge in the complex cut of the sleeve, which must derive from an expert pattern-drafter.

How fashionable was it? Dating a garment relies on subtle points of observation and differentiation. Here, the amount and positioning of the pleating and the fullness in the sleeve head are the best date indicators. The key stylistic points are the popular high collar, slightly flared cut of the skirts and sleeve-heads getting a little fuller, with the fullness moving from the top shoulder to further down the back. The high neck, puffed decoration and small amount of increase in the lower skirt also tally with garments (fig. 2.20) and engraved fashion plates included in magazines from this date. The decoration is restrained for a garment of the 1810s. A September 1813 morning dress plate published in *La Belle Assemblée* (fig. 2.19) shows

similar but more numerous ruched puffs adorning a pelisse on the collar and armholes, and demonstrates the relationship between ideal fashion and actual garments. Brown appears repeatedly in plates of fashionable dress from around 1800 onwards, and her 1801 and 1813 gowns (see pp. 45 and 85) show it was a colour Austen liked to wear.

The pelisse is hardly worn. If it was Austen's, she had no more than five years' use, including a year of illness when a fine pelisse would have been socially superfluous. The only alteration is the loss of a belt that was once stitched on at the central back seam and fastened under the bust at the front. The belt on the reconstruction in figure 2.21 takes its pattern from a similar pelisse in the Victoria and Albert Museum London (fig. 2.20), and its position and presence are indicated by minute evidence of stitching. The inch-wide (2.5 cm) white silk waist ribbon that secured the pelisse inside has also been torn from its place. Combined with this internal waist stay, the replica belt worked effectively to close the pelisse, at the right height, and solved a long-standing query about how to keep it closed, as the front opening has no fastenings of any kind, and neither are there discernible marks revealing the ghosts of brooches or pins past. With the belt in place, a small pin, brooch or ribbon would easily fasten the neckline.

The pelisse may have been worn with the fronts open like a revers collar, as seen in contemporary fashion plates and as displayed on some official images of the garment, but the internal finishing with large facing, and visible lining and stitching, does not suggest it was made to be seen. The yellow silk cording that runs all the way down both front sections does create a visible ridge through the fabric when one is placed underneath the other. I first questioned why the trimming was symmetrical when one edge would be hidden underneath, but trying the replica pelisse on moving figures reveals the lower fronts fall open when walking, so the cord creates a pleasing decorative visual equality while hiding the construction stitches.

A garment is where style and consumer cultures of an age manifest themselves, demonstrating how the wearer may have negotiated those cultures to reflect her own taste and situation in life. This pelisse is a material text as richly explicit as any of Austen's literary constructions. It, too, can be 'read' in the same way, through the process of unpicking and remaking to reveal a whole world of experience around the business of getting fashionably dressed.

2.19 Morning dress, 'a pelisse of the palest faun-colour sarsnet, ... the trimming, which is composed of crape, is ... a crape rosette slightly spotted with floss silk, and the heart of the rosette is a very small floss silk button of the most elegant workmanship: this trimming goes entirely round the pelisse', *La Belle Assemblée*, September 1813, no. 18

2.20 Red and blue shot silk sarcenet pelisse, English, 1805–10. © The Victoria and Albert Museum, London / Given by Miss M. D. Nicholson

2.21 Hilary Davidson, replica of Jane Austen's pelisse (see fig. 2.12), 2007. Courtesy of the author

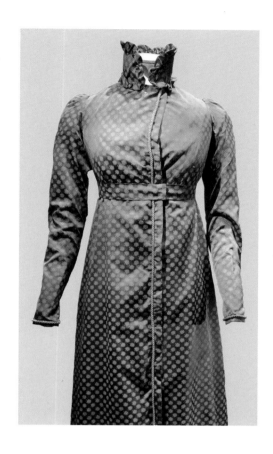

[13] Velvet was usually made from silk, but, as we have seen, Austen referred to it by the fabric.

[14] Hilary Davidson, 'Reconstructing Jane Austen's Silk Pelisse, 1812–1814', *Costume*, 49.2 (2015), pp. 198–223.

[15] Hilary Davidson, 'Jane Austen's Pelisse Coat', in *Jane Austen: Writer in the World*, ed. Kathryn Sutherland (Oxford: The Bodleian Library, 2017), pp. 56–75.

[16] Letter from Winifred Jenkyns, 7 November 1931.

[17] Hampshire County Council, 'Jane Austen's Pelisse Coat': http://www3.hants.gov.uk/austen/austen-pelisse.htm [accessed 7 May 2014].

[18] Letter from Winifred Jenkyns, 7 November 1931.

[19] Cited in Claire Tomalin, *Jane Austen: A Life* (London: Viking, 1997), pp. 108 and 111.

[20] Letter 33, 25 January 1801.

[21] Letter 86, 3–6 July 1813.

[22] Letter 116, December 1814, and Letter 1, 9–10 January 1796.

[23] Topham 1810.

[24] *The Repository of Arts*, vol. 41, May 1812 (London: R. Ackermann), p. 313.

2.22 Scarlet woollen hooded cloak, fronts bound with silk ribbon, collar quilted with pink silk lining, lined with scarlet and brown silk, English, 1800–20. Image courtesy of Manchester Art Gallery

2.23 Sir Henry Raeburn, *Portrait of Ellen Cochrane*, oil on canvas, 76.5 × 63.8 cm, *c.*1808. Philadelphia Museum of Art/ Gift of Mr and Mrs John Howard McFadden, Jr, 1952

2.24 Diana Sperling, *The Lord of the Manor & his family going out to a dinner Party at 5 o'Clock with a tremendous stile before them* (detail), watercolour on paper, September 1816. Private collection

1811
WALKING THINGS

Letter 75, Thursday 6 June 1811, Chawton

'I had just left off writing & put on my Things for walking to Alton, when Anna & her friend Harriot called in their way thither, so we went together.'

Austen was a good walker, and the letters reflect constant perambulations until the final illness slowly rendered her unable. The 'things' suitable for walking in a lady's wardrobe extend several possibilities for what Austen was putting on.

Besides good footwear (see p. 167), it was important to have an outer garment to keep out the wind and weather, even in summer. For walking Austen would have needed something stouter than her fashionable yet flimsy lace cloaks (see pp. 147 and 151), perhaps one of the bright red worsted or frieze cloaks (figs 2.22 and 2.23) that were common scarlet spots of colour amid English towns and villages, as foreigners noticed. In 1817, the Austen ladies' servant Sally 'got a new red Cloak, which adds much to her happiness', and they were notable for being worn across social classes in the countryside.[25] Austen may have worn something less vivid, more like the 'Grey Woollen' cloak costing ten shillings she ordered from Coleby in Alton the next year on behalf of Martha Lloyd, although that was in cold November.[26] Cloaks were convenient in that they threw on easily around any shape of ensemble underneath, had capacious hoods that would also cover headwear, and in the event of a sudden shower could be used to shelter bundles being carried.

Wool is the best fibre for water resistance, and also stays warm when damp. Austen may have had some kind of walking dress (meaning the ensemble, not a gown alone) of cloth, which at the time always meant a wool fabric. Austen's niece Fanny recorded such an outfit received 'On my birthday Jan'y 23rd 1808 when I was 15 … I had very handsome presents to viz: a new walking dress (Pelisse, bonnet & waist coat of the same grey kind of cloth) from Papa.'[27] The many appearances of 'walking dress' in fashion plates (see figs 1.24, 1.29, 1.85, 2.7, 2.8, 4.6, 4.9, 4.17, 4.18, 4.21 and 5.16) often contain outerwear covering the gown, and the accompanying texts detail the sturdier textiles involved in their making. A woollen pelisse, redingote or spencer worn over her garb would also be an effective garment for walking in, as Austen's kerseymere spencer was 'quite the comfort of our Eveng walks' three years earlier (see p. 99).[28] Redingotes in England were usually the feminine equivalent of men's great, riding or driving coats, a heavy outer coat to keep out the weather. The word, in fact, is a borrowing back into English from the French pronunciation of 'riding-coat' (fig. 2.6), while, confusingly, what the French called a 'redingote' in fashion plates was the English 'pelisse'. The shoulder capes so typical of the masculine coats found their way into the female garment also, providing extra layers to keep off the weather on the most exposed upper body. Wool cloaks for both sexes often had an extra shoulder cape, too. While some more sophisticated cloaks had wide sleeves, the tailoring and cutting involved in this detail increased the price.

Finally, Austen would have added a bonnet on her head to keep the sun off, or the heat in during colder seasons. The watercolours by her contemporary Diana Sperling show what the combined ensemble might have looked like, as she and her sisters of the same social level as Austen traipse through the countryside near their home (fig. 2.24).

[25] Letter 149, 23 January 1817.
[26] Letter 77, 29–30 November 1812.
[27] Fanny Knight's Diaries, U.951/F.24/1–69, Kent History and Library Centre. Recorded in *Rackham's Fashionable Repository*.
[28] Letter 55, 30 June–1 July 1808.

BAND BOX
HATS, CAPS
AND
BONNETS

1798
HAPPINESS HAT

Letter 10, Saturday 27 – Sunday 28 October 1798, Steventon

'I bought some Japan Ink likewise, & next week shall begin my operations on my hat, on which You know my principal hopes of happiness depend.'

Jane Austen had a large range of headwear, like all her peers. Besides the caps worn underneath hats, and at home (see p. 121), partaking of the latest novelty of headdress was an excellent way to engage with fashionable variety at lesser expense than whole garments. Fashion magazines often displayed pages only of caps, hats and bonnets (fig. 3.1), and these mutable accessories anchored changes of taste into genteel consumers' wardrobes.

Bonnets with a brim were quite a new kind of headwear for Regency women. They evolved from the eighteenth-century habit of pulling down a flat hat brim to hold it about the face; the back of the brim was soon lost. Bought either whole, or in parts, a bonnet comprised a front, a solid or fabric back, and a riot of trimmings of the kind proffered at milliners' shops: ribbons of all sorts and colours, flowers, edgings, cord, gimp and galloon. Trimmings and ribbons were usually pinned onto the bonnet base for ease of altering the decoration quickly to match a gown, as a new style, or to refresh an old bonnet, something Lizzy Bennet in *Pride and Prejudice* may be doing when she is found trimming a hat.[1] However, a bonnet could also mean a flatter-crowned, brimless soft hat, more like berets or tam o'shanters – a Scotch bonnet. The word 'hat' encompasses everything else, and in using it Austen gives little clue as to what style her happiness depended on, facetious though the comment is.

There is a clue, though, in her purchase of Japan ink. As Deirdre Le Faye identified, it was 'A superior kind of black writing ink, generally glossy when dry.'[2] The connection is that the liquid may have been used to touch up the brim or crown of a glossy black straw

or chip (wood strip) hat. The image in figure 3.2 is from the same year of Austen's letter, in the *Gallery of Fashion*. The high-crowned, round, brimless headwear is described as a 'Black straw patent hat, worked with chenille; white and pink military feather placed on the right side.' Austen's could have been any shape.

---

[1] *Pride and Prejudice*, vol. I, ch. ii.
[2] Letters, p. 360.

3.3 'Costume Parisiens', *Journal des Dames et des Modes*, 6 December 1801: '5. Demi-Paysanes, 6. Demi Bonnet garni en Tulle' [5. Half-peasant caps, 6. Half-bonnet trimmed with tulle], plate 348

3.4 *Capote à la Titus*, embroidered cotton batiste, 1800–10. Villa Rosemaine Collection, Toulon

3.5 Bertel Thorvaldsen, *Lady Elizabeth Vernon, née Bingham*, Carrara marble, 42.9 × 17.8 × 20.3 cm, modelled 1816 and/or 1817/1818, carved *c.*1821. National Gallery of Art, Washington, DC/Patrons' Permanent Fund

3.6 Back view of Bertel Thorvaldsen's *Lady Elizabeth Vernon, née Bingham* (see fig. 3.5). National Gallery of Art, Washington, DC/ Patrons' Permanent Fund

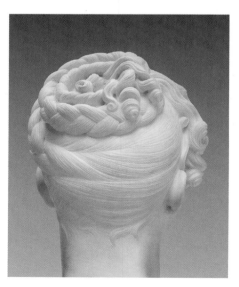

1798
EVENING CAPS

Letter 13, Saturday 1 – Sunday 2 December 1798, Steventon

'I have made myself two or three caps to wear of evenings since I came home, and they save me a world of torment as to hairdressing, which at present gives me no trouble beyond washing and brushing, for my long hair is always plaited up out of sight, and my short hair curls well enough to want no papering.'

Caps were an essential part of Regency gentry women's lives. The getting of caps and their style appear in Austen's letters more than any other garment, conjuring their usefulness, as well as their smaller size and affordability, as sites of novel fashion response. Everyone, including teenage girls, wore caps in the morning, as borne out by their constant presence in fashion plates for morning dress. Periodicals give caps of satin and lace, or lace and muslin, as suitable for morning dress (fig. 3.3), and ladies' heads tended to be covered even in domestic privacy. In a sense, this was also a practical response to the 'world of torment as to hairdressing' in the everyday setting. It was much easier to tuck one's hair up under a cap than to curl and pin it. Evening caps were often more decorative and pretty than morning caps (fig. 3.4).

Wearing a cap in the evening instead of one's own beautifully arranged hair was a subtle gradation of adoption in line with getting older. The habitual wearing of evening caps denoted middle age. The Austen sisters notably espoused these earlier than usual – Austen was only 22 when she wrote this letter. Caroline Austen recalled in 1867 that '[Austen] always wore a cap—Such was the custom with ladies who were not quite young—at least of a morning but I never saw her without one, to the best of my remembrance, either morning or evening.'[3] 'There was little public recognition of [women's] "middle age" at all', historian Amanda Vickery explains. 'Rather, there was an alarming haemorrhage of youth from the late twenties with absolute "old age" in women appearing to arrive at least a decade earlier than today, around fifty.'[4] Caps were an effective way to manage the transition sartorially, and they hid many sins: greying, unwashed or undressed hair and locks cropped during illness.

Regency women's hair was divided approximately from ear to ear into front or short hair, and long or back hair (see fig. 5.13). The front hair was the site of innumerable hairstyling modes, often based around curls, appearing in almost every female image of the period. As the possessor of naturally curly hair, Austen could cut out another stage of hairdressing by not having to coax her tresses into fashionable lines with curling papers. The length of Regency women's remaining 'back' hair could be considerable. Another niece, Louisa Hill (née Knight), remembered Austen's long chestnut-brown hair as reaching to her knees.[5] Other rare depictions of undone hair show equally abundant waist-length or longer tresses. Statues showing the back of the head, as in figures 3.5 and 3.6, also reveal hair length through the number of coils achieved.

[3] Austen-Leigh 2008, p. 169.
[4] Amanda Vickery, *The Gentleman's Daughter* (London and New Haven, CT: Yale University Press, 2003), p. 859.
[5] As told to Lady Campbell in 1856: *Family Record*, p. 274.

3.7 Nicholas Heideloff, (left) 'casque bonnet of black velvet, trimmed across the crown with a black curled feather, and round it with a band of rose coloured velvet', (right) 'Bonnet à la Turque of black velvet', *Gallery of Fashion*, January 1798. Courtesy of the author

3.8 Nicholas Heideloff, 'Afternoon Dress… Black velvet bonnet hat with a white bugle band. One white ostrich feather', *Gallery of Fashion*, January 1799. Courtesy of the author

3.9 Nicholas Heideloff, 'Bonnet of white satin, trimmed with *coquelicot* cords; *coquelicot* silk handkerchief, arranged upon the hind part and tied under the chin; black and coquelicot military feather placed in front', *Gallery of Fashion*, November 1798. Courtesy of the author

1798
BLACK VELVET CAP

Letter 14, Tuesday 18 – Wednesday 19 December 1798, Steventon

'—I took the liberty a few days ago of asking your Black velvet Bonnet to lend me its cawl, which it very readily did, & by which I have been enabled to give a considerable improvement of dignity to my Cap ....'

An early letter demonstrates the kind of invention the Austen sisters employed in creating stylish clothes, and how the pair collaborated both ideas and materials. While Cassandra was away, Austen took the black velvet cawl, or soft back part covering a large part of the head, from an existing bonnet to adapt her own cap. While the word 'bonnet' now means headwear with a large brim around the face, styles in this mode were more popular in the 1810s onwards. In the 1790s, a bonnet was more of a soft, voluminous cap, as figures 3.7 and 3.8 show. Austen could interchange a bonnet cawl with that of her cap.

> —I shall wear it on Thursday, but I hope you will not be offended with me for following your advice as to its ornaments only in part—I still venture to retain the narrow silver round it, put twice round without any bow, & instead of the black military feather shall put in the Coquelicot one, as being smarter;—& besides Coquelicot is to be all the fashion this winter.—After the Ball, I shall probably make it entirely black.

There is a wealth of detail here. A narrow silver band would sparkle against deep black velvet. 'Coquelicot' is French for 'poppy', adding a luminous orange-red flash in a feather. Austen was showing her knowledge of current fashion, as *coquelicot* did indeed lend pops of colour to outfits in fashion plates in the late 1790s (occasionally spelled 'coclico'), and its appearance colouring ribbons in a hat in *Northanger Abbey* testifies to the novel's composition in the same period.[6] Nicholas Heideloff started publishing his beautiful *Gallery of Fashion* monthly fashion prints in 1794 as a 'collection of all the most fashionable and elegant Dresses in vogue'.[7] They ran until March 1802, and purported to document real ensembles that 'Ladies of rank and fashion' wore.[8] Coquelicot-coloured ribbons, feathers, cords, handkerchiefs and shawls bedeck plates from 1796, particularly increasing in 1798. Figure 3.9 shows a *coquelicot* detail from November 1798, a month before Austen wrote her letter.

But, these visions' certainty soon vanished. Once Austen continued writing the next morning, Cassandra was informed: '—I have changed my mind, & changed the trimmings of my Cap this morning; they are now such as you suggested;—I felt as if I should not prosper if I strayed from your directions, & I think it makes me look more like Lady Conyngham now than it did before, which is all that one lives for now.' Elizabeth, Marchioness Conyngham, was a contemporary beauty, later mistress to the Prince of Wales, the future George IV.

In whatever manner the trimmings were finally resolved, the arrangement was effective. On Christmas Eve 1798, Austen happily shared how 'My black Cap was openly admired by M[rs] Lefroy, & secretly I imagine by every body else in the room.'[9]

---

6. *Northanger Abbey*, vol. I, ch. vi.
7. 'Advertisement', *Gallery of Fashion* (London: N. Heideloff, 1794), vol. I [n.p. but 5].
8. 'Advertisement', *Gallery of Fashion* (London: N. Heideloff, 1794), vol. I [n.p. but 5].
9. Letter 15, 24 December 1798.

3.10 'Costumes et portraits … 8. Mamlouks' (detail), engraving on paper, 1817. Rare Book Division, New York Public Library

3.11 Nicholas Heideloff, 'Oriental cap of white and crimson velvet, ornamented in the front with small pearls', *Gallery of Fashion*, March 1800. Courtesy of the author

3.12 'Full Dresses… A Mamaluk turban, ornamented with beads, and a whit e ostrich feather', *The Fashions of London and Paris During the Years 1804, 1805 and 1806*, February 1804. Courtesy of Candice Hern/www. candicehern.com

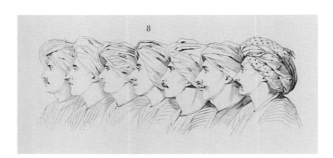

1799
MAMALOUC CAP

Letter 17, Tuesday 8 – Wednesday 9 January 1799, Steventon

> '—*I am not to wear my white sattin cap to night after all; I am to wear a Mamalouc cap instead, which Charles Fowle sent to Mary, & which she lends me.—It is all the fashion now, worn at the Opera, & by Lady Mildmays at Hackwood Balls—I hate describing such things, & I dare say You will be able to guess what it is like—.*'

Cassandra may have been able to guess what a Mamalouc cap was like, but we do not share her contemporary knowledge. Happily, the headwear was part of a swathe of 'Mameluke' or Egyptian-inspired looks sweeping through fashion after the Battle of the Nile fought between 1 and 3 August 1798 – a British victory over French forces led by Horatio Nelson, future hero of the Battle of Trafalgar – so we can piece together something of its style and wider topical popularity. Mamluks (spelled with heroic variety as mamaluke, mameluk, mameluke, mamlouk, mamluke, mamluq or marmeluke) were a military knightly class comprising non-Arab slave-soldiers and freed slaves across Muslim Mediterranean-bordering areas. In Egypt particularly, they held military and political power, and were in charge when Napoleon invaded as part of his ultimately unsuccessful 1798–1801 Egyptian campaign.

Lord Brabourne's first published compilation of some Austen letters (1884) printed 'mamalone' as the description, and it was Constance Hill in 1923 who guessed it to be 'mamalouc'. As she said, the Battle of the Nile 'had set the fashion in ladies' dress for everything suggestive of Egypt and of the hero of Aboukir. In the fashion-plates of the day we find Mamalouc cloaks and Mamalouc robes of flowing red cloth. Ladies wear toupées, somewhat resembling a fez, which we recognise as the "Mamalouc cap".'[10] Hill appears to have been drawing upon the *Gallery of Fashion* for her sources.

In January 1799 the publication included a 'Mamelouc robe, the sleeves ornamented with diamond buttons and the whole trimmed with sable', beside a 'Mamelouc cloak'. April the same year introduced a 'Jacket and petticoat of Mamaluke muslin'. The *Fashions of London and Paris* documented a red wool 'Mamaluke Mantle' in December 1798.[11] By 1804 the French language seems to have adopted 'Mameluck' as the name for a kind of robe, as in a fashion plate showing a 'Mameluck Bordé en Mousseline Turque', and it continued through the 1800s.[12]

Hill's 'recognition' of a Mamelouc cap as resembling a fez is misplaced. An 1817 drawing from life of actual 'Mamlouks' shows the men wearing turbans (fig. 3.10), a style manifesting in infinite variation in women's fashion from the mid-1790s (fig. 3.11). And this, it eventuates, is what Austen's borrowed cap may have looked like. A fashion plate from 1804 (fig. 3.12) describes the figure on the left as wearing 'A Mamaluk turban, ornamented with beads, and a white ostrich feather', suggesting Austen's was also in the turban style.

[10] Constance Hill, *Jane Austen: Her Homes and Her Friends* (London and New York: John Lane, 1923), p. 76, cited in *Letters*.
[11] *The Fashions of London and Paris During the Years 1798, 1799 and 1800*, vol. I (London: Richard Phillips, 1801), p. 12.
[12] 'Costume Parisien', *Journal des Dames et des Modes*, 3 August 1804, p. 572.

3.13 'London Head Dresses… 1. Bandeau of flowers and ribband. 2. White lace cap. 3. Silk and chip bonnet. 4. White crape cap with pink ribbands. 5. White crape turban. 6. Yellow crape dress cap, trimmed with lace. 7. White satin dress cap. 8. Black satin bonnet trimmed with green ribband. 9. Net crape cap with ribband bows', *The Fashions of London and Paris During the Years 1798, 1799 and 1800, June 1800*, engraving and watercolour on paper. Rijksmuseum, Amsterdam/ Purchased with the support of the Flora Fonds/Rijksmuseum Fonds

3.14 White satin cap trimmed with braid and tassels, 1800–10. Courtesy of the National Trust

3.15 'Costume Parisien', *Journal des Dames et des Modes*, 18 August 1804: 'Chapeau Moitié Paille sur un Bonnet' [Half-straw hat on a bonnet], plate 576

3.16 'London Head Dresses [detail] … 7. A bonnet made with crape net … lined with satin … Bow of ribband in front. 8. A bonnet, the cawl of which is made of chequed penny satin ribband, in purple and brown … The front of satin of the same colour… 9. Cap of lilac crape, with three silver bands', *The Fashions of London and Paris During the Years 1798, 1799 and 1800*, May 1800 (detail), engraving and watercolour on paper. Rijksmuseum, Amsterdam/Purchased with the support of the Flora Fonds/Rijksmuseum Fonds

1799
WHITE SATIN CAP

Letter 17, Tuesday 8 – Wednesday 9 January 1799, Steventon

'—I am not to wear my white sattin cap to night'

Austen's neglected satin evening cap has been similarly overshadowed in histories of dress by the Mamalouc cap she *did* wear in early 1799 (see p. 125). The item she discarded for something more immediately fashionable deserves some attention. The word 'cap' could refer to a multitude of styles, including bonnets (without brims at this point), turbans, close-fitting informal wear tied under the chin (like Austen's evening caps; see p. 121), items of cotton or linen worn under brimmed bonnets or any unstructured soft headwear. We have quite a free rein to imagine what this one looked like, as figure 3.13 shows in its selection of fashionable headwear.

Pursuing fashionable images gives several offerings. White satin was a standard fabric for evening wear (fig. 3.14), and it was the style, construction and decoration which distinguished the fashion moment that the headwear embodied. The bonnet 'trimmed with *coquelicot* cords' that the *Gallery of Fashion* depicted in 1798 is made of white satin (see fig. 3.9). Two months later, in January 1799, is another 'bonnet of white satin'.

Both of these looks are daywear, however, and Austen was contemplating adornment for a ball at Kempshott. Her Mamalouc cap was almost certainly a turban style, and in *Northanger Abbey* fashion-obsessed Isabella Thorpe mentions how she had put on a turban to wear at a concert.[13] It may be that Austen's 'cap' was more in this mode, as seen in style 5 in figure 3.13.

[13] *Northanger Abbey*, vol. II, ch. xii.

1799
STRAW AND PURPLE RIBBON HAT

Letter 20, Sunday 2 June 1799, Bath: 13 Queen Square

'—Eliz: has given me a hat, & it is not only a pretty hat, but a pretty stile of hat too— It is something like Eliza's— only instead of being all straw, half of it is narrow purple ribbon.'

Elizabeth Austen, wife of Jane's brother Edward, was the donor of this pretty hat. We can decipher some of its arrangements from the descriptions, for once, and with pictures may be able to flatter ourselves that we understand a little more of it than Cassandra might have from the letter alone.

The hat of 'Eliza' that Austen compares it to could be either Austen's friend Mrs Fowle's, or her cousin and sister-in-law Mrs Henry Austen's. Eliza's hat being all of straw conjures something with a brim, which could allow half of it to be made from ribbon (fig. 3.15). Figure 3.13 shows a pretty lilac hat from 1800 looking like latticed ribbons – brim, crown and all. On the same page is a green hat with a chip brim, and a soft silk crown festooned with ribbons. Perhaps even closer is a different range of fashionable headwear seen in figure 3.16. The idealised ladies wear purple bonnets and a cap, and the one at the far left has a satin brim or front, and a cawl made of ribbons.

3.17 'A bonnet of white chip turned up on one side, and lined and ornamented with pink', *The Fashions of London and Paris During the Years 1801, 1802 and 1803*, July 1801. Yale Center for British Art, New Haven

3.18 Nicholas Heideloff, 'Black and white chip bonnet, black feather placed on the left side', *Gallery of Fashion*, April 1801. Courtesy of the author

3.19 'Fig. 7.—A hat of white chip … the crown covered with white crape. Fig. 8.—A large straw bonnet … Fig. 9.—The Obi hat, of straw or chip', *The Fashions of London and Paris During the Years 1801, 1802 and 1803*, July 1801. Yale Center for British Art

1801
WHITE CHIP BONNET AND STRAW BONNET

Letter 35, Tuesday 5 – Wednesday 6 May 1801, Bath: The Paragon

'—My Mother has ordered a new Bonnet, & so have I;—both white chip, trimmed with white ribbon.—I find my straw bonnet looking very much like other peoples & quite as smart.'

'Chip' was an inventive material used for hats from at least the eighteenth century. It was made from long, thin, pliable strips of wood, then plaited together, like straw was, to form a durable material (see fig. 3.29). Being made of wood, the final finish was chunkier than more delicate straw, but it could be painted or dyed – black or white was common (figs 3.17 and 3.18). The word 'chip' was mis-transcribed as 'strip' in early editions of the Austen letters, causing some confusion until Deirdre Le Faye's correction in 1995.

A few days later, on 13 May, Austen mused, '[we] were not so very stupid [at Mrs Lillingstone's] as I expected, which I attribute to my wearing my new bonnet & being in good looks'.[14] It would seem her white chip bonnet had arrived in time to buoy up Austen's social elan with the buzz of a new hat. She already had some fashionable headwear to swan around Bath in, as 'my straw bonnet' – one she already possessed – was evidently doing good service in both style and condition (fig. 3.19). Her last straw bonnet mentioned was the purple ribbon one two summers earlier (see p. 127), but it is unlikely to have been the same item, given how fast fashionable styles moved, and how easy headwear was to update.

Austen's existing and new hats still did not satisfy all desire for summer headwear. She concluded this passage by informing Cassandra: '—Bonnets of Cambric Muslin on the plan of L[ad]y Bridges' are a good deal worn, & some of them are very pretty; but I shall defer one of that sort till your arrival.' This suggests that when her sister arrives, the pair will again shop together for matching headwear. It is also worth noting that Austen is observing what styles are in fashion, and who the fashion leader they are inspired by is, and she desires what other people are wearing. Looking 'very much like other people' was clearly a concern; to be sitting in the comfortable gentry middle ground of being neither too forward nor too behind in the fashion stakes.

[14] Letter 36, 12–13 May 1801.

3.20 Cassandra Austen, portrait of Jane Austen from behind (detail; see fig. 1.41), pencil and watercolour on paper, 1804. Private collection, reproduced with permission

3.21 Nicholas Heideloff, 'Bag bonnet of blue striped sarcenet, chip front, trimmed with lace; black-edged yellow sarcenet riband', *Gallery of Fashion*, June 1800. Courtesy of the author

3.22 Silk bonnet (side view), 1805–20. The Metropolitan Museum of Art, New York/Isabel Shults Fund, 2008

3.23 Front and side view of silk bonnet (see fig. 3.22). The Metropolitan Museum of Art, New York/Isabel Shults Fund, 2008

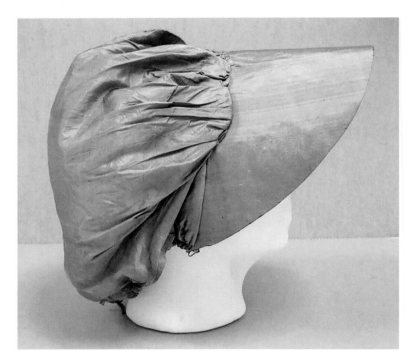

1804
BLUE BAG BONNET

Cassandra's portrait of Austen seated, from behind (see p. 56), is distinguished in headwear terms by the view it affords of her blue 'bag' bonnet (fig. 3.20). This phrase is based on a description of a similar bonnet in the *Gallery of Fashion* in June 1800, shown in figure 3.21, made of 'blue striped sarcenet [silk], chip front, trimmed with lace; black-edged yellow sarcenet riband'. The appellation is a literal explanation of the headwear's construction, being made with a brim attached to a 'bag'.[15] As we saw in 1799, when Austen took Cassandra's bonnet's cawl to adapt (see p. 125), the soft back part of a bonnet could be made of fabric alone, a kind of a bag caught in to the 'front', or bonnet brim. The 1800 example is made of white chip, or thinly shaved and plaited wood, of the kind Austen buys in 1801 (see p. 129), slightly chunkier yet sturdier than straw. The painted crisp front curve of the brim reveals its stiffening structure which has been covered with fabric. There are creases or gathers at the join with the softer back piece made from the same fabric, either a cotton or silk, shown in a real bonnet of the period in figures 3.22 and 3.23. No previous bonnet mentioned in the letters matches the style of this one, once again showing how much clothing is missing from the textual record. Cassandra doubtless had similar headwear. Their niece Anna Lefroy remembered 'their bonnets: because though precisely alike in colour, shape & material, I made it a pleasure to guess, & I believe always guessed right, which bonnet and which Aunt belonged to each other'.[16]

Cassandra has carefully depicted the blue of the bonnet as not quite matching the dress, being a little fresher and less grey in hue. The clarity of her technique also reveals more details of how the headwear was constructed. What their niece Anna called 'bonnet strings' is actually a long piece of white fabric, either in two parts or continuous, which winds around the base of the 'bag', is formed into two puffs or a bow at the centre back of Austen's neck, then comes partly round the brim again to form the ties going under the chin.[17] Looking closely, Cassandra has even included the little pin holding the fabric there. Using pins to attach bonnet decorations

was common, as it made changing the embellishments much easier than having to snip and undo sewing stitches, as seen on many surviving examples of historic bonnets.

[15] I have made a replica of this bonnet for Jane Austen's House.
[16] Austen-Leigh 2008, p. 157.
[17] Anna Lefroy to James-Edward Austen Leigh, 20 July 1869, National Portrait Gallery archive, quoted in National Portrait Gallery, 'Jane Austen', *Regency Portraits Catalogue*: https://www.npg.org.uk/collections/search/portraitExtended/mw00230/Jane-Austen [accessed 23 May 2021].

3.24 'Head Dresses, Sept.ʳ 1805', *The Fashions of London and Paris During the Years 1804, 1805 and 1806*, 1805, engraving and watercolour on paper. Courtesy of the author

3.25 Black silk bonnet, upper part of the crown of thin slats of wood over a support of woven cane; the rest of the crown is formed by a paper cylinder; the brim is also made of paper, which is reinforced along the edge with metal wire, *c.* 1815–20. Rijksmuseum, Amsterdam

3.26 'Costume Parisien… Chapeaux, Capotes et Cornette de Virginie et de Lévantine' [Hats, Caps and Cornette in Virginie and Levantine style], *Journal des Dames et des Modes*, 30 April 1811, plate 1140. Rijksmuseum, Amsterdam/Purchased with the support of the F. G. Waller-Fonds

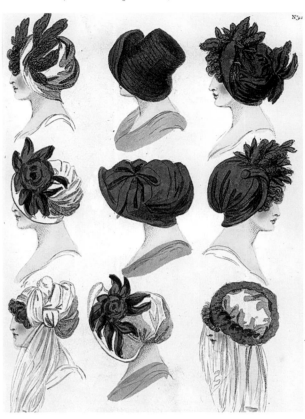

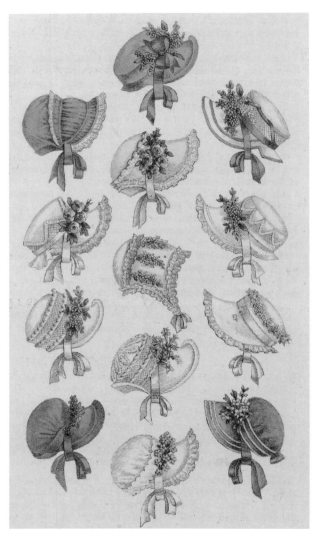

1808
MOURNING BONNET

Letter 59, Saturday 15 – Sunday 16 October 1808, Southampton: Castle Square

'—*One Miss Baker makes my gown, & the other my Bonnet, which is to be silk covered with Crape.*'

Having looked at the prevalence of bombazine and crape for mourning in the discussion of the bombazine mourning gown this hat was worn with (see p. 65), we now turn to the bonnet itself. The combination of silk and crape in headwear was also of long standing. A letter responding to mourning for the death of George II in 1760 talks of deep mourning in women's hats being signified by 'plain black silk with crape around the crown, with a bow knot'.[18]

Austen's 'covered with Crape', therefore, can be read as the mourning textile adorning a silk base, rather than obscuring it wholly. As fashion plates such as figure 3.24 show, the requirements of materialised grief in no way needed to concede any fashionability. These 1805 examples are as varied and full of novelty as their non-sable equivalents. Austen could have made use of the requirements of mourning to acquire a nice new hat. As we know she already wore a black velvet cap (see p. 123), and had a black velvet pelisse (p. 103), it is reasonable to assume that by changing the crape for ribbons, flowers or other trimmings, she could easily have converted it into fashionable attire, like the splendid yet sombre slightly later bonnet of the late 1810s in figure 3.25.

1811
MISS BURTON'S BONNET

Letter 70, Thursday 18 – Saturday 20 April 1811, London: Sloane Street

'—*Miss Burton has made me a very pretty little Bonnet*'

Nothing more can be gleaned from the letters about what the bonnet Miss Burton made Austen may have looked like. She was in London, and doing quite a lot of shopping for herself and Cassandra, including a straw riding hat (see p. 135), a pelisse (p. 105) and a spotted muslin (p. 73). We can therefore give imagination full licence to speculate about its style and colour. The French fashion plate in figure 3.26 shows straw hats in bonnet shapes, and linen and cotton caps. Given that Austen appears to be doing some investment in her wardrobe, it is likely this bonnet was in current taste, and was acquired as a fashionable article rather than one of practicality which she could purchase at home in Hampshire.

This is a middling period for bonnet styles. The flat crown and wholly face-enclosing brim popular in 1800s bonnets had mainly fallen away in favour of the style of crown that reached more vertically, and shorter brims sitting more openly around the face. Only three years later, in 1814, would the tall crowns of fashionable bonnets start to resemble chimneys, inspired by the headwear of the Grand Duchess of Oldenburg as she accompanied her brother, the Emperor of Russia, around Europe in a tour somewhat premature in celebrating Napoleon's defeat.

[18] Lou Taylor, *Mourning Dress: A Costume and Social History* (London: Routledge, 2009), p. 81.

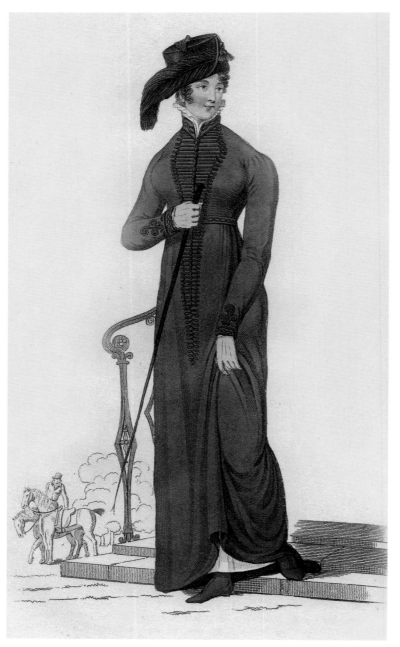

1811
STRAW RIDING HAT

Letter 70, Thursday 18 – Saturday 20 April 1811, London: Sloane Street

*'—& now nothing can satisfy me but I must have a straw hat, of the riding hat shape, like M*rs *Tilson's; & a young woman in this Neighbourhood is actually making me one. I am really very shocking; but it will not be dear at a Guinea.'*

This desire for a straw riding hat comes immediately after Austen's information about Miss Burton's bonnet (see p. 133). Apparently Miss Burton's skills did not lie in straw work, which may be a matter of specialisation, or perhaps stiff straw abused the fingertips and made them too rough for work with muslin and other fine textiles. Instead, another artisan nearby to Sloane Street, where Austen was staying with her brother Henry at his latest town residence, was creating a fashionably shaped hat for the author. This month she was revising the proofs of her first published novel: *Sense and Sensibility* would appear in October 1811. Austen was still buying this hat on her normal income, and it is interesting that she considers a guinea a reasonable cost. This amount does appear to be a normal price for bonnets and other headwear, as seen in numerous account books and milliners' bills.

The influence of men's riding clothing on men's fashionable dress had been growing since the late eighteenth century. In the 1790s, the influence started transferring significantly to women's dress also, along with a new military styling from the increasing European conflicts. These details included horizontal braid decorations, sometimes called 'Brandenburgs' in the 1810s (fig. 3.27), shoulder capes on outdoor coats, fur trimmings, bonnets in the shapes of jockey hats, and much more.

Women's riding habits – the wool cloth bodice and skirt combination worn on horseback, while travelling, or as casual dress – had long paralleled male clothing, and were the only part of the female wardrobe regularly made by male tailors, used to working with and shaping woollen cloth. Figure 3.27 shows 'A habit of bright

green ornamented down the front and embroidered at the cuffs *à la militaire* with black', accessorised with a 'Small riding hat of black beaver fancifully adorned with gold cordon and tassels, with a long ostrich feather of green in the front'.[19]

The 'riding hat' shape was a particular silhouette which developed in the early nineteenth century. Women had always worn hats for riding; the riding hat in this case took inspiration from the military shako, especially the version worn with Hussar uniforms. It resembled a top hat in the height and cylindrical shape of the crown, only dispensing with the brim or shrinking it to a stylistic detail. The lady's beaver riding hat in figure 3.28 was made by an American hatter somewhere around 1810, and shows the more delicate proportions and decorative details characterising the style by comparison to male headwear. The man's chip straw top hat in figure 3.29 shows how the texture of Austen's finished hat may have looked.

---

19 'Fashions for June 1812', *La Belle Assemblée: or, Bell's Court and Fashionable Magazine* (London: J. Bell, 1812), p. 265.

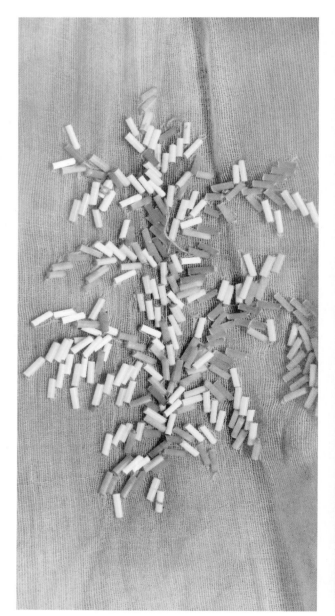

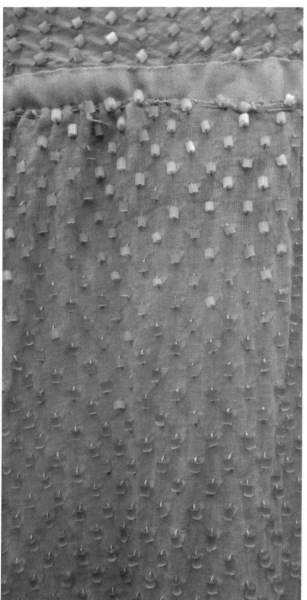

1811
BUGLE BAND HEADDRESS

Letter 72, Tuesday 30 April 1811, London: Sloane Street

'—My head dress was a Bugle band like the border to my gown, & a flower of Mrs Tilson's.'

Austen was describing her dress for a party on 23 April at her brother Henry's house in Sloane Street, where she was staying, hosted by her sister-in-law Eliza, with sixty-six guests, which went on until after midnight. Her description appears to be in response to a query of Cassandra's about what she wore, as the previous letter goes into some detail about the event itself.[20] This also got written up in a newspaper report: 'On Tuesday, Mrs. H. AUSTIN [sic] had a musical party at her house in Sloane-street' (*Morning Post*, 25 April, the day Austen wrote her previous letter).[21] Austen informed Cassandra at the start of this one that 'I had sent off my Letter yesterday before Yours came, which I was sorry for; but … your questions shall be answered'.

Austen, then, was in evening dress. She had headwear matching her gown's border, both made from bugle beads, shaped as long thin glass tubes (fig. 3.30). The beads were a popular Regency adornment, and often appear in fashion descriptions for full dress from the 1800s and 1810s (see also fig. 3.12). A 'full or opera dress' of January 1807 included 'a rich border of embossed velvet, terminating at the extreme edge with a narrow Vandyke, or fringe of bugles … the front of the vest made high, and formed in irregular horizontal gathers; confined with two narrow bands of bugles'.[22] At the king's birthday celebrations later that year, Lady Molyneux wore a 'white crape petticoat, with a rich embroidered border of bugles' under her lilac crape gown, while Mrs Lawrell attended in 'A dress of green satin and gauze, richly trimmed with chains and fringe of green bugles'.[23] The bead's weight contrasted with light gauzes, muslins and silk crapes, and gave them more heaviness and

drape, as is seen in the fabric detail of a fully bugled gown in figure 3.31.

While there is no mention in previous letters of a specific evening gown that could have been worn here, it appears the headdress, and perhaps the gown's bugle border, were recent acquisitions. On Wednesday 17 April, Austen and her sister-in-law's servant Manon visited the cheap haberdashery Grafton House (see p. 181). Although they waited half an hour to be served, once they were, 'I was very well satisfied with my purchases, my Bugle Trimming at 2/4ᵈ.'[24] Buying a bugle trimming a week before she wears a bugle headdress implies it was a new purchase. Perhaps she bought it to match the gown. The price indicates this bugle was not the one trimming the gown. In March 1813 in London, widow and regular shopper Mrs Mary Topham bought two and a quarter yards of bugle trimming, which cost her 3s.4½d, or 1s.6d per yard. At roughly that cost, Austen could have bought about a yard and a half for what she spent, only enough to wrap the head. Grafton House was famously cheap and she may have got a little more trim for her tuppence— say, two yards at 1s.2d per yard – but still not enough to border a gown. If her flower was Mrs Tilson's, it was borrowed and therefore faux.

[20] Letter 71, 25 April 1811.
[21] Letter 71, 25 April 1811.
[22] 'Mourning Full or Opera Dress', La Belle Assemblée: Or, Bell's Court and Fashionable Magazine (London: J. Bell, 1806), p. 611 [1807 fashions for January published in December 1806].
[23] 'Fashions for July, 1807 King's Birthday', La Belle Assemblée: Or, Bell's Court and Fashionable Magazine (London: J. Bell, 1807), pp. 335–6.
[24] Letter 70, 18–20 April 1811.

3.32 Satin and figured silk bonnet, 1810. Brooklyn Museum Costume Collection at The Metropolitan Museum of Art/Gift of the Brooklyn Museum, 2009/Gift of Mrs John Wells Parrish, 1953

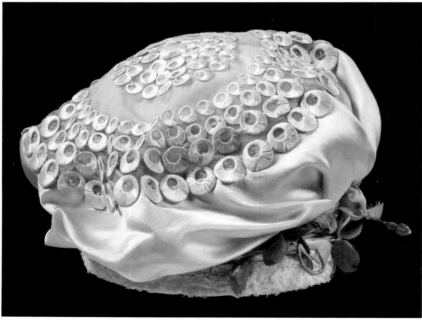

3.33 A full cap of white satin gathered into a headband, inset with white net embroidered in circles; headband of white satin edged with white silk plush; trimmed on one side with artificial flowers, 1818–23. © Victoria and Albert Museum, London/Given by Henry Curtis

1812, 1813
WHITE SATIN AND LACE CAPS

Letter 87, Wednesday 15 – Thursday 16 September 1813, London: Henrietta Street

'4 o'clock.—We are just come back from doing Mrs Tickars, Miss Hare, and Mr Spence. … Miss Hare had some pretty caps, and is to make me one like one of them, only <u>white</u> sattin instead of blue. It will be white sattin and lace, and a little white flower perking out of the left ear, like Harriot Byron's feather. I have allowed her to go as far as £1–16.'

When Austen spent money on clothes in London, she wrote about them more, for which we are grateful. This pretty cap is fifteen shillings over a guinea – a reasonable price for a London cap, as emphasised in dozens of accounts. The 'allowed her' shows how the headwear's cost comprised both the making and the component costs. Austen was permitting Miss Hare to decorate her cap with up to a certain combined value, and according to the milliner's taste, like the white gown ordered at the same time (see p. 77, where the Mayfair businesswoman is also discussed further). Figure 3.32 shows a fashionable satin cap or bonnet of around the time. See also figure 5.16 for an 1813 style called 'Lady Wellington's cottage hat' made from white satin and lace.

Miss Hare was prompt in her making. The next letter was written after dinner on Thursday 16th, relating that 'My Cap is come home & I like it very much, … My Cap has a peak in front. Large, full Bows of very narrow ribbon (old twopenny [7/16 in./ 1 cm wide]) are the thing. One over the right temple perhaps, & another at the left ear.'[25] The reference to Harriet [*sic*] Byron is from *Sir Charles Grandison* by Samuel Richardson (1753), a novel Austen loved. Richardson's full description is: 'A white Paris sort of cap, glittering with spangles, and encircled by a chaplet of artificial flowers, with a little white feather perking from the left ear, is to be my headdress.'

The Austen sisters had 'Sattin & Lace caps' from the winter of 1812, as Austen reveals in comparison with the shape of a new cap their niece Fanny bought on the same expedition. In September 1813, this earlier cap appeared to be still holding up: 'I assure you my old one looked so smart yesterday that I was asked two or three times before I set off, whether it was not my new one' – presumably the one she bought here.[26] The same September letter conveyed both Cassandra's and Martha Lloyd's approval of the new cap. Fanny, alas, was 'out of conceit' with hers already.

There is no mention of the handmade luxury laces such as Brussels, Valenciennes or Mechlin in Austen's letters, which were usually identified as such in texts. The lace decorating her cap, like the trimming on her cloaks (see pp. 147 and 151), would have been the machine-made lace proliferating through the early century, like the net on the cap in figure 3.33.

[25] Letter 88, 16 September 1813.
[26] Letter 89, 23–24 September 1813.

SHELVES

SHAWLS TIPPETS, CLOAKS AND SHOES

4.1 Muslin and cotton shawl,
early 19th century. Jane Austen's
House, Chawton

1788–1810
MUSLIN SHAWL

The muslin shawl held at Jane Austen's House is one of the two surviving pieces of clothing associated with the author (fig. 4.1).[1] Family history says Austen embroidered it. Since the only confirmed example of her excellent sewing skills is the embroidery on Cassandra's pocket handkerchief (see p. 186), it is hard to compare the stitching on this textile with a wider set of samples and decide whether the object bears out the tale. What is notable is that in a Regency context, the embroidery is not particularly fine. While both the handkerchief and shawl are embellished using satin stitch, the shawl's pattern of small crosses or four-petalled flowers (fig. 4.2) is less fine than the handkerchief. Nonetheless, it would still have required a lot of skill and experience to work quite a thick cotton thread into such an exact design on a gauzy fabric with threads that pull at the slightest tension. Another possibility is that it was embroidered in India. The delicate cloth is handwoven Indian muslin, and the assured embroidery is comparable in style and technique with many other examples of Indian whitework from this time.

The shawl has a border of small crosses all the way round, and a scattering of crosses of the same size across the main ground fabric. The length is created by joining together two muslin panels with a strip of cotton lozenge net, embroidered in a similar thick thread with zigzags along the edges and an X in the centre at every second point (fig. 4.3). It is long and rectangular ($101\frac{1}{2} \times 19\frac{3}{4}$ in./258×50 cm), imitating woollen Kashmiri shawls, but narrower. Although it is likely she had at least one wool shawl, no trace remains in Austen's letters of these items, which quickly became an integral part of women's wardrobes from the 1790s (see figs 1.62–1.64, 1.75 and 1.86), first through imports and then through local manufacture of cheaper versions.[2]

Shawls could also be square, as Austen described of young Mary Whitby in Bath, whose 'turn is actually come to be grown up & have a fine complexion & wear great square muslin shawls'.[3] A beautiful example of a late eighteenth- or early nineteenth-century square shawl is seen in figure 4.4. As pages 147 and 151 discuss,

a garment Regency people described as a 'cloak' could also be long and narrow. Henry Tilney in *Northanger Abbey* enumerates 'a cloak' as one of the things spare muslin could be turned into. In 1789, the fourteen-year-old Austen dedicated the story 'Frederic and Elfrida' to Martha Lloyd, then her new neighbour in the Deane parsonage, as 'a small testimony of the gratitude I feel for your late generosity to me in finishing my muslin Cloak',[4] perhaps making the novel's reference something of an in-joke. There is a slight possibility this shawl may be Austen's teenage muslin cloak.

However and whenever the shawl found its way into Austen's wardrobe, what is clear from the repairs seen in figures 4.3 and 4.5 is that it was a valued item of clothing, and its owner took great care of it. The careful, precise sewing on the fine $\frac{1}{16}$ inch (2mm)-wide hems, lace strip, darns and patches show a highly skilled needlewoman at work.

[1] Alison Larkin has made a sewing project inspired by this shawl. See Jennie Batchelor and Alison Larkin, *Jane Austen Embroidery: Authentic Embroidery Projects for Modern Stitchers* (London: Pavilion, 2020), pp. 108–13.
[2] For more on Austen and shawls, see Davidson 2019, pp. 272–4.
[3] Letter 44, 21–23 April 1805.
[4] *Family Record*, p. 69.

4.2 Detail of cross embroidery on muslin
and cotton shawl (see fig. 4.1). Jane Austen's
House, Chawton

4.3 Detail of embroidery on shawl, showing muslin panels joined by a strip of cotton lozenge net (see fig. 4.1). Jane Austen's House, Chawton/Courtesy of the author

4.5 Detail of repairs on muslin and cotton shawl (see fig. 4.1). Jane Austen's House, Chawton/Courtesy of the author

4.4 Muslin embroidered shawl, late 18th/early 19th century. The Hopkins Collection, London

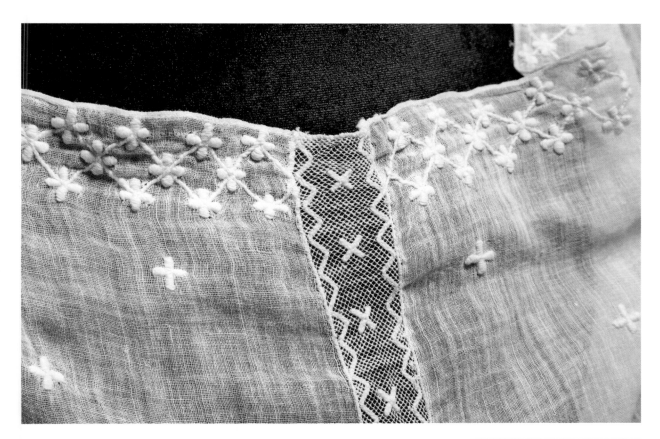

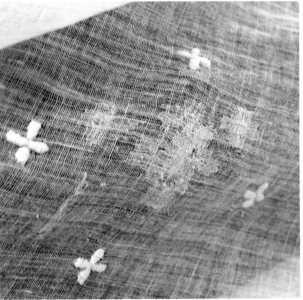

4.6 'London Walking Dress', *The Lady's Magazine*, June 1799, engraving and watercolour on paper. Rijksmuseum, Amsterdam/Purchased with the support of the Flora Fonds/Rijksmuseum Fonds

1799
LACE CLOAK

Letter 20, Sunday 2 June 1799, Bath: 13 Queen Square

'My Cloak is come home, & here follows the pattern of its' lace. —*If you do not think it wide enough, I can give 3ᵈ a yard more for yours, & not go beyond the two Guineas, for my Cloak altogether does not cost quite two pounds. —I like it very much …'*

The word 'cloak' now recalls a loose outer garment gathered or cut in a semi-circle, fastening around the neck and falling to the knees or lower, like the distinctive red worsted cloaks (see p. 114). In this period, however, 'cloak' also meant a garment more like a long shawl or scarf, trimmed with frills, and sometimes gathered together at the centre back. Fashion illustrations abound with these cloaks (figs 4.6 and 4.7) and show how they were worn around the shoulders with the long ends clasped together at the front or crossing over. The contemporary description is 'drawn and tied in the front, the two ends hanging down very low'.[5] This is the kind of cloak Austen bought, and the lace is therefore the frill, or the frill and the main body itself. Austen continued, 'I saw some Gauzes in a shop in Bath Street yesterday at only 4s a yard, but they were not so good or so pretty as mine', meaning hers was likely gauze trimmed with lace, like that depicted in the *Gallery of Fashion* in 1798 (fig. 4.8).

Austen, aged 24, is dressing to a fashionable trend for the time – a practice she continues by buying another lace cloak only 18 months later. Machine-made lace, such as this cloak was made of, was a relatively recent invention, as page 151 explores. Black lacy cloaks had made regular appearances in the *Gallery* since its inception in 1794, and were particularly fashionable around this time and into the 1800s. The main part of the cloak is recorded as made variously of 'figured gauze', 'black silk', and 'netted … trimmed with a full plaiting [pleating] of lace'. As Austen told Cassandra from Bath in May 1801, 'Black gauze Cloaks are worn as much as anything',[6] following

up later that month by telling her cloaks 'are very much worn here, in different forms—many of them just like [Martha's] black silk spencer, with a trimming round the armholes instead of Sleeves;—some are long before, & some long all round like C[atherine]. Bigg's'.[7] Other fashion plate publications of the time often show lace cloaks and they are usually black, or in a dark colour like the December 1799 purple cloak for 'London Walking Dress' (fig. 4.9). Cloaks spring out of fashion pages and paintings (fig. 4.10).

A 1798 reference to a 'black velvet cloak, trimmed with very broad lace' sheds some light on Austen's question to Cassandra about the width of the lace desired for her cloak – once again, the sisters are matching clothes.[8] Three pennies a yard would obtain lace a little wider to make a broad frill and attain a little further towards an epitome of fashion at the time. Two pounds to two guineas was quite a large purchase, especially for something which, while it looks like a wrap, does not add much utilitarian warmth to an outfit. The sisters are splashing out for fashion, not function.

[5] *Gallery of Fashion*, September 1794, vol. I, fig. XXV.
[6] Letter 35, 5–6 May 1801.
[7] Letter 37, 21–22 May 1801.
[8] *Gallery of Fashion*, January 1798, vol. IV, fig. CLXV.

4.9 'London Walking Dress',
*The Fashions of London and Paris
During the Years 1798, 1799
and 1800*, December 1799.
Rijksmuseum, Amsterdam/
Purchased with the support of the
Flora Fonds/Rijksmuseum Fonds

4.10 'Costume Parisien',
Journal des Dames et des Modes,
19 April 1799, plate 102.
Rijksmuseum, Amsterdam/
Purchased with the support
of the F. G. Waller-Fonds

4.11 Anne Frankland Lewis, 'Collection of English Original Watercolour Drawings', March 1806, plate 31, watercolour on paper, 36.8 × 25.7 cm. Los Angeles County Museum of Art/Costume Council Fund/ www.lacma.org

4.12 James Stanier Clarke, portrait of a woman, identified as Jane Austen by Richard Wheeler, watercolour on paper, 1810s. Private collection

4.13 Detail of double-press point lace edging in black silk, 1797–1800. Nottingham Trent University Lace Archive/Photograph by Gail Baxter

4.14 Detail of double-press point lace edging in black silk, 1797–1800. Nottingham Trent University Lace Archive/Photograph by Gail Baxter

1800
ANOTHER LACE CLOAK

Letter 24, Saturday 1 November 1800, Steventon

'My Cloak came on tuesday & tho' I expected a good deal, the beauty of the lace astonished me.—It is too handsome to be worn, almost too handsome to be looked at.'

In the same parcel as the gown of uncertain taste (p. 37), Cassandra sent other items she had purchased on behalf of Austen, including two pairs of stockings (p. 217), some hair combs (p. 179), and two pairs of shoes (p. 161). Austen was also 'glad that I have still my Cloak to expect'.[9] Four days later, it arrived. It had only been eighteen months since she bought a new cloak with lace in June 1799 (see p. 147). This one could have been made entirely of lace, or merely trimmed with it (figs. 4.11 and 4.12).

Austen's lifetime encompassed significant technological developments in lace-making. The textile form had been made by women's and children's hands for centuries, and embodied huge amounts of skill, labour and time. Lace's cost was correspondingly expensive. Industrial innovations were revolutionising spinning and weaving from the 1760s, and engineers across England soon turned their attention to machines for mass-manufacturing lace, especially in Nottingham, a traditional handmade-lace production centre. Thomas Taylor patented a point net machine in 1778 that created a hexagonal net from loops, adapted from knitting machines. The Hayne brothers improved on this to produce double-press point net, like modern tulle (the French name for silk net) (fig. 4.13).[10] Their big innovation was to create a net that did not run when cut, unlike the original point net looped from a single thread which unravelled easily. This success stimulated further lace-making innovations during the 1790s, creating 'edgings, insertions, borderings, flouncings; also veils, scarfs, and every description of articles suited to the varying fashions of the time'.[11]

Taylor's patent (and others') gave the common name 'patent net' to these looped net productions. One of the problems with patent net was its need to be stiffened to maintain the hexagonal ground appearance. If it got even damp, the textile 'shrunk into a fabric looking like crape'.[12] Perhaps lace for cloaks was unstiffened to begin with, allowing for a soft wrapping around the body seen in fashion plates.

The lace in this cloak, then, would have been of silk, the ground made by machine, the decoration applied by hand by one of the hundreds of thousands of women around Britain employed in 'lace running' – putting spots on point net, decorating it with needle-run and tamboured embroidery (a chain stitch created by a tambour hook), or applying some of the other numerous techniques for creating lace on a net ground.[13] The machine-made ground did not preclude the necessity of hand labour (fig. 4.14).

John Heathcoat's second bobbin-net machine of 1809 perfected a cotton machine-made net, and reproduced exactly the twisted (not looped) net ground of handmade bobbin lace. After this, lace in Regency fashion proliferates remarkably, especially from 1815 when bobbin-net manufacture superseded point net.

[9] Letter 23, 25–27 October 1800.
[10] Santina M. Levey, 'Machine-Made Lace: The Industrial Revolution and After', in *The Cambridge History of Western Textiles*, ed. D. T. Jenkins, II vols. (Cambridge: Cambridge University Press, 2003), II, p. 846.
[11] William Felkin, *A History of the Machine-Wrought Hosiery and Lace Manufactures* (London: Longmans, Green, and Co., 1867), pp. 139–40.
[12] Felkin 1867, p. 137.
[13] Levey 2003, p. 851.

4.15 Jean-Auguste-Dominique
Ingres, *Mademoiselle Caroline Rivière*,
oil on canvas, 100 × 70 cm, 1805.
Musée du Louvre, Paris

4.16 'Morning Walking Dresses'
(detail), *La Belle Assemblée*, October
1808, hand-coloured engraving on
paper. Los Angeles Public Library

1808
A BOA

Letter 52, Wednesday 15 – Friday 17 June 1808, Godmersham

'We were rather crowded yesterday, though it does not become me to say so, as I and my boa were of the party'

As its serpentine name evokes, a boa was a long, slender stole or scarf, usually made of some fluffy material such as fur, swansdown or silk pile, in a range of tones matching that of natural fur. It can be hard to capture a clear example visually, as at this point the word 'tippet' was quite interchangeable in fashion descriptions. In 1812, Austen wrote to Martha Lloyd proposing she make a present of a shawl to Miss Benn, as 'Her long Fur tippet is almost worn out'.[14] As the century progressed, a tippet (see p. 155) would more usually mean a short cape, wider stole or structured capelet. The splendidly clear painting in Ingres's 1806 portrait of Mademoiselle Caroline Rivière (fig. 4.15) includes the inside of a white fur boa or tippet, and shows that, in this case at least, the rounded shape was made by simply letting the skin side turn in on itself.

Boas are often seen in fashion plates wound around the neck, as if in imitation of their namesakes (fig. 4.16). The accessory is universally shown in an elegant but distinctly thin length, suggesting Austen's comment about the space hers takes up is somewhat tongue in cheek. The same plates appear to favour them for winter wear, accompanying snug woollen pelisses and capes, themselves often trimmed with fur. Austen could have worn hers with the kerseymere spencer mentioned three letters later, in the manner of figure 2.2. As with Mademoiselle Rivière, boas are also seen accompanying evening or other light dress, and acting then something like a shawl. As Austen was writing in high summer, she is perhaps using hers this way.

An article two decades later in *The Lady's Monthly Museum* writes of *boas* (in italics, indicating it might be a French term).[15] A 'superb *boa*' of ermine 'went three times round the neck and shoulders'. In the same fashion reportage is related the tale of a new bride who wears 'a triple row of sable' around her neck, causing her mother's satisfaction that 'no more colds, nor sore throats, nor cricks in the neck' were to be dreaded in a moment when 'fashion combined the interests of health with those of good taste'. Alas, as the young woman progresses through the season, she moves to a single knot, then a few weeks later, 'no longer as an appendage of winter', the boa 'escape[s] from the neck' to reach the shoulders, and as far as the sleeves. At this point her mother hunts out throat pastilles for the cold her daughter has caught.

[14] Letter 77, 29–30 November 1812.
[15] 'The Parisian Toilette, March 19th, 1827', *The Lady's Monthly Museum* (London: Dean and Munday, 1827), vol. XXV, pp. 232–3.

1814
ERMINE TIPPET

Letter 98, Saturday 5 – Tuesday 8 March 1814, London: Henrietta Street

'Edward & Fanny [Knight] stay another day, & both seem very well pleased to do so. … You cannot think how much my Ermine Tippet is admired both by Father & Daughter. It was a noble Gift.'

A tippet was very like a boa (see p. 153), being a long kind of scarf, often made of fur, though the name was also applied to cape-like garments worn around the shoulders. Whatever the name or form, the purpose was to keep warm – a function ermine fur would have filled admirably and luxuriously.

Ermine is the pure white winter fur of the European stoat or short-tailed weasel (*Mustela erminea*). It is represented in images from the Middle Ages onwards the way it was fashioned, with the black tail tip added to provide a contrast on the snowy ground, as seen on the pelisse trimming and lining in figure 4.18. Austen's may have been of the long form, or more resembled the shorter wrap in figure 4.17. There are no other clear references to fur in her letters, but its fashionable popularity suggests the material's presence was highly likely.

There are many fur-lined or trimmed garments in Regency dress. Fashion plates and portraits are full of them, and ermine was noticeably popular in the early 1810s (figs 4.19 and 4.20). Austen's favourite niece Fanny, the one mentioned in the quote, recorded in her diary in November 1804 how she went into Canterbury with her father from their estate at Godmersham, Kent. There she had her ears 'bored' (pierced), bought 'a bear [fur] long tippet[,] ordered a black beaver hat … & a Pelisse of Lady's cloth trimmed with bear'. Five days later the pelisse was finished, delivered (on a Sunday), and found to be too small. It was returned to the mantua-maker, possibly after pinned alterations had been made at home, and by 5 December, a month after ordering, the coat had arrived 'and just fitted me'.[16] How warm these garments must have kept the nearly twelve-year-old girl in the ensuing winter.

While it is clear the Knight relatives are admiring Austen's ermine, who gave it to her? She was writing to Cassandra, so it may well have been a sisterly present. The letter came from Henrietta Street, where she was staying with her brother Henry and maybe it was his generosity enrobing Austen.

Opposite
4.17 Dark cinnamon coloured silk pelisse lined with padded buff silk with large down feather collar, *c*.1815. Fashion Museum, Bath/ Bridgeman Images

[16] Fanny Knight's Diaries, U.951/F.24/1–69, Kent History and Library Centre. Recorded in *Lady's Daily Companion*.

4.18 'Walking Dress', *The Lady's Magazine*, October 1816. Courtesy of the author

4.19 'London Dresses for April' (detail), *The Lady's Monthly Museum*, 1 April 1811. Courtesy of the author

4.20 'Walking & Morning Dress' (detail), *The Repository of Arts*, November 1810. Los Angeles County Museum of Art/Gift of Charles LeMaire/www.lacma.org

4.21 Henry Mutlow, 'Paris Dresses' (detail), *The Ladies' Magazine*, November 1800. © The Trustees of the British Museum

4.22 'Costume Parisien', *Journal des Dames et des Modes*, 14 January 1799: plate 84 (detail), engraving and watercolour on paper. Rijksmuseum, Amsterdam/Purchased with the support of the F. G. Waller-Fonds

4.23 Pair of woman's shoes of green leather with cut-out decoration on vamp, 1790s. © Victoria and Albert Museum, London

4.24 Side view of woman's shoe of green leather with cut-out decoration on vamp (see fig. 4.23). © Victoria and Albert Museum, London

1799
GREEN SHOES

Letter 17, Tuesday 8 – Wednesday 9 January 1799, Steventon

'I wore my Green shoes last night'

As the waistline of women's gowns rose through the 1790s, the heels of their shoes lowered with equal rapidity. Already a smaller, delicate size and shape than decades previously, by 1799 heels had started disappearing to become flat (figs 4.21 and 4.22) and would not emerge again until the 1850s. They have a connection rooted in Enlightenment ideas that had become more concerned with the natural body. As columnar dresses made of light washable cottons came to dominate, no longer relying on heavy stays to shape the torso, so heels that did not make the wearer 'trip and totter' gained the upper hand and aided a more natural gait.[17] As Austen said in a letter a few months later, 'I am not fond of ordering shoes, & at any rate they shall all have flat heels.'[18]

At this time, the predominant toe shape of women's fashionable footwear was pointed. It would become rounder as the nineteenth century progressed, moving towards an almond shape by the end of the 1810s, which heralded the blunt or square toes of the 1820s. Another prevailing construction detail was a lower throat (the top front line of a shoe), allowing the foot to slip in without then requiring a pair of latchets, or straps, fastened with a buckle to close it (figs 4.23 and 4.24). This made it easier for shoes to slip off again, especially while dancing, hence the adoption of ribbons to secure them (see fig. 4.25; the ribbons here are modern to show how the lacing would originally have looked). Shoes were also made on straight lasts, meaning they came from the maker with no left and right. The wearer could choose to shape them into each side, or, more usually, swap the feet regularly to prevent too much wear in the same places on the sole and uppers.

Shoes were a more fluid clothing item for Regency consumers. Leather soles wore out fast, no matter how well made, and required frequent replacement. Shoes were consumables, constantly entering and departing the wardrobe, made to eke out longer by frequent cobbling and repairs. Light ladies' shoes had a short life, especially those worn to dance in, just as Austen wore this pair to a ball along with her Mamalouc cap (see p. 125). The examples in the pictures are not dancing shoes, which would have looked more like the pair in figure 4.31, and were often made of satin or the finest leather.

[17] Giorgio Riello, *A Foot in the Past: Consumers, Producers and Footwear in the Long Eighteenth Century* (Oxford and New York: Pasold Research Fund/Oxford University Press, 2006), p. 83.
[18] Letter 20, 2 June 1799.

4.25 Edward Hogg, pair of leather,
silk and linen shoes, 1795–1800.
© Victoria and Albert Museum,
London/Given by Messrs Harrods Ltd

1800
PINK SHOES

Letter 23, Saturday 25 – Monday 27 October 1800, Steventon

'The Pink Shoes are not particularly beautiful, but they fit me very well—the others are faultless.'

The two or more pairs of shoes are part of a commissioned glut of purchases Cassandra made for her sister in London (see also pp. 37, 151 and 179). They had not arrived when she started her letter on 25 October (in lovely synchronicity, the feast day of Crispin and Crispinian, patron saints of shoemakers), but the parcel had turned up by the letter's completion on Monday 27th. We can assume that Cassandra tried on the shoes herself to test their fit, based on Letter 59, where upon sending mourning clothing to Cassandra in Godmersham, Austen told her, 'I hope the Shoes will fit; Martha & I both tried them on.'[19] The sisters evidently and conveniently had the same size feet.

We have no information as to shoe sellers the Austens may have patronised or preferred. Cassandra had visited London with their brother Edward on a trip from her home at Steventon to Godmersham in the middle of October. Edward ordered a hat from Lock & Co (today still in their original premises in St James's Street) to be sent to the Blenheim Hotel in New Bond Street, so Cassandra was presumably staying there with him in the heart of the West End, amid a plethora of attractive retail opportunities.[20] Given the prettiness of pink shoes from this period (figs 4.25–4.27), one wonders what made this pair 'not particularly beautiful', and what a 'faultless' shoe meant to Austen.

That Cassandra was able to test the fit also tells us how she bought them: ready-made from a shop or warehouse, instead of bespoke from a shoemaker. The label inside the pair in figure 4.25 proclaims them to come from Edward Hogg's 'Cheap Shoe Warehouse' at 25 Jermyn Street, St James's (fig. 4.28). A warehouse in the Regency period merely meant a large shop; a house of wares. People paid for existing goods with ready money, instead of on a credit system, and took

them home straight away, instead of waiting for their manufacture – part of the shift to a product- instead of a service-based consumer relationship.[21]

A well-established outwork system flourished from the mid-eighteenth century, supplying warehouses and wholesale dealers who 'provided readymade shoes in direct competition with the traditional system' centred on the cordwainer's workshop.[22] An 'army of small shoemakers' supplied these outlets. Although warehouses' reputation was initially for low-cost, low-quality goods, by the 1790s such large-scale retailers were proffering fashionable footwear to the gentry and middle classes, and became 'an integral part of middle-class shopping practices' by the mid-1810s.[23]

[19] Letter 59, 15–16 October 1808.
[20] *Chronology*, p. 244.
[21] Riello 2006, p. 13.
[22] Riello 2006, p. 157.
[23] Riello 2006, pp. 100–1.

4.26 Stencilled pink leather shoes made by Hoppe, London, 1795–1805. With permission of Royal Ontario Museum, Toronto/© ROM

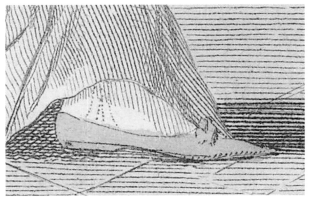

4.27 'Costume Parisien', *Journal des Dames et des Modes*, 17 August 1799: plate 148, engraving and watercolour on paper. Rijksmuseum, Amsterdam/ Purchased with the support of the F. G. Waller-Fonds

4.28 Detail of maker's label in shoe (see fig. 4.25). © Victoria and Albert Museum, London/ Given by Messrs Harrods Ltd

4.29 Woven black wool list boot, front-laced, with added leather sole, European, 19th century. Courtesy Bally Shoe Museum, Schönenwerd

4.30 One of a pair of early 19th-century man's list slippers. © HS2 Ltd

4.31 Marianne Knight's evening shoes of white silk satin and leather, 1820s. Jane Austen's House, Chawton

4.32 Rolinda Sharples, The Cloak-Room, Clifton Assembly Rooms (detail), oil on canvas, 73 × 88.2 cm, 1818. Bristol Museums, Galleries and Archives/ Bridgeman Art Gallery

1809
LIST SHOES

Letter 66, Tuesday 24 January 1809, Southampton: Castle Square

'Your silence on the subject of our Ball, makes me suppose your Curiosity too great for words. We were very well entertained, & could have staid longer but for the arrival of my List shoes to convey me home, & I did not like to keep them waiting in the Cold.'

List shoes or list slippers were soft, thick, warm footwear made from list – the selvedges of woollen textiles cut off as industrial waste and thriftily rewoven into a new textile (fig. 4.29). Selvedges were tightly woven and did not unravel, especially after finishing processes such as fulling and napping, so the discarded strips functioned more like tape than offcuts. As an eighteenth-century shoemaker explained, 'The cloth is three, four or five threads wide, depending on whether they are wanted fine or coarse', to make 'Plaited shoes and quarter slippers of cloth or list … Inside they are lined with baize, closed with binding, fastened on the outside, and soled.'[24] During the Napoleonic wars, French prisoners in England were set to producing list shoes, their leather soles sewn on by people around Norwich. Other Regency makers of list shoes and slippers were poor women and children, convicts and the blind, as the footwear was straightforward to assemble and simple in cut. Old Bailey records indicate list shoes' value as being between 1s and 3s a pair.

Their production did not make for fashionable footwear. Soft, soundless list shoes and slippers were popular wear when quiet was needed, as in a house during illness. Their silence was also exploited for sneaking around and out of houses and checking up on servants, if Regency literature is to be believed. Country people, prisoners, thieves, spies, the old, the stay-at-home, coach travellers, ship's gunners and exercisers were all to be found in list footwear. An 1820s French 'Book of Politeness' includes list shoes in its description of 'vulgar shoes' one 'ought not to be in the habit of wearing' in common life, and never when visiting, perhaps like that in figure 4.30, worn by a London gentleman later in his life, and buried with him in 1832.[25] A traveller in France during 1814–15 recorded French gentlewomen resplendent at night, yet found during the day in 'complete dishabille' of bedgowns, papered hair and 'their handsome ancles [*sic*] covered by coarse list slippers'.[26] So when were list shoes or slippers appropriate? The shoemaking manual explains a similar kind of footwear as being worn 'in winter because of their warmth, not just indoors, but also outside, and on journeys, as overshoes or alone, with or without soles', although they were not good for long walks.[27] This is Austen's context on a January night. Her list shoes would have been worn over delicate dancing slippers (fig. 4.31), protecting them from the journey to and from the ball, and keeping her feet warm. Rolinda Sharples's painting of a ballroom shows a servant helping a woman to change her shoes (fig. 4.32), and the parcels the Sperling girls carry also look as if they contain shoes (see fig. 2.24).

[24] François-Alexandre Pierre de Garsault, *M. de Garsault's 1767 Art of the Shoemaker: An Annotated Translation*, trans. D. A. Saguto (Williamsburg, VA: The Colonial Williamsburg Foundation, in association with Texas Tech University Press, 2009), p. 141.
[25] 'The Gentleman and Lady's Book of Politeness'/'Manuel Complet de la bonne companies', trans and ed. Frances Grimble, in *The Lady's Stratagem: A Repository of 1820s Directions for the Toilet, Mantua-Making, Stay-Making, Millinery and Etiquette* (San Francisco, CA: Lavolta Press, 2009), p. 570.
[26] Archibald Alison, *Travels in France, During the Years 1814–15* (Edinburgh: Macredie, Skelly, and Muckersy, 1816), p. 298.
[27] Garsault 2009 (1767), p. 139.

4.33 Leather shoes, possibly British, 1805–15. Brooklyn Museum Costume Collection at The Metropolitan Museum of Art, New York/Gift of the Brooklyn Museum, 2009/Gift of Herman Delman, 1954

4.34 'Toe-tology – versus – phrenology' (detail), litho-engraving and watercolour on paper, c.1820. Wellcome Collection, London/Attribution 4.0 International (CC BY 4.0)

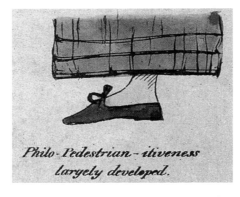

Philo-Pedestrian-itiveness largely developed.

4.35 Pair of woman's striped brown cotton half-boots with front lacing and low heel, buff leather toecap, 1815–20. © Victoria and Albert Museum, London

4.36 Wood and wrought-iron pattens, 25.4 × 9.5 cm, 1810s. Philadelphia Museum of Art/Gift of Mrs William D. Frishmuth, 1903

1811
WALKING SHOES

Letter 75, Thursday 6 June 1811, Chawton

'I had just left off writing & put on my Things for walking to Alton, when Anna & her friend Harriot called in their way thither, so we went together.'

What Austen may have worn to walk to town is discussed on page 115. Like her outerwear, there were several possibilities for how she shod her feet for the exercise. Austen would need good footwear. Country roads were unpaved, muddy in winter or after England's frequent rain, dusty in summer when the letter was written and full of stones and horse droppings. The walking route from Chawton into Alton, the nearest town, still avoids a lot of the road, and would then also have gone on a trail through grass. As Austen wrote in 1813, 'I walked to Alton, & dirt excepted, found it delightful'.[28] Shoes for walking were common, and advertisements and account books are full of such 'walking shoes' (figs 4.33 and 4.34) made in plain leather.

The growing popularity of half-boots during this period also provided another option for walking footwear. Laced up the centre front, or down the inside, ankle-height boots were as fashionable as shoes during the day. Those especially for walking were 'galoshed' with a leather lower half or front, often using a robust textile such as jean or nankeen for the upper part (fig. 4.35). In both *Persuasion* and her unfinished novel *The Watsons*, Austen emphasises the 'stout' and 'thick' qualities of boots fit for country walking. A double or triple sole on walking footwear would survive longer and make replacing it easier once worn down.

Leather soles can be slippery to begin with, and walking gave them a patina which increased their sliding glaze. One solution was to hammer nails in to provide more grip on grass and trackless vegetation – another advantage of a thicker walking sole. Surviving wooden clogs from throughout the nineteenth century also show this technique in use. In addition, the soles of Regency

shoes and boots easily absorbed damp and cold in their untreated state, nailed or not. Early nineteenth-century beauty manuals strongly advised taking off the shoes one wore outside at home, 'even where there is very little mud', to give them a chance to dry out and not keep cold around the feet, leading to illness.[29]

A good twenty years before the invention of vulcanisation created rubber footwear, pattens and other strategies such as cork soles or separate clogs made to match the shoe helped buffer feet from the ground. Pattens were wooden overshoes raised on an iron ring (fig. 4.36) that gave some protection from mud through elevation. The sisters 'walked in wintry weather through the sloppy lane between Steventon and Dean[e] in pattens, usually worn at that time even by Gentlewomen', so they may have been one of the things Austen put on, as she definitely wore them.[30] Pattens were useful but not fashionable. Like scarlet cloaks (see p. 114), their functional qualities transcended class differences, and working and gentry people alike wore the raised shoes.

[28] Letter 80, 4 February 1813.
[29] Grimble 2009, p. 83.
[30] Austen-Leigh 2008, p. 157.

DRESSING TABLE

GLOVES, FANS, FLOWERS, TRIMS AND HANDKERCHIEFS

5.1 Louis-Léopold Boilly, *The Card Sharp on the Boulevard* (detail), oil on wood, 24 × 33 cm, 1806. National Gallery of Art, Washington, DC/ Gift of Victoria and Roger Sant

5.2 Sir Thomas Lawrence, *Portrait of Lady Frances Hamilton* (detail), black and red chalk on paper, 55.6 × 32.1 cm, 1804

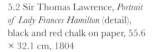

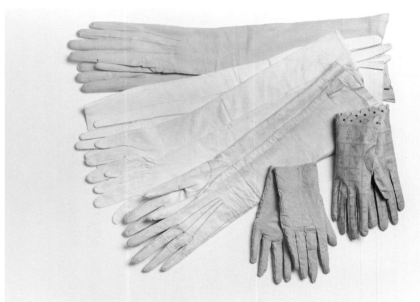

5.3 Women's gloves (from top): yellow chicken-skin gloves made by Lyons of Limerick and elbow-length white kid evening gloves, both pairs belonging to Princess Charlotte, 1815–17; elbow-length white cotton gloves, cut on the bias for stretch, 1800–15; elbow-length white kid gloves, 1820; Spanish wrist-length leather gloves with decorative prints, 1800–20; wrist-length chicken-skin gloves, 1800–10. Museum of London/ Photograph by John Chase

Letter 1, Saturday 9 – Sunday 10 January 1796, Steventon

'all my money is spent in buying white gloves and pink persian'

Gloves were a ubiquitous accessory for Regency women. They kept hands warm and gave protection from the elements and dirt, in an age when facilities to wash one's hands were not necessarily easily available.[1]

As women's sleeves grew shorter in the 1790s, their gloves grew longer, reaching over the elbow and held up there by 'Ribands [ribbons] or other fastenings of gloves above the elbow', which a doctor complained of as being bad for the circulation (fig. 5.1).[2] A coloured ribbon was another way to complement a gown colour. Looking at accounts of spending, the most popular kinds of gloves for genteel women were plain white kid, worn wrist-length during the day or with long-sleeved gowns (fig. 5.2), and Austen was likely purchasing something of this kind. Kid leather has a finer grain and more elasticity than skins made from older animals, allowing it to fit the hand and arm closely and smoothly. Comparing two pairs in the Museum of London (fig. 5.3) shows the considerable difference between a pristine new pair of white kid leather gloves and the creasing and grime caused by wear.

Long gloves were awkward to remove. Taking the tips of the fingers out for use at home was a practical solution for keeping warm yet enabling practicality, as shown in the pair of late eighteenth-century knitted cotton gloves in figure 5.4. We do not know what kind or colour of gloves Austen bought in 1798 when she told Cassandra, 'I have unpacked the Gloves & placed yours in your drawer.—Their colour is light & pretty, & I beleive exactly what we fixed on.'[3] Cotton, linen (usually called 'thread'; fig. 5.5), jean, nankeen, worsted and silk gloves were all possibilities, as well as the standard York tan and Limerick gloves, which a fashion magazine said were 'far more genteel than those of kid the colour of bonnets'.[4] As Austen's gloves were coloured, they may be to match gowns or bonnets or to complement an ensemble, as in figure 5.6.

The final mention of Austen's own gloves in the letters concerns the serendipity of a cheap pair found in London:

> I was very lucky in my gloves, got them at the first shop I went to, though I went into it rather because it was near than because it looked at all like a glove shop, & gave only four Shillings for them;—upon hearing which, every body at Chawton will be hoping & predicting that they cannot be good for anything, & their worth certainly remains to be proved, but I think they look very well.[5]

Gloves were such a staple that they were to be had at many shops selling all sorts of goods. Was four shillings cheap? It depends what kind of gloves they were. Prices range so much in accounts, depending on material, place and quality, that we must take Austen's word for it. She appears to be buying only one pair. Two or three pairs were often bought at once by middle-class consumers. The glove purchases of Eliza Jervoise of the Herriard estate (whose husband Colonel George Purefoy Jervoise danced with Jane Austen in 1799) in Basingstoke and Salisbury through 1801 give an idea of the variety available just in Austen's own locality. A pair of kid gloves was 3s.6d, as was a pair of 'Long Tan Mitts', while two pairs of 'Gray Gloves' and of 'Open Cotton' gloves both cost 7s each set. 'A pair of Short Mitts' was 2s; five pairs of 'Tan Beaver Gloves' 17s.6d, but a pair of 'Grey Beaver Habits' was only 2s. '1 Pr Silk Habit Gloves' came in at 4s.6d; '2 pr Black Silk Gloves' was 13s, and one pair of 'Silk Gloves was a whole 7s.'[6] The facility with which small, portable gloves went astray also underlies the Regency practice of buying multiple pairs to allow substitution of lost or besmirched singles, as with stockings.

5.4 Pair of machine-knitted cotton
gloves with open fingers, 1800–20.
The Hopkins Collection, London

5.5 Linen gloves cut on the bias,
with embroidery in ivory silk floss
and silver filé, now tarnished, and
silk tassels, never worn, 1800–20.
The Hopkins Collection, London

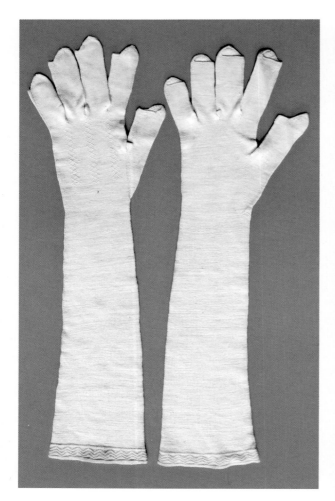

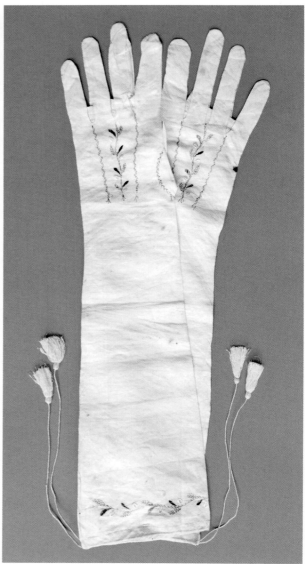

[1] The post-pandemic world has perhaps a greater appreciation of this sanitary use of gloves than previously.
[2] William Buchan, *Advice to Mothers, on the Subject of Their Own Health; and on the Means of Promoting the Health, Strength, and Beauty, of Their Offspring*, 2nd edn (London: Cadell and Davies, 1811), p. 129.
[3] Letter 10, 27–28 October 1798.
[4] *La Belle Assemblée: Or, Bell's Court and Fashionable Magazine* (London: J. Bell, 1807), issue 3:21, September 1807, p. 115, cited in Liza Foley, '"An Entirely Fictitious Importance"? Reconsidering the Significance of the Irish Glove Trade: A Study of Limerick Gloves, 1778–1840', *Costume*, 48.2 (2014), p. 165.
[5] Letter 84, 20 May 1813.
[6] Jervoise of Herriard Collection.

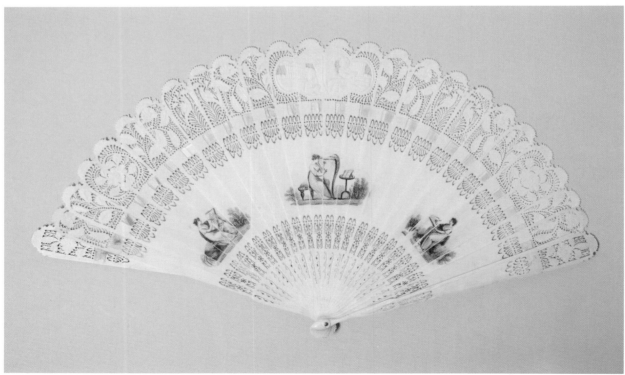

1799
WHITE FAN

Letter 17, Tuesday 8 – Wednesday 9 January 1799, Steventon

'I … took my <u>white fan</u> with me; I am very glad he never threw it into the River.'

One's curiosity is piqued by who may have been threatening to throw Austen's fan in the river. She had been to 'The Ball at Kempshott' on Tuesday evening and wrote to Cassandra on the Wednesday. This is the event to which she wore the Mamalouc cap (see p. 125), along with her green shoes (p. 159).

Fans were an essential evening accessory. Although women's dress for balls at this time had short sleeves and was leaving increasing quantities of back and décolletage bare, the heat in the rooms could be intense. At this ball, 'There were more Dancers than the Room could conveniently hold.' A crush of active bodies, in modest rooms lit entirely by candles emitting their own radiant heat, rapidly built up a swelter. Fans then came into their own to create an individual breeze and cool off the 'glow' ladies acquired (presumably men perspired manfully within their woollen suits and made discreet use of handkerchiefs). Any language of flirtation was certainly secondary to the practical function. As Austen said in *Northanger Abbey*, 'But in dancing … the agreeableness, the compliance are expected from him, while she furnishes the fan and the lavender water', the latter also used to cool a flushed head.[7]

Austen's white fan could have been made of all sorts of materials. The most common way to construct a folding fan was using sticks, held together by a curved 'leaf' of paper, silk or sometimes lace, which unfurled to display a pattern or decorative scene. The second was to make the fan wholly from decorative sticks, interlaced by a ribbon, in the style now called 'brisé'. These fans imitated Chinese wood or ivory examples imported en masse by the East India Company (fig. 5.7), and saw an increased popularity in the early nineteenth century, in another Asian addition to the Regency wardrobe. Solid fans were a little more durable and compact than those

with leaves, so survive in greater numbers. They further complemented the general Regency fashion trends of simpler decoration and smaller scale. Historic examples are largely made of materials which could be described as white, particularly bone, horn and ivory. Brisé sticks were frequently embellished by highly intricate carved or pierced designs in filigree or lace patterns, and had additional embellishment through grisaille prints, painted panels and decoration, sequins, spangles and metal piqué work (fig. 5.8). Austen's fan could have had any or all of these aesthetic elements.

[7] *Northanger Abbey*, vol. I, ch. x.

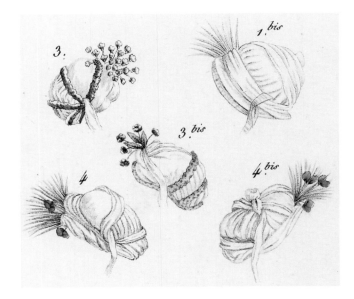

5.9 'Costumes Parisiens', *Journal des Dames et des Modes*, 15 May 1800: 'Capotes' (detail), plate 216. Bibliothèque nationale de France, Paris

5.10 Silk cap, French, *c.*1800. The Metropolitan Museum of Art, New York/Purchase, Irene Lewisohn Trust Gift, 1991

5.11 Detail of faux wheat adorning the front of the silk cap (see fig. 5.10). The Metropolitan Museum of Art, New York/ Purchase, Irene Lewisohn Trust Gift, 1991

1799
FAKE FLOWERS

Letter 20, Sunday 2 June 1799, Bath: 13 Queen Square

'—Flowers are very much worn, & Fruit is still more the thing.—Eliz: has a bunch of Strawberries, & I have seen Grapes, Cherries, Plumbs & Apricots. … —A plumb or green gage would cost three shillings;—Cherries & Grapes about 5 I beleive—but this is at some of the dearest Shops'

Austen wrote to Cassandra from Bath, the next most influential style centre outside London, telling her of the fashion there for decorating headwear with faux fruits and flowers (fig. 5.9). Cassandra may have requested an item to partake of this mode, as Austen continued in her letter: 'My Aunt has told me of a very cheap one near Walcot Church, to which I shall go in quest of something for You.' A little over a week later, on 11 June, Austen recounted to her sister: 'We have been to the cheap Shop, & very cheap we found it, but there are only flowers made there, no fruit—& as I could get 4 or 5 very pretty sprigs of the former for the same money which would procure only one Orleans plumb, in short could get more for three or four Shillings than I could have means of bringing home, I cannot decide on the fruit till I hear from you again.' 'Again' infers Cassandra's letters have been discussing which fruit to buy or how best to spend their limited budget. The practical consideration of the amount of flowers purchasable for the same cost as one fruit is further enhanced by a very Austen observation that 'I cannot help thinking that it is more natural to have flowers grow out of the head than fruit.'[8] These imitations of nature were all handmade by women and children outworkers, many of them French post-Revolutionary émigrés.

A French hat or bonnet of around 1800 made from satin, ribbon and net has faux wheat adorning its front (figs. 5.10 and 5.11). One wonders where grains would fit in Austen's scheme of naturalness. An 1825 guide for ladies' maids reflected on this as 'a very singular whim of fashion', when flowers were succeeded by 'grass, dog's grass, barley, wheat, acorns &c.'[9] The same source considered that 'imitations of natural flowers will always be more or less fashionable as ornaments of dress' and 'flowers … recall so many pleasing ideas, that a handsome woman adds to her attractions when she admits to her toilette these charming children of Spring and Summer'.[10] In terms of being part of Austen's physical wardrobe, a French manual advised ladies to hang their fake flowers upside down by means of a hook in the wire stem, to avoid them being crushed.[11]

[8] Letter 21, 11 June 1799.
[9] *The Duties of a Lady's Maid* 1825, pp. 160–61.
[10] *The Duties of a Lady's Maid* 1825, pp. 159–60.
[11] Grimble 2009, p. 123.

5.12 Blond imitation tortoiseshell hair
comb with seventeen plain, narrow, slightly
curved-back teeth, 7.5 × 9.5 × 1.5 cm, early
19th century. Rijksmuseum, Amsterdam/
A. J. Enschedé Bequest, Haarlem

5.14 Brock family artist, *Elizabeth Brock*,
American, watercolour on paper, 1810s.
Courtesy of Jeffrey S. Evans & Associates

5.13 Cassandra Austen, portrait
of Fanny Knight (detail), watercolour
on paper, 3 September 1805. Jane
Austen's House, Chawton

5.15 Diana Sperling,
self-portrait (detail), plate 40,
watercolour on paper, 1816.
Private collection

1800
COMBS

Letter 23, Saturday 25 – Monday 27 October 1800, Steventon

'—*The Combs are very pretty, & I am much obliged to you for your present; but am sorry you should make me so many.*'

Hair combs were functional and decorative ornaments useful to the Regency woman for styling her hair (fig. 5.12). While overall, there was a distinct change from large tumbling powdered curls fashionable in the 1790s, to the more natural, antique-inspired styles resembling chignons of *c*.1800 and into the nineteenth century, the variations were legion. Fashion plates show all sorts of hairstyles, some of them held up with combs. But combs' efficacy and how Austen may have used them are better visualised in less formal portraits, conveying a more intimate sense of convenient daily hairdressing.

Cassandra's watercolour sketch of her niece Fanny painted in 1805 (fig. 5.13) shows how the twelve-year-old girl was using a comb to style her hair in a chignon, while her childhood shorter haircut grew out. The image shows the distinct line between the 'short' or 'front' hair and the 'long' or 'back' hair, approximately over the centre of the head between the ears. The fringe (or bangs), as we would now call it, covered not only the forehead but reached right round to the back of the ear. This was the section that was curled or frizzed for more formal styles, unless, like Austen, a woman was lucky enough to have hair that 'curls well enough to want no papering'.[12] With her long hair out, and short hair over up to half her head, the Regency lady's hairstyle resembled that bastion of 1980s hairstyling, the mullet – a look that is yet to make it to a screen adaptation.

As an adult woman, during the day Austen's long hair was 'always plaited up out of sight' under caps, as she records in 1798.[13] Pictures of young women like the American Elizabeth Brock in figure 5.14 help show off the sizes and uses of combs. Not only does Brock have a large comb curved to her head holding up her bun, but she also has the small comb near her centre parting sometimes seen in early to mid-nineteenth-century portraits, whose function appears to be keeping the hair smoothed away from the parting, or controlling where the first curl sits. What happened when a comb no longer gripped is charmingly illustrated (fig. 5.15) in an 1816 self-portrait watercolour by Essex gentry lady Diana Sperling, losing her comb and thus her coiffure while out riding one 'dark, muddy, raining and windy day in November'.[14]

[12] Letter 13, 1–2 December 1798.
[13] Letter 13, 1–2 December 1798.
[14] Sperling 1981 (1812–23), plate 40.

Morning & Evening Dresses.

1813
PLEATING LACE

Letter 88, Thursday 16 September 1813, London: Henrietta Street

'We must have been 3 q^{rs} of an hour at Grafton House, Edward sitting by all the time with wonderful patience. …— The Edging there is very cheap, I was tempted by some, & I bought some very nice plaiting [pleating] Lace at 3.4.'

We have seen Austen shopping at Grafton House in 1811 (see p. 137) and now turn our attention to the attractions of the place, and why she kept returning, in this instance for some 'plaiting' lace. During the Regency period, 'plait' was the usual spelling of 'pleat', starting to change much later in the century. The fashion plate in figure 5.16 shows such pleating lace in use to trim around the top of the bodice and at the lower hem of the robe. Lace's preformed holes made it much easier to run a thread along them and create even pleats for applied trim decorations. This type of lace is also seen in the 'broad lace pleated lappet' finishing a bonnet in figure 5.17. Austen could have been buying some of the popular pale ecru silk lace called 'blonde' (figs 5.18 and 5.19) found adorning many Regency garments.

Grafton House has been tentatively identified as the linen draper's Wilding and Kent, at 164 New Bond Street on the corner of Grafton Street, Mayfair. But there was a second Grafton Street in London in Austen's day, between Litchfield Street and West Street in Soho, now built over and so hidden from researchers. At number 15 was a large, cheap haberdashery and hosiery store run by Thomas Flint and John Ray, who married Flint's sister Elizabeth in 1809.[15] The couple lived on the premises, known variously as Flint's, Flint and Ray, or Grafton House. The names appear together in many historical documents, whereas Wilding and Kent's are never connected with a Grafton House. Furthermore, Bond Street was the home of luxury shopping, not the inexpensive goods and crowded premises that Austen's letters convey, more applicable to Soho merchants. This

second establishment is the one Austen patronised.

Grafton House was one of the first large-scale drapery shops established on the principle of ready-money payment instead of credit, meaning the customer paid then and there instead of requiring approval for an account that let bills accumulate and be paid quarterly or more. Anyone could shop at Flint's and the prices reflected this new egalitarianism of consumption. As was written of the store in 1830, 'Everybody has heard of Grafton House, where Mr. Flint sells his haberdashery goods ten times cheaper than any man in the "whole world" and therefore cannot afford to wrap any purchase in a piece of paper.'[16] The business had moved to 8 and 9 Soho Square by about 1825. Flint and Ray had a second establishment at 10 Fish Street Hill in the City of London, slightly south of the Monument, which insurance records describe as 'mercer, hosier, laceman, linen draper and haberdasher'.[17]

The renowned cheapness attracted many shoppers, so the store was always busy. Austen mentions in this letter that 'by going very early' to Grafton House 'we got immediate attendance & went on very comfortably'. The previous letter tells us 'early' is 9 o'clock in the morning, to 'get that over before breakfast', which was easy as Henrietta Street was about seven minutes' walk from the place.[18] The tactical timing was based on experience. In 1811, 'We set off immediately after breakfast & must have reached Grafton House by ½ past 11—, but when we entered the Shop, the whole Counter was thronged, & we waited full half an hour before we c^d be attended to.'[19] The early shopper caught the free attendant

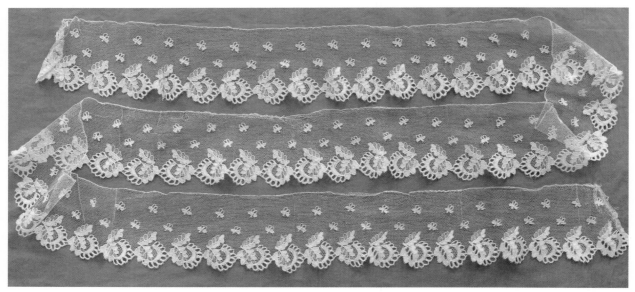

without whom she could not buy. Before department stores, goods were kept behind counters and brought out individually for each customer. In 1815, Austen alluded to 'encountering the miseries of Grafton House' while shopping for someone else.[20]

Her brother Edward's 'wonderful patience' is contrasted by an 1821 description of a man shopping at 'Flint's with your wife or sister … scolding her for delay, abusing shops and shopping, fashions and flounces, dress and dressers, tapping your stick incessantly on the ground, looking at your watch every three minutes, and interrupting by your impatience and complaints a pending decision between a *gros de Naples* and a *Zephyreene*'.[21] Some things, it appears, do not change.

[15] Philanthropist and lace merchant George Moore married John and Elizabeth's daughter, Eliza Flint Ray.

[16] Lucia Elizabetta Vestris, *Memoirs of the Life of Madame Vestris* (privately printed, 1830), p. 53.

[17] Sun Insurance Records, 'Insured: Thomas Flint Junior 10 Fish Street Hill mercer, hosier, laceman, linen draper and haberdasher', 6 April 1820, London Metropolitan Archives: City of London, MS11936/478/966146.

[18] Letter 87, 15–16 September 1813.

[19] Letter 70, 18–20 April 1811. At this date, Austen was probably walking to Grafton House from Henry Austen's old home at 64 Sloane Street, which takes about 45 minutes in modern London.

[20] Letter 128, 26 November 1815.

[21] *The New Monthly Magazine and Literary Journal* (London: Henry Colburn, 1821), vol. I, p. 676.

5.20 George Engleheart, *Portrait of a Lady*, watercolour and gouache on ivory, 8.3 × 6.7 cm, 1801. Yale Center for British Art, New Haven, CT/ Paul Mellon Collection

5.21 Pink kerchief with black and yellow stripes and fringe, silk gauze with plain-weave stripe, European, 74.6 × 75.9 cm, early 19th century; worn by donor's great-aunt Caira Robbins (1794–1881). Museum of Fine Arts, Boston/ Gift of Miss Ellen A. Stone/ Photograph © 2023 Museum of Fine Arts, Boston

1813
WHITE SILK HANDKERCHIEF

Letter 88, Thursday 16 September 1813, London: Henrietta Street

'—it was bought at Grafton House … —I only forgot the one particular thing which I had always resolved to buy there—a white silk Handkf—& was therefore obliged to give six shillings for one at Crook & Besford's'

For this shopping trip, Austen had ventured further west into London from the home of her brother Henry at 10 Henrietta Street, right by Covent Garden and St Paul's Church. Grafton House was in Grafton Street in Soho (see p. 183). Crook and Besford, haberdashers and hosiers, were a fifteen-minute walk away at number 104 Pall Mall (the address has been the home of the Reform Club since 1837).

We encounter one of Austen's decorative handkerchiefs before her plainer pocket and neck kerchiefs (see pp. 187–89). From its cost and textile, the kind she purchased was one of those more like a modern scarf. Being of silk, as in figure 5.20, would make this one suitable for women's evening wear and requiring of some more care to clean and maintain. Austen wrote of attending a ball in her 'aunt's gown and handkerchief' in November 1800.[22] Different ways of wearing the item are seen in figures 1.62, look 11 in 3.1, 3.9, 3.15 and 3.18.

There were myriad kinds of these scarf-like large, decorative handkerchiefs available for Regency consumers (fig. 5.21). The account books of Mrs Mary Topham, Austen's contemporary (although older and widowed), show a wide range of expenditure on handkerchiefs of all kinds and qualities. Her silk purchases included a colourful 'purple and amber Silk Handkerchief' (5s in 1816), 'a blue Barcelona Hand[kerchief]' (4s.6d in 1817) and 'a Brocaded 1/2 Hand[kerchief]' in 1816 for a luxurious 14s. Half-

handkerchiefs were triangular, and had a neater fit because of the lack of doubled material, meaning they were often more decorative as all of the embellishment would be shown when worn. The 12s cost of a silk handkerchief of unknown colour in 1816 shows how the brocading added to the expense. Nearer to the style of Austen's purchase were a 'White Silk Hand[kerchief]' in 1818 for only 4s, plus another for 3s.6d in 1819 – almost half the cost of Austen's six years earlier. Topham also bought a 'white figured Barcelona Hand[kerchief]' in 1815 (5s).[23] These handkerchiefs could be made plain, check or with fancy patterns, but were always made from twilled silk, first manufactured in Spain, hence the name. We can see a decorative kerchief in use tied around Austen's neck in the blue dress painting by Cassandra (see fig. 1.41).

[22] Letter 27, 20–21 November 1800.
[23] Topham 1810.

5.22 Cassandra Austen's handkerchief, linen embroidered in satin stitch, 73 × 73 cm, 1800–17. Jane Austen's House, Chawton

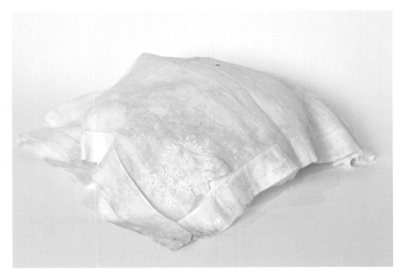

5.23 Detail of Cassandra Austen's handkerchief (see fig. 5.22). Jane Austen's House, Chawton

1814
POCKET
HANDKERCHIEF

Letter 112, Tuesday 29 November 1814, London: 23 Hans Place [to Anna Lefroy]

'Acting seldom satisfies me. I took two Pocket handkerchiefs, but had very little occasion for either. She is an elegant creature however & hugs Mr Younge delightfully.'

Pocket handkerchiefs were one of the useful, universal squares of textiles everybody in the Regency had about their person. Austen took two to the theatre against the possibility of tears, but they were carried and used for all sorts of purposes. In a time without disposable paper goods or easily accessible public running water, small washable pieces of cloth were handy at home and away for cleaning, wiping, carrying and wrapping.

They also made very good presents, both as useful gifts and to demonstrate affection between friends and family. Austen hemstitched some pocket handkerchiefs as a wedding present for her friend Catherine Bigg in summer 1808, and on 26 August added a verse to go with them:

> Cambrick! With grateful blessings would I pay
> The pleasure given me in sweet employ.
> Long may'st thou serve my friend without decay,
> And have no tears to shed but joy.[24]

In October of the same year, Austen 'finished a Handkf. for Mrs James Austen'.[25]

A surviving handkerchief is also the bearer of an example of Austen's excellent needlework. She made the linen handkerchief in figures 5.22 and 5.23 for her sister, and embroidered it with Cassandra's initials in satin stitch, held within a wreath. The fine, high quality of the embroidery backs up the opinion of her niece Caroline Austen that 'she was a great adept at overcast and satin stitch—the peculiar delight of that day'.[26]

Her nephew James Edward Austen-Leigh also considered 'Her needlework both plain and ornamental was excellent and might almost have put a sewing machine to shame.'[27] Austen was fond of 'work', as plain and decorative needlework was called, and spent a lot of time at it, especially when entertaining visitors in the drawing room. She also used the thinking time gained while her hands were occupied as an aid to writing her prose.[28] This handkerchief is the only verified example of Austen's needlework, which is as fine, precise and controlled as her handwriting and writing.

[24] *Family Record*, p. 167.
[25] Letter 56, 1–2 October 1808.
[26] Caroline Austen, *My Aunt Jane Austen: A Memoir* (1867), in Austen-Leigh 2008, p. 171.
[27] Austen-Leigh 2008, p. 77.
[28] See Davidson 2019, p. 95.

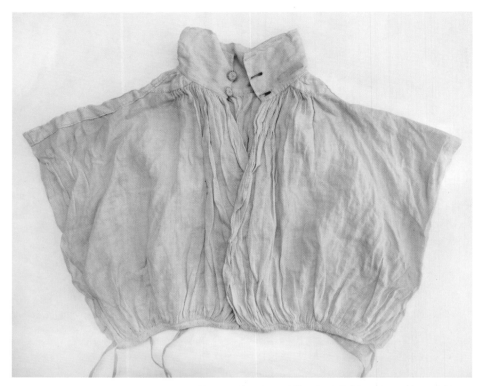

5.24 Woman's linen collared neck-handkerchief or chemisette, early 19th century. © Victoria and Albert Museum, London/ Courtesy of the author

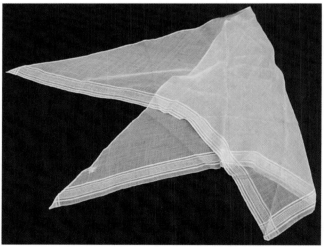

5.25 Neckerchief or half-handkerchief, American, cotton, 1804–14. The Metropolitan Museum of Art, New York/Gift of Mrs Alice Baker Furst, 1942

1815
NECK
HANDKERCHIEF

Letter 128, Sunday 26 November 1815, London: 23 Hans Place

'The Parcel arrived safely, & I am much obliged to you for your trouble. ... In the 3 neckhandfs. I include the one sent down before.'

A neck handkerchief is what the French called a *'fichu'*, and under this name has attracted more attention in histories of dress (see fig. 1.5). The word 'handkerchief' encompassed a variety of purposes for Regency dressers. It was a generic term for any large piece of fabric, generally a square, hemmed or fringed, which could be put to uses from the pocket handkerchief we are most familiar with today, to being large and voluminous enough to act as a shawl. Indeed, when the first proper woollen shawls with elaborately woven edges were being introduced to Britain from their native Kashmir, a fashion magazine of 1790 described the item as 'a type of unusually ample handkerchief'.[29] Austen's scarf-like silk version is discussed on page 185. Handkerchiefs of all sorts, shapes, sizes and textiles are so ubiquitous that they appear in at least half the depictions of Regency dress across all social classes.

Handkerchiefs of the larger sort tended to take the width of the fabric off the roll as their measure. A yard square (36 in./91 cm) was common, usually made of fine linen or cotton textiles such as muslin, cambric and lawn. The kind of neck handkerchief Austen refers to in this letter probably means a square of fabric folded diagonally and worn over the shoulders and décolletage, tucked into the front of a gown and pinned to secure it (fig. 5.25), as Austen 'tucked Mrs. Lance's neckerchief in behind and fastened it with a pin' at a ball in 1809.[30] They could also be called a double handkerchief. When describing the construction of an 1801 gown (see p. 53), Austen explained, 'there is to be a frill ... to put on occasionally [tucked into the front bodice neckline] when all one's handkerchiefs are dirty'. Neck handkerchiefs kept warm on cold days the open expanse of chest revealed by lower-necked gowns, protected them from the sun and the associated tanning at warmer times of year, and aided in modesty. Confusingly, chemisettes or other sewn chest coverings, especially those with collars, could also be called neck handkerchiefs, or shirt handkerchiefs (fig. 5.24).

Although Austen would have worn neck handkerchiefs all her life, at the time of writing she was forty – high time, in Regency consideration, for more of her skin to be covered up. Society was intractable about ageing women's need to retreat into increasing layers of textiles (see fig. 1.31).

29 *Journal de la Mode et du Goût*, 5 June 1790, cited in Alice Mackrell, *Shawls, Stoles, and Scarves* (London and New York: Batsford, 1986), p. 38.
30 Letter 66, 24 January 1809.

JEWELLERY BOX

NECKLACES, RINGS AND BRACELETS

1801
TOPAZ CROSS
PENDANT

Letter 38, Tuesday 26 – Wednesday 27 May 1801, Bath: The Paragon

'—[Charles] has received 30£ for his share of the privateer & expects 10£ more—but of what avail is it to take prizes if he lays out the produce in presents to his Sisters. He has been buying Gold chains & Topaze Crosses for us;—he must be well scolded.'

The youngest Austen sibling, Charles, born four years after Jane in 1779, joined the navy in 1791 like his older brother Francis, and was made lieutenant in 1797 and captain in 1804. Capturing an enemy ship resulted in prize money, where the value of the ship and its contents was divided among the victorious crew by established and diminishing proportion according to rank. The captain got two-eighths and the admiral one-eighth of the assessed value, but every hand received something. Charles Austen received a percentage of the one-eighth share of the spoils allotted collectively to the master and lieutenants.

The topaz cross pendants (fig. 6.1) that Charles spent his spoils on as gifts for his sisters are made from five pieces, one with baguette cut stones, and the other with facetted oval cut stones. The accompanying gold chain (fig. 6.2) is 30 inches (76 cm) long. Topaz and other gemstone crosses were popular accessories throughout the late eighteenth and nineteenth centuries. Figure 6.3 shows a similar topaz cross owned by Edward (Austen) Knight's wife, Elizabeth. While the pendant itself was a pretty ornament, full sets of topaz necklaces and crosses were even more resplendent (fig. 6.4). How these looked in use is seen in figure 6.5, a French fashion plate.

Though Austen willed all her possessions to Cassandra, it has been suggested that her cross was given to their dear friend Martha Lloyd, based on an identification in a picture traditionally said to be of Lloyd. However, the clothing in the image and the ambrotype technique used to make it are both dated to the 1850s – well after Lloyd's 1843 death. At some point, both crosses were returned to Charles Austen's family after both ladies' deaths, accompanied by the letter mentioning them, and from there they ended up for sale in the Brick Row Book Shop in New Haven, Connecticut. American collector Charles Beecher 'Beech' Hogan bought them in 1927, and after promising the items as a bequest, eventually presented the pendants, chain and letter directly to the Jane Austen Society in 1974. They now remain in the collection of Jane Austen's House, in Chawton Cottage in Hampshire, where Austen lived between 1809 and 1817, and where she wrote and published her six completed novels. Replicas of the straight-edged cross adorned the necks of the actresses playing Elizabeth Bennet in the 1995 television drama *Pride and Prejudice* and Emma Woodhouse in the 2020 film production of *Emma*.

Austen borrowed the topaz crosses and their gold chain for *Mansfield Park*. Fanny Price's beloved brother William is a midshipman and brings her 'a very pretty amber cross' from Sicily (there is no record of where Charles Austen obtained his gifts).[31] Desiring to wear 'the almost solitary ornament in her possession' to her first real ball, Fanny is distressed she has 'nothing but a

193

6.2 Topaz cross and gold chain,
1801. Jane Austen's House,
Chawton/Photograph by
Peter Smith

bit of ribbon to fasten it to'. Mary Crawford offers her a necklace from her own collection, urging upon the girl one 'of gold, prettily worked' given by her brother Henry, who has a romantic interest in Fanny.[32] She accepts with some reluctance. Soon after, Fanny's cousin Edmund, whom her heart prefers, offers her 'a plain gold chain, perfectly simple and neat' to accompany the cross, which she accepts with delight as 'the very thing, precisely what I wished for! This is the only ornament I have ever had a desire to possess. It will exactly suit my cross. They must and shall be worn together.'[33]

Note Austen's delicate distinction between a necklace, adorned and intended for wear in its own right, and a plain chain, made to support a pendant. Austen's heroine chooses what Austen's brother gave, and what Fanny's fictional brother intended, wanting 'to buy her a gold chain too, but the purchase had been beyond his means'.[34] The emotional dimension of such gifts and the joined chain and cross is extolled in fiction: 'those memorials of the two most beloved of her heart, those dearest tokens so formed for each other by everything real and imaginary'.[35] Such must have been some of the feelings of Charles's sisters when wearing his thoughtful presents.

6.3 Topaz and gold cross pendant once belonging to Elizabeth Austen, wife of Edward Austen, 7.5 × 4 cm, 1790–1808. Jane Austen's House, Chawton/ Photograph by Peter Smith

---

[31] *Mansfield Park*, vol. II, ch. viii.
[32] *Mansfield Park*, vol. II, ch. viii.
[33] *Mansfield Park*, vol. II, ch. xix.
[34] *Mansfield Park*, vol. II, ch. viii.
[35] *Mansfield Park*, vol. II, ch. ix.

6.4 Pink topaz collet necklace with cross-shaped
pendant, length approx. 40.5 cm, early 19th century.
Courtesy of Sotheby's

6.5 Georges Jacques Gatine, engraving after drawing
by Louis Marie Lanté, *Incroyables et Merveilleuses*,
1818, *Merveilleuse No. 33* (detail), 1818. Rijksmuseum,
Amsterdam/Purchased with the support of the
F. G. Waller-Fonds

6.6 Turquoise and gold ring owned
by Jane Austen. Jane Austen's House,
Chawton/Photograph by Peter Smith

6.7 Inside view of turquoise and gold
ring owned by Jane Austen (see fig.
6.6). Jane Austen's House, Chawton/
Photograph by Peter Smith

1760-80 TURQUOISE RING

This pretty, elegant and simple gold ring (figs. 6.6 and 6.7) is set with a cabochon natural turquoise in an oval bezel (⅝ × ⅜ in./17.5 × 8 mm). It was probably made in the eighteenth century, in the 1760s or '70s, perhaps before Austen's birth in 1775. The date reflects its similarity with other rings of the same period. The ring was altered with a device to reduce the size of the band, in the late nineteenth or early twentieth century (fig. 6.8). The blue stone was first identified as odontolite, but has since been confirmed as turquoise. The box currently housing the jewellery is a nineteenth-century rectangular leather case bearing the name of T. West, goldsmith of Ludgate Street, London, but the jewellery sits loosely, which suggests the box is not original (fig. 6.9). Thomas West was at that location no earlier than 1815, and the family retained the business until at least the 1860s. The ring fits with what seems to have been Austen's preference for plain simplicity. In 1813, she bought a locket for Cassandra: 'neat and plain, set in gold'.[36] A turquoise engagement ring that Percy Bysshe Shelley gave to Harriet Westbrook in 1811 is fussier and finer, more in keeping with Regency taste (fig. 6.10).

Austen's ring came into Cassandra's keeping on her sister's death in 1817. As Eleanor Austen (née Jackson) explained in the accompanying autograph note (fig. 6.11) of November 1863, 'It was given to me by your Aunt Cassandra as soon as she knew that I was engaged to your Uncle' – Henry Austen, marrying for the second time in 1820. From 1816 Henry was curate of Chawton, and Eleanor was the niece of Revd Papillon, the rector of Chawton and known to the family for many years. She bequeathed the ring shortly before her death in 1864 to her niece Caroline Mary Craven Austen, to whom the note is addressed. Caroline and her brother James-Edward Austen-Leigh were children of James Austen, Jane's brother, and Caroline contributed childhood memories of her aunt to her sibling's invaluable book, *A Memoir of Jane Austen and Other Family Recollections* (1871). In her turn, Caroline passed the ring either to James-Edward's daughter Mary A. Austen-Leigh or his wife Emma Austen-Leigh. From there it descended to Mary

Dorothy Austen-Leigh, who gave the ring to her sister Winifred Jenkyns on 27 March 1962. Mrs Jenkyns was also the keeper of the brown silk pelisse (see p. 107). The ring stayed within the Austen family until it was put up for auction at Sotheby's in London in 2012, and what transpired afterwards made this little ring arguably now the best-known piece of Austenalia.

As one scholar put it, 'The ring was little known to the present generation of Austen scholars and entirely unknown to the great majority of her readers when its auction was announced.'[37] The guide price in the catalogue was £20–30,000. It sold on 10 July 2012 for £152,450 (including the premium) to Kelly Clarkson, an American singer and long-time fan of Austen. Jane Austen's House was interested in acquiring the ring, but was unable to raise the funds to meet the greatly increased hammer price. However, given the importance of the ring to British history and culture, and the rarity of personal Austen effects on the market, it was placed under a temporary export ban under the Waverley Criteria, 'used to measure whether an object should be considered a national treasure on the basis that the object's departure from the UK would be a misfortune', specifically Criterion Three, having 'outstanding significance for scholarship either on its own account or on account of its connection with a person'.[38] The ban stopped the ring being allowed to leave the country and gave the museum until 30 September to raise the purchase cost and 'show a serious expression of interest to buy the ring'.[39] A 'Bring the Ring Home' fundraising appeal began in August and was immediately boosted by an anonymous £100,000 donation. Thousands of Austen fans globally were able to contribute the rest to comprise a serious counter-offer, which was accepted. The turquoise ring finally entered the museum's permanent collection in 2013. Clarkson was gracious about her loss. Instead, she was seen shortly afterwards wearing a replica of the ring, which her fiancé had made for her, with diamonds added around the band.

The auction prompted a wave of discussion and investigation around the ring. Richard Edgcumbe, a

6.8 Later addition of sizing bar to turquoise and gold ring owned by Jane Austen (see fig. 6.6). Jane Austen's House, Chawton/ Photograph by Peter Smith

6.9 Turquoise and gold ring owned by Jane Austen in its later 19th-century box. Jane Austen's House, Chawton/Photograph by Peter Smith

senior curator at the Victoria and Albert Museum in London, wrote in his report for the export reviewing committee: 'It is precisely because Jane Austen understood so minutely the pains and pleasures of a jewel, and because jewellery has such potency as an intimate possession, that a gold and turquoise ring with a reasonable claim to have been owned by her aroused such interest … Whether the ring was a gift from an older relative or a younger friend remains pleasant speculation.'[40] Wherever Austen acquired it, the ring's history has taken it through a meandering path back to the home she owned and wore the jewellery in.

6.10 Turquoise and gold engagement ring given to Harriet Westbrook by Percy Bysshe Shelley in 1811. New York Public Library

6.11 The ring in its box, with provenance documentation. Jane Austen's House, Chawton/ Photograph by Peter Smith

[36] Letter 85, 24 May 1813.
[37] 'Reviewing Committee on the Export of Works of Art and Objects of Cultural Interest (RCEWA): Statement of Richard Edgcumbe, Senior Curator, Sculpture, Metalwork, Ceramics and Glass Department, Victoria and Albert Museum', Annex A, Case 4 (2013–14).
[38] Department for Culture, Media & Sport, 'Export Controls on Objects of Cultural Interest', March 2015.
[39] Press release, 'Museum successful in bid to bring Jane's ring home', Jane Austen's House Museum, undated.
[40] 'Reviewing Committee', Annex A, Case 4 (2013–14).

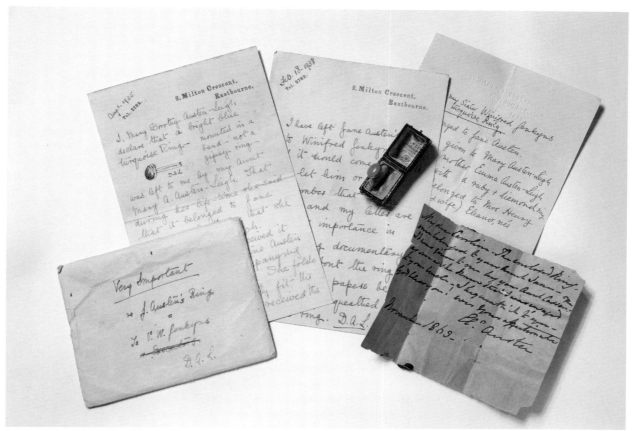

6.12 Turquoise, ivory and pinchbeck bracelet owned by Jane Austen, early 19th century. Jane Austen's House, Chawton/Photograph by Peter Smith

6.13 Bracelet, chain band strung with wooden beads, with coloured gold clasp with enamel decoration, possibly made in England, *c*.1805. © Victoria and Albert Museum, London

6.14 Thomas Lawrence, The Wellesley-Pole Sisters [daughters of William Wellesley-Pole, 1st Baron Maryborough, and 3rd Earl of Mornington (1763–1845)], black and red chalk, pink wash on paper, 48 × 38.4 cm, 1814. Christies/Wikimedia Commons

1810–16 TURQUOISE BEAD BRACELET

The final piece of jewellery belonging to Jane Austen is a turquoise glass and ivory bead bracelet with a gilt metal box clasp, 6½ inches (16.5 cm) long (fig. 6.12). The bead size is between 18° and 22°, referring to the number of beads that could line up in 1 inch (2.5 cm). The association is not quite as secure or traceable as the turquoise ring (see p. 199) and topaz cross (p. 193). It was donated to Jane Austen's House in 1973 by Helen Wilder, who decided it should belong with the other artefacts. As scholar and author Hazel Jones explains, 'Writing to [the] President of the Jane Austen Society, she thanked him for accepting her donation – "It is only of sentimental value as it is of beads but it is a charming thing" – and said how happy she would be to think of it at Chawton. She continued, "My Father took me to see Cousin Mary Augusta Austen Leigh at Roehampton in 1914. I think it was in May but am not absolutely certain of the month & she gave me the bracelet telling me it had belonged to Jane Austen".'[41]

The connection is unclear from Austen to cousin Mary, who also possessed the turquoise ring for a time. Cassandra does not mention such a bracelet in her 1843 testamentary letter, but it might have been among the 'other items' to be 'ticketed for the beneficiaries'.[42] She may have given it directly to her five-year-old great-niece Mary, who remembered Cassandra as 'a pale, dark-eyed old lady, with a high arched nose and a kind smile, dressed in a long cloak and large drawn bonnet' from a childhood meeting, probably also in 1843.[43] The bracelet could also have gone to Caroline Austen. In her will of 1878, she directed some wearing apparel and 'trinkets' to be divided between three of her nieces, including Mary. 'Given that the bracelet had little monetary value … it would have counted as a mere "trinket" albeit one of great sentimental worth', continues Jones.[44]

The bracelet is not high quality, like the bracelet with simple wooden beads in figure 6.13, and has proved difficult for experts to date. The clasp design of flowers arranged around a rectangle with a symmetrical foliage motif is the strongest element for basing a date on. The patterning has some similarities with dated jewellery of c.1810–15, within Austen's lifetime, but also to later, more Romantic-style pieces from the 1820s. So, if it was hers, the bracelet must have been somehow acquired late in her life. Deirdre Le Faye speculated that Austen 'could have bought it for herself locally, using a bit of her royalties money', and mused on the matching turquoise colour of ring and bracelet, feeling 'sure the[y] … are significant – she might have bought/been given the one to match the other, to be worn on special occasions'.[45] Austen had at least four blue dresses, so the colour was one she liked to wear and perhaps co-ordinate with. Coincidentally, turquoise and topaz are now birthstones for December, or Austen's star sign Sagittarius, although they appear not to have been such in her lifetime. Le Faye also put forward that the bracelet may be the lone survivor of a pair, given contemporary fashions for wearing two over long sleeves (fig. 6.14). Given how often the sisters' possessions matched, and that Cassandra had 'a pair of small gold bracelets', a pair is possible.[46]

[41] The information here is indebted to Hazel Jones's research and report on the bracelet ('Austen-Leighs, Wilders and Jane Austen's Bracelet'), and I am grateful to her detailed work on the subject.
[42] *Chronology*, p. 663.
[43] *Family Record*, pp. 270–71.
[44] Jones, 'Austen-Leighs, Wilders and Jane Austen's Bracelet'.
[45] Deirdre Le Faye, personal commentary, cited in Jones, 'Austen-Leighs, Wilders and Jane Austen's Bracelet'.
[46] *Chronology*, p. 664.

6.15 Brooch: scroll-shaped
gold frame set with pearls and
enclosing plaited hair under rock
crystal, English, 2.2 × 3 × 1 cm,
1775–1800. © Victoria and Albert
Museum, London

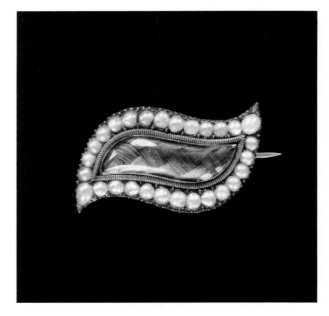

6.16 Memorial ring, English,
gold, enamel, pearls and hair, 2.2
× 2 cm, c.1804–5. The Walters Art
Museum, Baltimore

6.17 Robert Roskell, casemaker
Thomas Hilby, gold and enamel
pocket watch, made in Liverpool,
1802–3. The Metropolitan Museum
of Art, New York/Gift of Miss
Elizabeth M. Greenfield, 1910

1808
OTHER JEWELLERY

Letter 62, Friday 9 December 1808, Southampton: Castle Square

'The Bracelets are in my possession, & everything I could wish them to be.'

Deirdre Le Faye considers that these bracelets were presumably some memento once belonging to their recently deceased sister-in-law Elizabeth, wife to Edward. Cassandra owned a 'pair of small gold Bracelets with Topaze Clasps' in the mid-nineteenth century. She bequeathed these to Catherine Hubback, a daughter of Frank Austen, in her testamentary letter of Tuesday 9 May 1843.[47] Given the symmetry of their wardrobe, Austen may have owned something similar.

Personal items were popular as mementi mori. As a mourning token, Austen and Cassandra each received a 'Single Brilliant Centre Ring', valued at 5 guineas the pair, upon the death of their wealthy relative, the Hon. Mary Leigh of Stoneleigh Abbey, in 1806 (Cassandra's was a diamond set in blue enamel).[48] Cassandra had the sad task of distributing some of Austen's own pieces after her death on 18 July 1817. Ten days later, Cassandra wrote to Austen's friend, Anne Sharp, with enclosures. The letter reads:

> I have great pleasure in sending you the lock of hair you wish for, & I add a pair of clasps which she sometimes wore & a small bodkin which she had had in constant use for more than twenty years. I know how these articles, trifling as they are, will be valued by you & I am very sure that if she is now conscious of what is passing on earth it gives her pleasure they should be so disposed of.[49]

The bodkin was a sewing tool, used to pull tape or cords through channels. The clasps are less clear as to their purpose.

The day after, on 29 July, Cassandra further wrote to their dearest niece Fanny Knight. Among Austen's papers her sister had found 'Memorandums' directing further jewellery bequests. She desired 'that one of her gold chains may be given to her God-daughter Louisa & a lock of her hair be set for you. You can need no assurance my dearest Fanny that every request of your beloved Aunt will be sacred with me. Be so good as to say whether you prefer a broche or ring.'[50] This chain may be the one that Charles Austen gave his sister along with her topaz cross, or something similar (see p. 194). As only one gold chain accompanies the topaz crosses now (see fig. 6.2), that one may have belonged to Cassandra. The practice of setting locks of hair into jewellery to remember the deceased would become a staple of nineteenth-century mourning practices. The hair was often beautifully woven, as the 'broche or ring' set with hair centrepieces in figures 6.15 and 6.16 evoke.

We get one last view of Austen's accessories through Cassandra's bequests, when she gave 'My gold Watch & Chain, which was dear Jane's … for my Brother Henry,–these articles all came from him'. Figure 6.17 shows a plain gold English pocket watch of 1802–3.[51] And this most devoted sister herself memorialised Austen through jewellery: she always wore a ring containing Jane's hair, set with pearls, which she left to their niece Cassy Esten Austen, Charles's daughter.

[47] *Chronology*, p. 663.
[48] *Chronology*, p. 332.
[49] Letter CEA/2. From Cassandra Austen to Anne Sharp, 28 July 1817.
[50] Letter CEA/3. From Cassandra Austen to Fanny Knight, Tuesday 29 July 1817.
[51] *Family Record*, p. 270.

DRAWERS

UNDER-
GARMENTS
AND
NIGHTWEAR

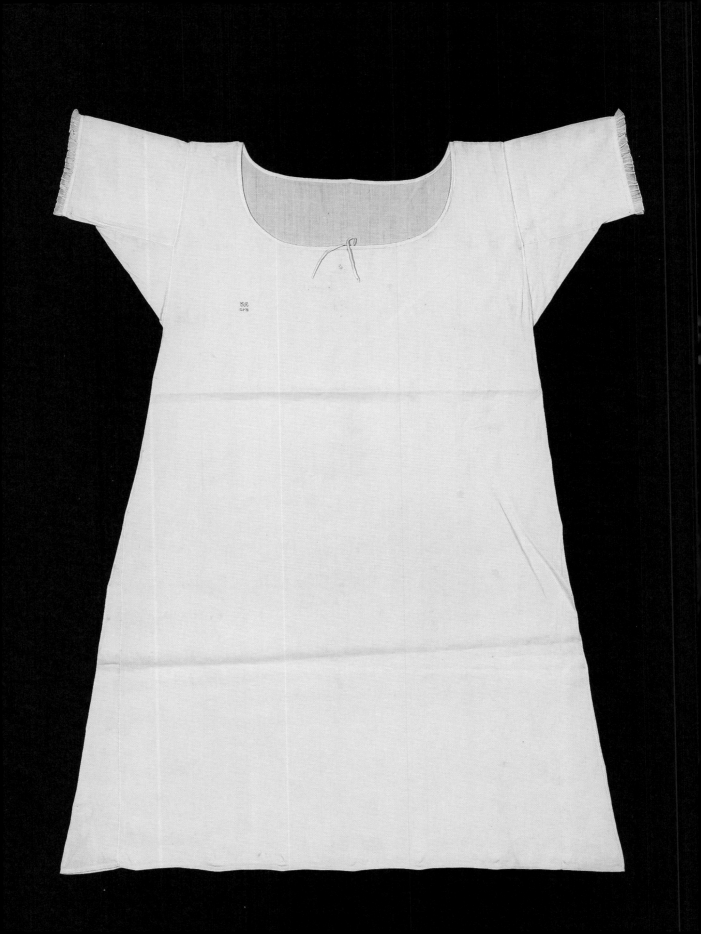

1798, 1813
SHIFTS

Letter 12, Sunday 25 November 1798, Steventon

'The Overton Scotchman has been kind enough to rid me of some of my money, in exchange for six shifts and four pair of stockings. The Irish is not so fine as I should like it; but as I gave as much money for it as I intended, I have no reason to complain. It cost me 3s. 6d. per yard. It is rather finer, however, than our last, and not so harsh a cloth.'

The shift was a linen knee-length tunic that women wore as the first layer next to their body (fig. 7.1). It was often called a 'chemise' in the Regency period, as the French word slowly began to replace the centuries-old English one. Shifts were made roughly T-shaped by a series of rectangles and triangles cut from a length of linen with no wastage, and sewn together carefully with strong run and fell seams to ensure long wear. Regency shifts generally had round scoop necklines, sometimes with a small drawstring or ribbon to hold them to the décolletage (fig. 7.2, also showing a small petticoat worn over the shift). Women usually made shifts themselves and in batches – six or a dozen at a time, cut from long pieces of fabric, such as Austen is buying in this quote. 'Irish' was a common shorthand for Irish linen. When she refers to buying six shifts, she means fabric enough to construct the garments. Cutting and sewing multiple garments allowed the needlewomen to cut the fabric most economically and to set up a more efficient production-line assembly. Austen's use of 'our last' suggests Cassandra might get some of the material for her own wardrobe. Middling-sorts women of Austen's milieu did a lot of seamstressing (constructing soft linen pieces using plain sewing, as opposed to dressmaking of outer clothing) this way, making body garments and accessories for themselves and their families. In Regency dressing, ideally at no point should a gown or other outer garment touch the body. Instead, linen undergarments provided a buffer between the body and more expensive, less cleanable materials such as silk, wool and leather.

Linen is a fibre with many qualities that make it excellent for undergarments (fig. 7.3). It can absorb a lot of moisture – more than cotton – when the wearer is warm and perspiring, and it is stronger than cotton because it is made from the stem of a plant instead of the fluffy top boll. The strength allows it to endure much tougher cleaning treatments, too, such as the hard soaking, boiling and beating laundry processes which kept Regency clothes clean. Washing procedures were another reason for having many shifts in rotation. Each garment was marked either by embroidery or colourfast ink with the wearer's initials and a number, allowing the prudent housekeeper to record and keep track of which pieces had been washed when, to ensure she always had a clean supply, and that no one garment got used or washed too much. The finer quality Austen has bought means the linen would feel more comfortable against the skin and compress slightly better to the body under her other clothes.

Worn-out shifts still had a long life ahead of them. In 1813, Austen wrote of donating 'an old Shift' to 'Dame G[arnet]' in the area local to Chawton, possibly a widow, and certainly with 'well-behaved, healthy, large-eyed Children'.[1] Linen softens more the longer it is worn, so Austen may have been donating her old undergarments to Mrs Garnet for wearing, as a source of lovely soft textiles for dressing her children, or to use as nappies for babies.

page 208
7.1 Woman's shift or chemise, American, linen with neck casing, lawn sleeve ruffles, and 'CR/ N12' embroidered in reverse chain stitch in blue thread, 119.4 × 87.9 cm, early 19th century; worn by donor's great-aunt Caira Robbins (1794–1881). Museum of Fine Arts, Boston/Gift of Miss Ellen A. Stone/Photograph © 2023 Museum of Fine Arts, Boston

7.2 Louis Vaslet, 'Scene II', *The Spoiled Child* (detail), watercolour with ink and wash, 1802. Yale Center for British Art, New Haven, CT/Paul Mellon Collection

7.3 Linen chemise, American, 1780–1800. The Metropolitan Museum of Art, New York/Irene Lewisohn Bequest, 2005

Austen's vendor was an itinerant trader originating in the town of Overton, about 17 miles (27 km) from Chawton. A 'scotchman' was a pedlar carrying fabrics and drapery goods round the countryside for doorstep sales. With no necessary relationship to the northern country, the name instead comes from the traders' practice of keeping accounts by 'scotching' (cutting notches in) tally sticks for their often unlettered buyers.

[1] Letter 78, 24 January 1813.

7.4 Detail of unbleached wool flannel, 1800–20. Courtesy of the author

7.5 Cream wool flannel nightgown, short length, worn by Thomas Coutts, 1800–22. © The Victoria and Albert Museum, London/Given by Mr Francis Coutts

7.6 Woman's linen unboned soft corset or waistcoat, 1790–1800. The Metropolitan Museum of Art, New York/Isabel Shults Fund, 2006

1798
FLANNEL

Letter 10, Saturday 27 – Sunday 28 October 1798, Steventon

'—I gave 2ˢ/3ᵈ a yard for my flannel, & I fancy it is not very good; but it is so disgraceful & contemptible an article in itself, that its' being comparatively good or bad is of little importance.'

Austen does not mention what the wool flannel fabric she bought is intended for, but its uses for the Regency consumer were endless, and all for underwear, nightwear or other private dress. Wool flannel was a soft, plain-weave textile, usually in its creamy natural state from white sheep (fig. 7.4). The weave could be quite open, and at least one side usually had a raised, fluffy nap. It was soft, washable, warm, light and comfortable. In the later nineteenth century, manufacturers imitated it in cotton to make flannelette, still popular today for nightwear and often abbreviated back down to 'flannel'.

Austen was probably buying a 'piece' of flannel in one length, common for the quotidian textiles for underwear like linen, as she bought shifts from an itinerant trader (see p. 211). Men and women used flannel for warm undergarments and intimate wear, often resorting to its ease during illness to keep cosy without too much weight in their dress. Austen reported the next year that 'my uncle is still in his flannels, but is getting better again'.[2] It was a popular choice for dressing gowns (see p. 223), as seen in surviving male garments (fig. 7.5). The fabric's plebeian nature is partly why Austen was so dismissive. Flannel had no glamour or fashion whatsoever and was, as Marianne Dashwood complains in *Sense and Sensibility*, 'connected with the aches, cramps, rheumatisms, and every species of ailment that can afflict the old and the feeble'.[3]

While Marianne misreads Colonel Brandon's military flannel as infirmity, for women the textile was a useful warming layer underneath thinner gown textiles.[4] Flannel was the stolid counterpoint to lightweight muslin's popularity. Among women, flannel petticoats were everywhere, from hills to ballrooms. For the gentry, an underskirt or two made of the textile, simply pleated into a waistband, was a discreet way to add warmth around the legs in colder periods, substituting for the eighteenth century's popular, more visible quilted petticoats.

Like men, women also wore flannel upper-body garments often called waistcoats, a simple wraparound bodice, closing down the front, with gores for hips and bust, of which the linen garment in figure 7.6 is an example. The 'waistcoat' Austen's sister-in-law Fanny bought for 12s.6d in 1814 is probably this kind of underwear (though they were also made of calico).[5] Austen's sort-of neighbour Eliza Jervoise regularly sent a flannel waistcoat for washing among her personal linen.[6] Flannel further appears in female wardrobes in loose, baggy bathing dress, for taking to the water at seaside or spa. Austen's purchase could have had any of these garments as its destination, and perhaps other everyday useful ends for this contemptible article, now lost to history through their very ordinariness.

[2] Letter 22, 19 June 1799.
[3] *Sense and Sensibility*, vol. I, ch. viii.
[4] For more on martial flannel, see Davidson 2019, pp. 231 and 255.
[5] Kindred 2017, p. 143.
[6] Jervoise of Herriard Collection.

1796–1815
STOCKINGS

Letter 1, Saturday 9 – Sunday 10 January 1796, Steventon

'You say nothing of the silk stockings; I flatter myself, therefore, that Charles has not purchased any, as I cannot very well afford to pay for them'

Stockings were the only thing enveloping women's legs between knee and ankle, and so formed the final important buffer there against damp, wind and cold, while maintaining respectable coverage. Stockings reached just above the knee and were held up by garters tied around the thigh or under the knee, depending on the activity (fig. 7.7). Under the knee held better for walking and dancing.

Like most Regency garments, stockings' use and quality depended on the niceties of their materiality. They were available in wool, worsted, thread (linen), cotton and silk, all knitted on framework machines. The stretch in this construction made them cling close to the leg, but the lack of any stretchy yarn meant even the finest quality 'elastic' silk stockings would wrinkle a little. Silk was the most desirable and expensive fibre, creating a smooth, sheeny appearance with a very fine knit, of the kind Austen's family friend Charles Fowle was buying for her (fig. 7.8). (It turned out that Charles had purchased some after all and was told off by Austen in the next letter: 'What a good-for-nothing fellow Charles is to bespeak the stockings!—I hope he will be too hot all the rest of his life for it!)[7] Silk stockings were the most decorative and could have lace patterns or embroidered 'clocks', the long triangular shaping gusset running up from the ankle to the calf. They were worn at dinner, in the evening and to balls, sometimes over cotton stockings for extra warmth and a smooth finish.

Austen's legwear reappeared two years later in 1799, along with her 'best gown' (see p. 35), when she thanks Cassandra for 'marking my silk stockings', showing that her sister has been plying her needle in the form of adding initials or numerals to Austen's stockings in order to keep track of them when going for laundry, as seen at the top of figure 7.8.[8] In November 1815, Austen also sent down '4 pr of Silk Stockgs' from London to Chawton with the note 'but I do not want them washed at present'.[9] While Austen does not mention how much these silk stockings cost, there are plenty of records from other accounts. She bought '3 pr silk Stockgs' for a little less than 12./S. a pr' in 1811, but it was at notably cheap Grafton House (see p. 181).[10] Her niece Fanny Knight also thought 12 shillings was a 'great bargain' for silk stockings bought in London in 1813.[11]

At the same time, Fanny purchased cotton pairs at 4s.3d each. Cotton stockings (fig. 7.9) bought in bulk were most common for the gentry class. Prices varied between around tuppence per pair, bought by the dozen, to at least the 5s per pair which Austen's contemporary Mrs Mary Topham paid in 1815.[12] However, these were a comparatively new invention from the later eighteenth century, and formed what has been called a 'semi-luxury', 'less expensive than fashionable silks, but more expensive than equivalent products made from other fibres'.[13] The same spinning innovations that helped push British cotton textiles to the global fore allowed the fibre to finally be spun as fine as silk, creating a product that 'could reproduce the pure white of fashionable silk stockings, but at a small fraction of the cost', while being easier to wash. Although they became generic as the nineteenth century progressed, for Regency consumers cotton stockings were still something of a class marker compared with the wool or linen worn by plebeian people.

Stockings wore out quickly and needed constant darning to remain wearable, so they were purchased often and, like gloves, in multiple pairs so a damaged one could

page 214

7.7 Unknown artist, *Le Coup de vent*, etching and watercolour on paper, 18.8 × 27.7 cm, 1802. Art Library/Fashion Image Collection, Kunstbibliothek der Staatlichen Museen zu Berlin/© bpk Bildagentur

7.8 Pair of woman's frame-knitted silk stockings, English, 64.8 × 13 cm, early 19th century; worn by donor's great-aunt Caira Robbins (1794–1881) and embroidered with her initials. Museum of Fine Arts, Boston/Gift of Miss Ellen A. Stone/Photograph © 2023 Museum of Fine Arts, Boston

7.9 Pair of women's machine-knitted cotton stockings with a decorative panel in an openwork knit, 1800–29, England or France [record shot]. © Victoria and Albert Museum, London

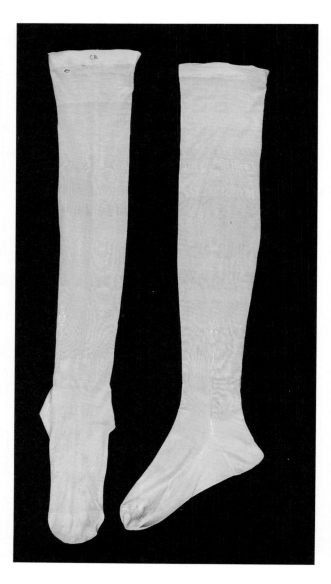

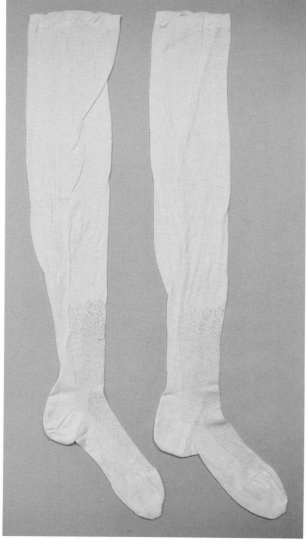

be easily substituted. Unlike fancywork, darning intimate apparel was not considered a suitable occupation while in company. 'Mrs Armstrong sat darning a p^r of Stockings the whole of my visit', observed Austen in 1804. 'But I do not mention this at home, lest a warning should act as an example.'[14] We have already read of Austen buying 'four pair of stockings' from the Overton Scotchman in 1798 (see p. 209).[15] Stockings were available to Regency consumers in a multitude of ways, ranging from these itinerant salespeople, to lending libraries, drapers, milliners, local stores such as Austen immortalised as Ford's in *Emma*, up to dedicated hosiers of every sort and condition in major cities. London hosiery retailers proclaim their wares from the advertising pages of many a contemporary magazine. Cassandra went shopping there for Austen in 1800 and bought her stockings she liked 'very much & greatly prefer having only two pair of that quality, to three of an inferior sort'.[16] Presumably a superior quality wore better and lasted longer through frequent washings. Austen sent her trunk separately when she travelled to London with her brother Henry on 2 March 1814. When it failed to arrive that evening, she wrote to Cassandra the next day, supposing 'it will [come] this morn^g; if not I must borrow Stockings & buy Shoes & Gloves for my visit. I was foolish not to provide better against such a Possibility. I have great hope however that writing about it in this way, will bring the Trunk presently.'[17] We have no record of its arrival, or whether she had to beg the loan of such essential items.

The other mention of stockings in the letters is as part of the extended discussion of mourning clothing after the death of Elizabeth Austen (see pp. 65 and 103). Austen wrote from Southampton telling Cassandra, 'I shall send you such of your Mourning as I think most likely to be useful, reserving for myself your Stockings.'[18] The sisters may have kept some black stockings especially for periods of mourning. While white and pale colours were most common for the legwear, stockings came in a variety of colours, from practical deep or drab hues for walking, to silk dyed in myriad hues to match fashionable colours of the moment.

[7] Letter 2, 14–15 January 1796.

[8] Letter 19, 17 May 1799.

[9] Letter 128, 26 November 1815.

[10] Letter 70, 18–20 April 1811.

[11] Letter 88, 16 September 1813.

[12] Topham 1810 (22 April 1815).

[13] John Styles, 'Re-Fashioning Industrial Revolution: Fibres, Fashion and Technical Innovation in British Cotton Textiles, 1600–1780', *La moda come motore economico: innovazione di processo e prodotto, nuove strategie commerciali, comportamento dei consumatori / Fashion as an Economic Engine: Process and Product Innovation, Commercial Strategies, Consumer Behavior*, 2022, p. 67.

[14] Letter 39, 14 September 1804.

[15] Letter 12, 25 November 1798.

[16] Letter 23, 25–27 October 1800.

[17] Letter 97, 2–3 March 1814.

[18] Letter 59, 15–16 October 1808.

7.10 Silk petticoat or slip, *c.*1805–10, British. The Metropolitan Museum of Art, New York

7.11 Starched white cotton petticoat, with bodice, sleeves and cutwork embroidered hem; drawstrings in the back waist, round the back neck and separately round the front neck, tying at one side, 1815–25. The Hopkins Collection, London

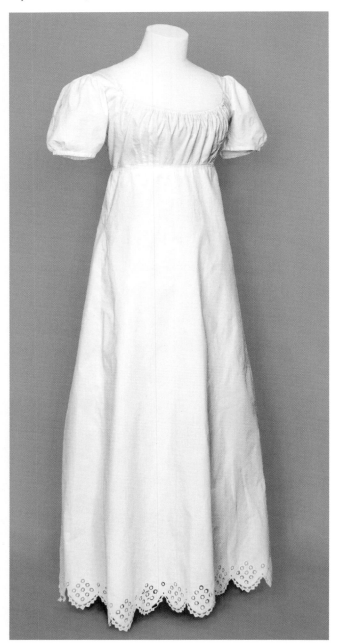

7.12 Woman's petticoat, American, cotton plain weave, cotton embroidery, cotton twill tape, linen plain-weave tape, centre front 117.5 cm, early 19th century; worn by Mehetable Stoddard Sumner (Mrs Benjamin Welles, 1784–1826). Museum of Fine Arts, Boston/Gift of Emily Welles Robbins (Mrs Harry Pelham Robbins) and the Hon. Sumner Welles, in memory of Georgiana Welles Sargent /Photograph © 2023 Museum of Fine Arts, Boston

Letter 17, Tuesday 8 – Wednesday 9 January 1799, Steventon

'—I am much obliged to you for meaning to leave my old petticoat behind You; I have long secretly wished it might be done, but had not courage to make the request.'

The word 'petticoat' covered a range of garments for Regency women. First, they were an essential and common feminine undergarment, going straight over the shift and stays or corset to cover the hips and legs. Figure 7.2 shows a semi-transparent short petticoat worn over the shift. These under-petticoats were made of linen or cotton textiles (more of the latter as the nineteenth century progressed) and were underskirts rather than underwear, meaning it was expected that they may be seen (see figs 1.35, 1.41 and 1.43). Like shifts, quotidian petticoats withstood tough laundering. Washing bills for this service show 'coat' is shorthand for a petticoat, and the same thing may be called either, depending on who wrote the bill. Plain white petticoats could be pin-tucked at the bottom for extra length and letting out. As outer skirts became more frequently gored, so did underwear petticoats.

The gleefully cavalier attitude that Austen displays to the loss of her petticoat insinuates it is an underskirt, rather than another type, which is any kind of skirt worn under the main gown. These petticoats could be of fine material equal to the gown, and sometimes matched its fabric as part of a set – especially in the 1790s, with its open-fronted robes and gowns. This kind continued through the 1800s but were disappearing by the 1810s. Such petticoats could also be made of old outer garments worn thin, a strategy Austen contemplated as a means of using up one of her muslin gowns of which she was 'tired & ashamed' the year before in 1798 (see p. 29). They often appear underneath robes to form most of the skirt (see fig. 1.10). The most visible petticoats were coloured 'slips' (fig. 7.10) in many hues intended to be seen under increasingly translucent gowns of diaphanous muslin

gauzes, lace and openwork. Clever rotations of slips could change an overdress's appearance. Visible petticoats increased during the 1810s as the hemlines widened and allowed more space for fashionable decoration, especially after 1815 (fig. 7.11). Petticoats with frills and flounces added bulk and visual interest to the bottom of skirts.

In spring 1814, Austen wrote to Cassandra from Henrietta Street in London, informing her, 'I have read the Corsair, mended my petticoat, & have nothing else to do.'[19] Again, there is no indication about which kind of petticoat she may have repaired. Later the same year, she wrote one of her most detailed fashion commentaries about 'coloured petticoats with braces' as fashionable outerwear.[20] Her comment highlights a third meaning for Regency petticoats: any skirt, even those with bodices. No wonder it can be hard to disentangle what a garment might look like from textual references.

As waistlines remained high, the bodiced under-petticoat, sometimes with an upper of coarser material, became practical for holding the undergarments up to the right level under the bust without bulky waist ties (figs 7.11 and 7.12). Some surviving petticoats and petticoat-skirts, especially in the later teens and 1820s, have merely two straps or tapes running beside the bust over the shoulders to hold the garment up. Sometimes even garments that now look like sleeveless dresses are called petticoats, though they are effectively functioning as gowns (see fig. 1.62).

[19] Letter 98, 5–8 March 1814.
[20] Letter 106, 2 September 1814, to Martha Lloyd.

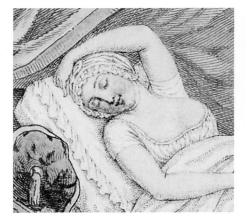

7.13 'Costume Parisien, Intérieur d'Appartement', *Journal des Dames et des Modes*, 1800: plate 163 (detail). Rijksmuseum, Amsterdam/Purchased with the support of the Flora Fonds/Rijksmuseum Fonds

7.14 Louis Vaslet, 'Scene II', *The Spoiled Child* (detail), watercolour with ink and wash, 1802. Yale Center for British Art, New Haven, CT/Paul Mellon Collection

7.15 Plate 9 (figs. 1 and 2), in *The Workwoman's Guide, Containing Instructions in Cutting Out and Completing Articles of Wearing Apparel, by a Lady* (London: Simpkin Marshall and Co., 1840 [1838])

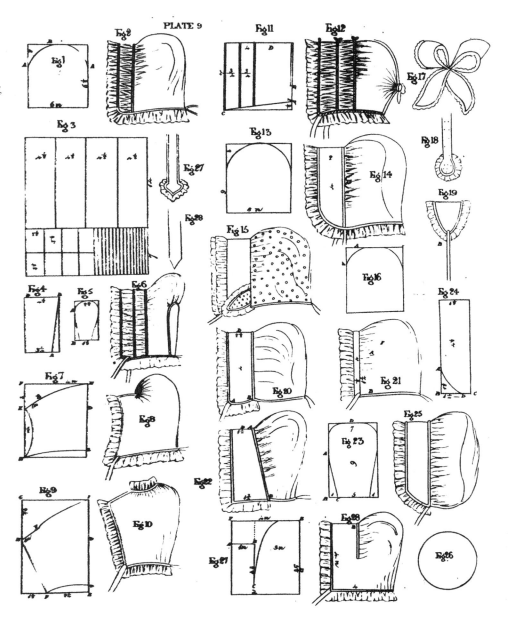

1805, 1813
NIGHTCAPS

Letter 45, Saturday 24 August 1805, Godmersham

'—I have found your white mittens, they were folded up within my clean nightcap, & send their duty to you.'

Small quotidian practical items such as nightcaps are one of the hardest kinds of garments to research in dress. They are private, intimate, generally out of the swing of fashion, but they were 'in constant wear' every day, or rather, night.[21] They kept the head warm, absorbed oil (thus keeping pillowcases cleaner), and, for women, helped their long hair not to become tangled while sleeping. Numerous modern conveniences, including central heating and the ability to wash hair regularly, have long since caused the common nightcap to disappear. As they were made of cotton or linen, and usually worn into nothingness, it is also hard to find surviving examples to indicate what Austen's nightcap might have looked like, though sometimes they appear in pictures (figs 7.13 and 7.14). She refers again to the article in 1813, writing, 'I had intended to beg you would bring one of my nightcaps with you, in case of my staying, but forgot it when I wrote on Tuesday.'[22]

The Workwoman's Guide, first published in 1838, is one of the first books that went into precise instructional detail about how to make a huge range of textile items, clothing and household linens. It is a wonderful resource for understanding early nineteenth-century clothing and to it we turn, even though it was published over twenty years after Austen's death. The anonymous female author included various designs and instructions for nightcaps, helping demonstrate their prevalence. The first instructions are for a 'Woman's day or night-cap', noting that 'this is a favourite shape for a day-cap among the poor' (nos. 1 and 2 on the plate in fig. 7.15).[23] This is followed by 'a very neat night-cap' to be 'made of checked muslin, with a border of corded muslin', and 'particularly comfortable for a night-cap, as it sets close to the head', and most economically made in sets of eight. One woman's collection of underclothes, dated 1818–36,

at the Gallery of Costume in Manchester, includes nightdresses, a chemise, a morning gown, neck frills and pockets, all with laundry numbers, that show the lady owned at least eighteen nightdresses, nine chemises and six plain striped cotton nightcaps. The latter could also be made of knitted textiles, though these seem to be more of a masculine choice. Making up basic garments in multiple sets was preferred for economy of cut, efficiency of construction, and the necessity of having clean clothes to last between laundry days, which could be weeks or even months apart.

Further on in *The Workwoman's Guide* there are directions for 'a favourite cap for ladies and poor women', listed as a night-cap in the index, and 'a neat comfortable day or night cap', noted as 'a shape particularly suitable for day-caps for young servants, or night-caps for any age or station'.[24] The difference is construction from 'clear or jaconet muslin' for day, and 'check [muslin] or calico' for night. The quality of textiles reinforces how important the material aspects of clothing were, and how a finer cloth could elevate a practical nightcap into something suitable for public, albeit servants', wear.

---

[21] Letter 89, 23–24 September 1813.
[22] Letter 93, 21 October 1813.
[23] A Lady, *The Workwoman's Guide, Containing Instructions in Cutting Out and Completing Articles of Wearing Apparel, by a Lady* (London: Simpkin Marshall and Co., 1840), p. 62.
[24] *The Workwoman's Guide* 1840, pp. 65–6.

7.16 Linen dressing gown, early
19th century. The Metropolitan
Museum of Art, New York/Gift
of Mrs Albert S. Morrow, 1937

1814
DRESSING GOWN

Letter 105, Tuesday 23 – Wednesday 24 August 1814, London: 23 Hans Place

'—be so good as to put up a clean Dressing gown which will come from the Wash on friday.'

In the sentence previous, Austen had asked Cassandra to send up her silk pelisse (see p. 107) and realised that, as a package would be sent up on Saturday, she may as well take the opportunity to obtain a clean dressing gown. The conveyor was the local coach, Collier's (or Collyer's), which ran a service to their nearest town, Alton, from the Bell Savage Inn on Ludgate Hill in London three times a week. Collier's Southampton coach also passed through Alton daily from the same inn, Sundays excepted.[25]

While men wore loose robes of many shapes and names around the house in informal situations, women's dressing gowns (fig. 7.16) were more intimate, and were worn only over the actual nightgowns in which they slept, before dressing and occasionally at breakfast. The difference to men's seems to be that women's dressing gowns were not to be seen by people outside the household or family. Elinor Dashwood uses the possibility of her sister Marianne being in her dressing gown as a way to try and put off a visit from the impertinent Steele sisters in *Sense and Sensibility*.[26] Caroline Austen visited Austen in the March before she died, when 'I had the first idea of her being seriously ill'. The niece described how Austen 'was then keeping her room, but said she would see us… She was in her dressing gown, and was sitting quite like an invalid in an arm-chair…'[27] She never saw her aunt again.

Austen's dressing gowns were likely of white cotton, implied by the example coming 'from the Wash', and as seen in an 1814 fashion plate (fig. 7.17). Linen was also a popular, washable fabric for the garment. A French linen dressing gown with beautifully finished self-striped muslin frill (fig. 7.18) shows the congruence between plate and reality. Warmer textiles were probably used for colder times, including the ever-useful wool flannel (see p. 213), which was also washable.

Sometimes there could be an elision between a morning gown and an open robe that functioned as a dressing gown. Figure 7.17 is described as a 'robe pelisse of Indian muslin, thrown quite open in front'. After exhausting herself with visits in 1802, author Fanny Burney 'rested upon a bed for the remainder of the day … in a close cap, my feet in their native, undrapieried state, hidden by a large, long, wrapping morning gown', sounding like the peignoir in figure 1.32 and looking like the woman reading in figure 7.19.[28] In *Pride and Prejudice*, Mrs Bennet calls for her housekeeper to 'put on my things in a moment', after languishing in her dressing-room for days, alluding to the idea that she is doing so in her dressing- or morning gown or other unstructured robe.[29] It is apt that the last garment in *Jane Austen's Wardrobe* is one she could wear to start, finish, or relax from a day of dressing in the myriad attires and accessories discussed in these pages. We leave the writer here in comfort, and end too this exploration of Austen's tastes, habits, life and times through what we know of her clothes.

[25] Thomas Hartwell Horne, *Crosby's Complete Pocket Gazetteer of England and Wales, Or Traveller's Companion* (London: Baldwin, Cradock & Joy, 1815), p. 12.
[26] *Sense and Sensibility*, vol. II, ch. x.
[27] Austen-Leigh 2008, p. 127.
[28] Fanny Burney, *Diary and Letters of Madame D'Arblay* (July 1791 to April 1802), ed. Charlotte Barrett and Austin Dobson, VI vols. (London: Macmillan & Co. Ltd, 1905), vol. V, pp. 221–2.
[29] *Pride and Prejudice*, vol. II, ch. vii.

7.17 'Morning Dress ... a loose robe pelisse of Indian muslin, thrown
quite open in front with a full gathered border of muslin or lace',
The Repository of Arts, January 1814, engraving and watercolour on paper.
Los Angeles County Museum of Art/Gift of Dr and Mrs Gerald Labiner/
www.lacma.org

7.18 Linen dressing gown, French, *c*.1802. The Metropolitan Museum
of Art, New York/Purchase, Irene Lewisohn Bequest, 1988

7.19 Henry Fuseli, *Woman Reading, Seated Before a Window*, pen and brown
ink on paper, 25.1 × 20 cm, 1805. Yale Center for British Art, New Haven,
CT/Paul Mellon Collection

RECOMMENDED READING

The following books are particularly recommended for those who wish to explore the world of Regency dress further, especially as connected with Jane Austen.

Batchelor, Jennie, and Alison Larkin, *Jane Austen Embroidery: Authentic Embroidery Projects for Modern Stitchers* (London: Pavilion, 2020)

Byrde, Penelope, *Jane Austen Fashion: Fashion and Needlework in the Works of Jane Austen* (Ludlow: Moonrise Press, 2008)

Davidson, Hilary, *Dress in the Age of Jane Austen: Regency Fashion* (London and New Haven, CT: Yale University Press, 2019)

Downing, Sarah Jane, *Fashion in the Time of Jane Austen* (Oxford and Long Island City, NY: Shire Publications, 2010)

Johnston, Lucy, *19th-Century Fashion in Detail* (London: V&A Publishing, 2016)

Le Bourhis, Katell, *The Age of Napoleon: Costume from Revolution to Empire, 1789–1815* (New York: Metropolitan Museum of Art, 1989)

O'Brien, Alden, ed., *'An Agreeable Tyrant': Fashion after the Revolution* (Washington, DC: DAR Museum, 2016)

Percoco, Cassidy, *Regency Women's Dress: Techniques and Patterns 1800–1830* (London: Batsford, 2015)

Ribeiro, Aileen, *The Art of Dress: Fashion in England and France 1750 to 1820* (New Haven, CT: Yale University Press, 1995)

GLOSSARY

apron-front *See* *fall-front.

band [bandeau] A headband, fillet or narrow piece of fabric or ribbon, sometimes decorated, worn on or around a woman's head.

Barcelona handkerchief A twilled silk handkerchief, plain, checked or with fancy patterns, and usually brightly coloured; handkerchiefs of this kind were first manufactured in Spain.

bib-front *See* *fall-front.

boa A long thin scarf usually made of fur or other warm, fluffy material. Also called a *tippet.

bobbin net [bobbinet, bobbinette] A machine-made lace, imitating fine bobbin or 'pillow' lace, plain woven in a hexagonal mesh of four sides twisted and two crossed over; it was usually made of silk and cotton. *Tulle is a kind of bobbin net.

bodice [body] (1) Any part of a woman's dress worn around the upper torso; the upper part of the gown, or the lining of that part. (2) A quilted or boned undergarment such as a *corset, jumps or *stays.

bombazine [bombasine, bombazin, bombazeen] A twilled fabric made of silk and wool worsted, of cotton with silk, or of worsted alone; it was often black, and in this colour was used for mourning dress.

bonnet (1) Structured women's headgear for outdoor wear, having a brim at the front and sides only; it was tied under the chin with 'strings' or ribbons. *See also* *cawl. (2) A soft, brimless cap made of fabric, or knitted.

bugle A straight, tubular glass bead, or decoration with such beads.

calico [callico] Originally a plain-weave cotton cloth, imported from India in many grades, and usually printed; the term soon came to mean any cotton imported from the East, and, eventually, any cotton fabric, including those of European manufacture, and those with warps of other fibres such as linen. Printed calico could be washed without the design's colour bleeding. Calico was used in morning and day dress, and for other informal or domestic clothing. (Unbleached calico is now called 'muslin' in American English.)

cambric [French lawn] A fine white linen or hard-spun cotton fabric, originally from Cambrai in France. When imported into Britain, it was known as French lawn.

cambric muslin A cotton fabric more densely woven and less transparent than muslin; it was popular for women's morning and day dress, and for small accessories.

cap A general term for any close-fitting headdress of soft material and structure, worn in informal domestic settings or by members of particular trades or professions. A woman's cap could also be worn out of doors, under a bonnet.

cape An elbow-length cloak, or the attached circular additions(s) falling from under the collar of a cloak or coat and draping over the shoulders to provide extra warmth.

cashmere The soft hair of the cashmere goat, and the light, warm and soft woollen cloth made from it.

cassimere *See* *kerseymere.

cawl [caul] (1) The soft fabric back part of a bonnet, taking the place of a structured crown, and attached to the brim or front. (2) The fabric cover applied over a bonnet foundation.

chemise *See* *shift.

chemisette A tabard covering the upper part of the body and filling in the neck of a gown, often appearing like a false shirt front with a collar; it fastened with a drawstring at the waist or under the bust. The term appeared in the later Regency period; earlier, the garment might be called a collared neckerchief (referring to the way a woman's neck handkerchief filled in the décolletage) or a habit-shirt.

China crape *See* *crape.

chintz A fabric of cotton, linen or combination-fibre calico, fast-printed or hand-painted in numerous colours with floral and other patterns, and usually glazed; it was imported from India.

chip Very thin strips of wood, plaited together to make material for hats; it was usually painted black or white.

cloak A loose outer garment, worn by both sexes over other clothing for warmth and protection outside. It was like a cape, but three-quarter or full length. Women's cloaks could also be made of light, decorative textiles, worn for style.

clock The shaping at the ankle of a stocking, tapering off up the leg; the clock was often knitted decoratively or embroidered.

clogs Wooden- or leather-soled overshoes, worn out of doors, to raise the wearer above dirt and wet ground.

cloud A textile technique where threads are dyed with a pattern before weaving, making the final design soft and fuzzy.

corset [corsette] (1) A close-fitting, soft undergarment, worn to support the breasts and shape the silhouette. Originally corsets were shorter and more lightly stiffened than *stays, using cording or whalebone, but from the early nineteenth century onwards the terms started to converge, as corsets were more commonly worn, became longer and had more boning in them. (2) In fashion, a kind of sleeveless, decorative waistcoat or bolero, worn over, and usually contrasting with, the gown.

crape (1) A light transparent fabric, woven from wool or gummed silk, in a plain weave with a distinctive, lightly crinkled surface achieved by extreme twisting of the fibres. Black crape was widely used for mourning dress. (2) China crape (now called crepe de Chine) was opaque and made of fine silk with more threads in the warp than the weft; it was used in evening dress.

crewel [cruel] Coloured embroidery yarn made of fine, loosely twisted two-ply worsted. Hence 'crewel-work' for embroidery done with this yarn.

dressmaker A woman engaged in the making of garments for other women; the term is synonymous with '*mantua-maker', and appeared c.1800.

evening dress A form of full dress, comprising clothing and accessories suitable only for evening events (cf. *morning dress).

fall-front [apron-front, bib-front, front fall, stomacher-front] An opening at the front of a gown consisting of a panel of fabric that pins or buttons onto the shoulder bands, covering the bust and hiding the overlapping bodice lining underneath. When unfastened, it falls down onto the skirt.

fichu A finished square or triangle of light linen or cotton, worn around a woman's neck, shoulders and chest for warmth and protection; it could be tucked into the gown or tied at the front. *See also* *handkerchief.

figured Of a fabric, ornamented with patterns or designs, often achieved by means of the weave, but also by printing or needlework.

flannel A somewhat loosely woven plain-weave or twilled cloth of undyed (cream) woollen yarn, of variable fineness, with a fluffy, raised nap; historically, it was called 'Welsh cotton' after its traditional place of manufacture.

frieze A coarse, warm woollen cloth with a rough nap, used for outer garments.

full dress An ensemble or a mode of dress appropriate for formal or public occasions in the afternoon or later, such as court dress, evening dress, or dress worn to the opera or formal dinners (cf. *half-dress).

galosh (1) In the upper of a shoe, a piece of leather running all round the shoe and attached to the sole; it was made of stouter material than the rest of the body of the shoe and protected the foot from cold and wet. (2) In later use, a protective overshoe made of impermeable material. In the Regency, 'galoshes' of this kind were unknown, and other kinds of outer footwear were worn to protect the shoes from dirt and wet (*see* *clog, *patten).

gauze A fine, thin, transparent, open-weave fabric, usually made of silk, but sometimes of linen or cotton; the dual warp threads are twisted around the weft to give firmness. It was popular for women's evening dress.

glazing A finishing process for textiles in which a glossy substance is applied to the fabric, which is then calendered (pressed), usually with rollers, to achieve a smooth, glossy surface; such cloth is described as 'glazed'.

gore A wedge-shaped or triangular piece of textile forming part of a garment, especially used to narrow a skirt at the waist and broaden it at the hem.

gown (1) The main woman's garment, a dress. (2) The length of fabric intended for making a dress.

half-dress An ensemble or a mode of dress appropriate for semi-formal public events, such as daytime functions or informal evening gatherings (cf. *full dress).

handkerchief A square of finished fabric, plain or decorated, worn around the head, neck or shoulders; a 'half-handkerchief' was a triangular piece of cloth used for the same purpose. A handkerchief worn around the neck was called a '*neckerchief'. A smaller piece, not worn but carried for various purposes, was called a 'pocket handkerchief'.

Irish Irish linen, used for nightwear, undergarments and many miscellaneous accessories.

jacket Any short, close-fitting, outer coat, for men or women, sometimes called a '*spencer'. For women, such a jacket was waist-length, in accordance with the fashionable waistline.

jaconet [jacconet, jaconet muslin] A thin cotton, of a weight between *muslin and *cambric; it was popular for women's morning dress.

jean (1) A stout, twilled cotton fabric, and (in the nineteenth century) also a twilled sateen. (2) A type of coarse twilled fabric of linen and cotton, used for a range of men's and women's clothing, and for linings.

kerseymere [cassimere, cassimer, casimir] An expensive, medium-weight, twilled woollen cloth, made of densely woven, very fine yarns, finished with a close nap and having a soft texture. First patented by Francis Yerbury of Bradford in 1766, it was used in tailored clothing.

latchet(s) The pair of long tabs at the top front of a shoe that overlap and pass through the buckle to fasten closed, or tie together with a lace without overlapping.

lawn A very fine, quite crisp, plain-weave linen or cotton, originally from Laon, France; it was widely used for undergarments, shirts, shifts and any other accessory that could be made of linen or cotton. For French lawn, *see* *cambric.

list (1) The cut-off selvedges of woollen textiles. (2) A fabric made from weaving the selvedges together.

mantua-maker In the eighteenth century, a maker of women's clothing; the name derives from the fashionable loose mantua gown. In the Regency period, the term was synonymous with 'dressmaker'. At all periods, a mantua-maker was usually female.

morning dress An ensemble or a mode of dress for informal day wear at home or outdoors in the hours before the afternoon. For women, indoor morning dress usually consisted of a high-cut, long-sleeved round gown; when layered with a bonnet and outer garment, such as a *pelisse, morning dress was also appropriate for walking, shopping, running errands and making informal visits (*cf.* *evening dress).

morning gown A gown worn as morning dress at home, often white with a high collar and long sleeves.

muslin A lightweight, semi-transparent, soft cotton fabric, of a plain, fairly open weave, usually white; it often had a pattern, either woven in, or applied after weaving through embroidery or *tambour work ('sprigged muslin'), and came in many different weights and finishes. It originated in India and was also manufactured in Britain during the Regency period. *See also* *calico, *cambric muslin, *jaconet.

nankeen [nankin] A fabric made from a yellow variety of cotton, resulting in a yellowish brown colour. Originally made in Nanjing (Nankin, Nanking), China, it was popular for men's dress, and also for women's shoes.

neckerchief [neck handkerchief] A square, finished piece of cloth, worn around the neck. Neckerchiefs were made in a huge variety of printed or woven coloured cottons and silks. *See also* *fichu, *handkerchief.

nightcap A cotton or linen cap worn in bed.

nightgown A loose gown worn in bed, especially by women.

Norwich crape A black, twill fabric of silk warp and worsted weft; it was the official fabric for court mourning. After 1819, also a fabric plain-woven with a glossy finish, similar to *bombazine.

Norwich stuff A general term for *worsted and worsted-blend fabrics manufactured in East Anglia.

Oldenburg bonnet A style of bonnet worn by the Grand Duchess of Oldenburg (1788–1819), with a very high crown and a wide brim that hid the face; it was popular throughout Europe after the grand duchess's tour of 1814.

open gown A gown with a skirt that opened down the centre front.

pasteboard Rolled and compressed paper, used for bonnet fronts.

patent net [patent lace, pattinet] A general term for machine-made lace.

patten An overshoe consisting of a wooden sole attached to a tall metal ring, held onto the foot by leather straps. Pattens were worn over normal shoes when walking outside, to raise the wearer above dirt and wet ground.

pelisse A woman's coat-dress, made from many kinds of material, from muslin to thick wool. It might be of any length from the knee to the ankle, and have any of various styles of collar, cape and sleeve; it was usually somewhat fitted, to follow the form of the gown worn underneath.

percale [perkale] A glazed, fine cotton cloth, similar to *cambric muslin, but less expensive; usually white or blue or printed, it was popular for morning dress.

persian A thin, light, soft, plain-woven silk, usually used to line garments; it was similar to, but lighter and cheaper than, *sarcenet.

petticoat A word with many applications. (1) Any skirt, whether visible or worn underneath a gown or other petticoats; in this sense, sometimes abbreviated to 'coat'. (2) The skirt of a dress, as distinct from the bodice, with which it could be coloured to match or contrast; it might be decorated with quilting or embroidery. (3) A skirted garment with its own bodice – usually sleeveless – to hold it up, worn under a gown (especially when made of transparent fabric), or, for informal wear, over a habit-shirt. *See also* *slip.

plain weave The simplest form of weave, in which the weft threads go over one warp thread and under the next, repeatedly (*cf.* *twill).

plait (1) Pleat. (2) A braided strip of straw or very thin wood, especially willow (*see* *chip), used in multiples to make hats and bonnets.

poke bonnet A bonnet with a crown fitting close to the head, and a long brim, cylindrical in shape, extending horizontally out over the face.

poplin A lightweight dress fabric with a dense silk warp and lighter worsted weft.

redingote A man's or woman's long, double-breasted and full-skirted greatcoat, with a prominent collar. A man's redingote sometimes had a short cape, and a woman's had a fitted body. The word is a French corruption of 'riding-coat', borrowed back into English.

ribbon [ribband] A length of narrow, fine fabric, usually of silk, used as edging or decoration on garments, millinery and soft furnishings, as a hair ornament and fastening, or to tether articles together attractively.

robe [half-robe] (1) In fashion, specifically, an evening gown open in front to display a decorative petticoat and having a train behind. A 'half-robe' was a low-necked, thigh-length tunic worn over a round gown. (2) Any loose garment (as in the modern sense).

round gown A gown with bodice and skirt in one; the skirt was closed all round, and not open in front to expose the petticoat. It emerged in the 1790s and continued to be worn through the Regency period.

sarcenet [sarsenet, sarsnet] A fine, soft silk, either plain or twilled, with a slight sheen; it was widely used for linings as well as outer garments, and could be woven with patterns.

shawl A rectangular or square piece of any textile, used as a covering for the shoulders, upper arms and torso, and sometimes worn over the head.

shift A woman's knee-length undergarment of plain linen or (especially after *c.*1820) cotton, worn next to the skin to protect outer clothing. The garment was also called by the older word 'smock', and in the Regency came to be called a 'chemise'.

slip A plain silk or satin undergown, white or coloured, worn under a transparent muslin, net or gauze gown.

spencer A short, close-fitting jacket without tails; the term is probably more common in modern usage than it was in the Regency period. Originally worn by men over a longer coat, the spencer then became popular with women and remained so throughout the Regency. The woman's spencer followed the form of the gown bodice over which it was worn.

sprig Any small flower or plant pattern, embroidered into or printed onto textiles.

stays A close-fitting undergarment, shaped and stiffened with whalebone, cording, canvas or a busk, closed with lacing, which shaped the wearer's torso. For women, it also supported the breasts. Female short stays reached from the bust to the waist; long stays consisted of a stiffened bodice, covering the hips and supporting the breasts, with a centre-front busk and shoulder straps. The term 'stays' started to converge with '*corset' in the early nineteenth century until the two became virtually synonymous.

stockings Leg coverings that were knee-length or extending above the knee; they were held up by garters.

stuff A general term for a plain- or twill-woven wool or worsted fabric, especially thin, light types of cloth, popular for women's day dress.

taffeta A crisp, plain-weave silk, woven with highly twisted threads, having a tight finish and a somewhat glossy surface.

tambour work A form of chain-stitch embroidery, worked in silk or cotton threads with a tambour hook, usually on translucent fabrics such as *muslin, net and *gauze.

thread Generally (when not otherwise qualified), a sewing thread or knitting yarn made from linen or flax, as in 'thread stockings' or 'a skein of thread'.

tippet A woman's stole or scarf, long and narrow, or triangular; it was generally worn for warmth and often made of fur or wool, though it could also be light and decorative. *See also* *boa.

tucker [chemise tucker] A separate edging of linen, *lawn, *muslin or some other fine material, worn around the top of a low-necked *bodice and tucked into it.

tulle [tule] Machine-woven, hexagonal net, first produced in 1768 in England; *see* *bobbin net. The name derives from the French town where the net was manufactured from 1817.

turban A round headdress, inspired by the headwear of various Eastern cultures; it consisted of a length of fabric sewn into shape or simply wound around the head. Turbans were most common as a form of women's headwear, and were very popular for evening wear.

twill A weave in which the warp thread passes over two or more weft threads before passing under (and vice-versa), producing regular diagonal ridges on the fabric's surface (*cf.* *plain weave).

twist Plied, stout silk thread, used for making buttonholes and other functional but decorative parts of dress.

undress [dishabille, negligee] Informal or ordinary dress. For women, this included *morning dress, walking dress and day dress. For men, it applied to morning wear and sporting clothing.

waistcoat As underwear, an upper-body garment, worn under or over the *shift for warmth. In this sense, the word could be used as a synonym for 'jumps', a quilted and boned garment.

worsted The combed, long-staple fibres of a fleece, smoother, shinier and more durable than the short-staple, fluffy wool; or any thread or fabric made from these fibres.

BIBLIOGRAPHY

ABBREVIATIONS

Chronology Le Faye, Deirdre, *A Chronology of Jane Austen and her Family: 1600–2000* (Cambridge: Cambridge University Press, 2013)

Family Record Le Faye, Deirdre, *Jane Austen: A Family Record*, 2nd edn (Cambridge: Cambridge University Press, 2004)

Letters Le Faye, Deirdre, ed., *Jane Austen's Letters*, 4th edn and online (Oxford: Oxford University Press, 2011)

MANUSCRIPTS

Austen, Mrs Cassandra, 'To Mary Austen', June 1811, 23M93/62/2/3, Hampshire Record Office

Fanny Knight's Diaries, U.951/F.24/1 *Lady's Daily Companion; Rackham's Fashionable Repository*. Kent History and Library Centre

Jervoise of Herriard Collection, Family and Estate Papers, 44M69/E13/13/3–4, Hampshire Record Office

Sun Insurance Records, 'Insured: Mary Hare, 6 Lower Grosvenor Street, Milliner', 1808, London Metropolitan Archives: City of London, MS 11936/440/812959

Sun Insurance Records, 'Insured: Thomas Flint Junior 10 Fish Street Hill mercer, hosier, laceman, linen draper and haberdasher', 6 April 1820, London Metropolitan Archives: City of London, MS 11936/478/966146

Topham, Mary, 'Lady's Account Book', 1810, Chawton House Library, 6641

PUBLISHED SOURCES

A Lady, *The Workwoman's Guide, Containing Instructions in Cutting Out and Completing Articles of Wearing Apparel, by a Lady* (London: Simpkin Marshall and Co., 1840)

Alison, Archibald, *Travels in France, During the Years 1814–15: Comprising a Residence at Paris During the Stay of the Allied Armies, and at Aix, at the Period of the Landing of Bonaparte* (Edinburgh: Macredie, Skelly, and Muckersy, 1816)

Ashmore, Sonia, *Muslin* (London: V&A Publishing, 2012)

Austen-Leigh, J. E., *A Memoir of Jane Austen and Other Family Recollections*, ed. Kathryn Sutherland, Oxford World's Classics (Oxford: Oxford University Press, 2008)

Batchelor, Jennie, and Alison Larkin, *Jane Austen Embroidery: Authentic Embroidery Projects for Modern Stitchers* (London: Pavilion, 2020)

Buchan, William, *Advice to Mothers, on the Subject of Their Own Health; and on the Means of Promoting the Health, Strength, and Beauty, of Their Offspring*, 2nd edn (London: Cadell and Davies, 1811)

Burney, Fanny, *Diary and Letters of Madame D'Arblay* (July 1791 to April 1802), ed. Charlotte Barrett and Austin Dobson, VI vols. (London: Macmillan & Co. Ltd, 1905), vol. V

Byrde, Penelope, and Ann Saunders, 'The "Waterloo Ball" Dresses at the Museum of Costume, Bath', *Costume*, 34.1 (2000), pp. 64–9

Cooper, Thomas, *A Practical Treatise on Dyeing, and Callicoe Printing: Exhibiting the Processes in the French, German, English, and American Practice of Fixing Colours on Woollen, Cotton, Silk, and Linen* (Philadelphia, PA: Thomas Dobson, 1815)

Davidson, Hilary, 'Dress & Dressmaking: Material Innovation in Regency Dress Construction', in *Material Literacy in Eighteenth-Century Britain: A Nation of Makers*, ed. Serena Dyer and Chloe Wigston Smith (London: Bloomsbury Academic, 2020), pp. 173–94

Davidson, Hilary, *Dress in the Age of Jane Austen: Regency Fashion* (London and New Haven, CT: Yale University Press, 2019)

Davidson, Hilary, 'Jane Austen's Pelisse Coat', in *Jane Austen: Writer in the World*, ed. Kathryn Sutherland (Oxford: The Bodleian Library, 2017), pp. 56–75

Davidson, Hilary, 'Muslin Shawl', Jane Austen's House, 2017: https://janeaustens.house/object/jane-austens-muslin-shawl/ [accessed 20 June 2022]

Davidson, Hilary, 'Reconstructing Jane Austen's Silk Pelisse, 1812–1814', *Costume*, 49.2 (2015), pp. 198–223

Department for Culture, Media & Sport, 'Export Controls on Objects of Cultural Interest', March 2015

The Duties of a Lady's Maid: With Directions for Conduct, and Numerous Receipts for the Toilette (London: James Bulcock, 1825)

Dyer, Serena, *Material Lives: Women Makers and Consumer Culture in the 18th Century* (London: Bloomsbury Publishing, 2021)

Fawcett, Trevor, 'Argonauts and Commercial Travellers: The Foreign Marketing of Norwich Stuffs in the Later Eighteenth Century', *Textile History*, 16.2 (1985), pp. 151–81

Felkin, William, *A History of the Machine-Wrought Hosiery and Lace Manufactures* (London: Longmans, Green, and Co., 1867)

Foley, Liza, '"An Entirely Fictitious Importance"? Reconsidering the Significance of the Irish Glove Trade: A Study of Limerick Gloves, 1778–1840', *Costume*, 48.2 (2014), pp. 160–71

Garsault, François-Alexandre Pierre de, *M. de Garsault's 1767 Art of the Shoemaker: An Annotated Translation*, trans. D. A. Saguto (Williamsburg, VA: The Colonial Williamsburg Foundation, in association with Texas Tech University Press, 2009)

Grimble, Frances, *The Lady's Stratagem: A Repository of 1820s Directions for the Toilet, Mantua-Making, Stay-Making, Millinery and Etiquette* (San Francisco, CA: Lavolta Press, 2009)

Hampshire County Council, 'Jane Austen's Pelisse Coat': http://www3.hants.gov.uk/austen/austen-pelisse.htm [accessed 7 May 2014]

Hart, Peggy, 'Cassimere: Hiding in Plain Sight', in *Textile Society of America Symposium Proceedings* (presented at the 17th Biennial; Hidden Stories/Human Lives, Lincoln: University of Nebraska, 2020): https://digitalcommons.unl.edu/cgi/viewcontent.cgi?article=2176&context=tsaconf [accessed 20 June 2022]

Horne, Thomas Hartwell, *Crosby's Complete Pocket Gazetteer of England and Wales, Or Traveller's Companion* (London: Baldwin, Cradock & Joy, 1815)

Hughes, Clair, 'Talk about Muslin: Jane Austen's Northanger Abbey', in Hughes, *Dressed in Fiction* (London: Berg, 2005)

Johnson, Barbara, *A Lady of Fashion: Barbara Johnson's Album of Styles and Fabrics*, ed. Natalie Rothstein (New York: Thames and Hudson, 1987)

Kindred, Sheila Johnson, *Jane Austen's Transatlantic Sister: The Life and Letters of Fanny Palmer Austen* (Toronto: McGill-Queen's University Press, 2017)

La Belle Assemblée: Or, Bell's Court and Fashionable Magazine; Containing Interesting and Original Literature, and Records of the Beau-Monde, November, issue 103 (London: J. Bell, 1817)

The Lady's Monthly Museum (London: Dean and Munday, 1827), vol. XXV

Le Faye, Deirdre, *A Chronology of Jane Austen and her Family: 1600–2000* (Cambridge: Cambridge University Press, 2013)

Le Faye, Deirdre, ed., *Jane Austen's Letters* (Oxford: Oxford University Press, 2011)

Le Faye, Deirdre, *Jane Austen: A Family Record*, 2nd edn (Cambridge: Cambridge University Press, 2004)

Levey, Santina M., 'Machine-Made Lace: The Industrial Revolution and After', in *The Cambridge History of Western Textiles*, ed. D. T. Jenkins, II vols. (Cambridge: Cambridge University Press, 2003), vol. II, pp. 846–52

Mackrell, Alice, *Shawls, Stoles, and Scarves* (London and New York: Batsford, 1986)

Miskin, Lauren, '"True Indian Muslin" and the Politics of Consumption in Jane Austen's Northanger Abbey', *Journal for Early Modern Cultural Studies*, 15.2 (2015), pp. 5–26

Montgomery, Florence M., *Textiles in America, 1650–1870* (New York: W.W. Norton & Co., 1984)

National Portrait Gallery, 'Jane Austen', *Regency Portraits Catalogue*: https://www.npg.org.uk/collections/search/portraitExtended/mw00230/Jane-Austen [accessed 23 May 2021]

O'Brien, Alden, ed., *'An Agreeable Tyrant': Fashion after the Revolution* (Washington, DC: DAR Museum, 2016)

Old Bailey Proceedings Online (www.oldbaileyonline.org, version 8.0, 24 February 2022), July 1800, trial of Ann Spencer (t18000709-86)

Old Bailey Proceedings Online (www.oldbaileyonline.org, version 8.0, 24 February 2022), 16 September 1801, trial of Ann Gill (t18010916-6)

Parliamentary Abstracts, Containing the Substance of All Important Papers Laid before the Two Houses of Parliament during the Session of 1825 (London: printed for Longman, Hurst, Rees, Orme, and Brown, 1826), vol. I

Priestley, Ursula, 'Norwich and the Mourning Trade', *Costume*, 27.1 (1993), pp. 47–56

Riello, Giorgio, *A Foot in the Past: Consumers, Producers and Footwear in the Long Eighteenth Century* (Oxford and New York: Pasold Research Fund/Oxford University Press, 2006)

Salisbury, Deb, ed., *Fabric à La Romantic Regency: A Glossary of Fabrics from Original Sources 1795–1836* (Abbott, TX: The Mantua-Maker Historical Sewing Patterns, 2013)

Smith, Elizabeth Grant, *Memoirs of a Highland Lady* (London: J. Murray, 1911)

Souter, John, *The Book of English Trades: And Library of the Useful Arts: With Seventy Engravings*, 7th edn (London: John Souter, 1818)

Sperling, Diana, *Mrs Hurst Dancing and Other Scenes from Regency Life 1812–23*, ed. Gordon Mingay (London: Victor Gollancz, 1981)

Stewart, J. A., *The Female Instructor; or, Young Woman's Companion: Being a Guide to All the Accomplishments Which Adorn the Female Character … With Other Valuable Information in the Branches of Domestic Economy* (Liverpool: Nuttall, Fisher and Dixon, 1817)

Styles, John, 'Re-Fashioning Industrial Revolution. Fibres, Fashion and Technical Innovation in British Cotton Textiles, 1600–1780', *La moda comemotore economico: innovazione di processo e prodotto, nuove strategie commerciali, comportamento dei consumatori / Fashion as an Economic Engine: Process and Product Innovation, Commercial Strategies, Consumer Behavior*, (Florence, Firenze University Press, 2022, pp. 45–71

Styles, John, 'Spinners and the Law: Regulating Yarn Standards in the English Worsted Industries, 1550–1800', *Textile History*, 44.2 (2013), pp. 145–70

Taylor, Lou, *Mourning Dress: A Costume and Social History* (London: Routledge, 2009)

The New Monthly Magazine and Literary Journal (London: Henry Colburn, 1821), vol. I

The Penny Cyclopædia of the Society for the Diffusion of Useful Knowledge (London: Charles Knight and Co., 1841), vol. XIX

The Repository of Arts, vol. 41, May 1812 (London: R. Ackermann)

Tomalin, Claire, *Jane Austen: A Life* (London: Viking, 1997)

Vestris, Lucia Elizabetta, *Memoirs of the Life of Madame Vestris* (privately printed, 1830)

Vickery, Amanda, 'Mutton Dressed as Lamb? Fashioning Age in Georgian England', *Journal of British Studies*, 52.04 (2013), pp. 858–86

Vickery, Amanda, *The Gentleman's Daughter* (London and New Haven, CT: Yale University Press, 2003)

Victoria and Albert Museum, 'Peignoir, 1812–14', *Collections:* http://collections.vam.ac.uk/item/O114688/peignoir-unknown/ [accessed 24 February 2022]

Whitlock, Tammy C., *Crime, Gender and Consumer Culture in Nineteenth-Century England* (London: Routledge, 2016)

ACKNOWLEDGEMENTS

I had the idea for this book during the first British lockdown for COVID-19 in 2020, in a cottage in rural Wales, and its creation has been shaped by the ongoing effects of the pandemic. My wonderful editor Sophie Neve turned the idea into reality with speed, enthusiasm and endless excellent support. Anjali Bulley once again worked miracles on the project management, while Jenny Wilson's copyediting was elegant, gracious and essential, Osborne Ross delivered beautiful layouts and Jo Walker produced a gorgeous jacket cover. My appreciative thanks to the constructive and very helpful feedback of the anonymous peer reviewers.

The book would not have been possible without the dedicated team at Jane Austen's House in Chawton, especially Sophie Reynolds. Sincere thanks to the staff of libraries, museums, archives and collections who contributed so much to the research: Rebekka Gerber, Bally Shoe Museum; Elizabeth Semmelhack, Bata Shoe Museum; Chawton House, Hampshire; Martina D'Amato, Cora Ginsburg LLC; Jacob Moss, The Fan Museum, Greenwich; Hampshire Record Office; Kent Family History Centre; Beatrice Behlen, John Chase, Sean Waterman and Lucy Whitmore, Museum of London; Louise Fowler and Andy Chopping, Museum of London Archaeology (MOLA); State Library of NSW; University of Sydney Library; Jenny Lister and Susan North, Victoria and Albert Museum, London; and Serge Liagre, Villa Rosemaine, France. Thanks also to Jennie Batchelor, Gail Baxter, Alison Carter, Jeffrey S. Evans, John Gagne, Mary Guyatt, Candice Hern, Sarah Howard, Hazel Jones, Lesley Miller, Robert Ross, Al Saguto, Mackenzie Scholtz, John Styles, Katie Szabo, and private individuals. Alden O'Brien, and Vanessa and Alan Hopkins, have been especially generous with their time and knowledge.

For moral and writing support during the book's genesis, many thanks to Cressida Barron, Adam Batenin, Albert Blaya Pérez, Robyne Calvert, Lizzie Chaikin, Craig Court, Alison Matthews David, Laurel Fox, Tony Harris, Donyale Harrison, David Hunt, Lynne Hulse, Veronica Isaac, Helen Johnson, Anna Vaughan Kett, Helene and Ted Markstein, Nicholas Marlowe, Jessie Ginsborg Newling, James Petersen, Sandra Leigh Price, Suzanne Rowland, Hannah Rumball, Nicola Scott, Emelia Simcox, Lorraine Smith, Lorraine Spring, Craig Stanton, Michelle Starr, Kate Strasdin, Alison Urquhart, Kim Wahl, Kylie Winkworth, Emma Zappia and the online Twitter community. Enormous thanks to Majella and Andrea Morello for their incredible hospitality. Mary Maddocks was a splendid comrade during interesting times. Especial love and thanks to Barbara Davidson, Gil Davidson, Mek Zwart, Connor Davidson, and Grace.

INDEX

Page numbers in **bold** refer to the illustrations